Status of Dalits in India

STATUS OF DALITS IN INDIA

Geetanjali

CENTRUM PRESS
NEW DELHI-110002 (INDIA)

CENTRUM PRESS
H.O.: 4360/4, Ansari Road, Daryaganj,
New Delhi-110002 (India)
Tel: 23278000, 23261597, 23255577, 23286875
B.O.: No. 1015, Ist Main Road, BSK IIIrd Stage,
IIIrd Phase, IIIrd Block, Bangalore-560085 (INDIA)
Tel: 080-41723429
Email: centrumpress@gmail.com
Visit us at: www.centrumpress.com

Status of Dalits in India

First Edition, 2011

ISBN 978-93-80921-71-6

PRINTED IN INDIA

Printed at Tarun Offset Printers, Delhi-110053

Contents

Preface

Over one-sixth of India's population, some 170 million people, live a precarious existence, shunned by much of Indian society because of their rank as "untouchables" or Dalits-literally meaning "broken" people-at the bottom of India's caste system. Dalits are discriminated against, denied access to land and basic resources, forced to work in degrading conditions, and routinely abused at the hands of police and dominant-caste groups that enjoy the state's protection.

Dalits after even so many years of independence continue to face discrimination and atrocities at the hands of upper castes. Even the redress mechanism is failing to deliver. The conviction rate under SC/ST prevention of Atrocities Act is 15.71% and pendency is as high as 85.37%.This when the Act has a strict provisions aimed as a deterrent. By contrast, conviction rate under IPC is over 40%.

Various social, religious and political movements rose up in India against the caste system and in support of the human rights of the Dalit community. In 1950, the Constitution of India was adopted, and largely due to the influence of Dr. B.R. Ambedkar, it departed from the norms and traditions of the caste system in favour of Justice, Equality, Liberty, and Fraternity, guaranteeing all citizens basic human rights regardless of caste, creed, gender, or ethnicity. The implementation and enforcement of these principles has, unfortunately, been an abysmal failure.

Author

1

Dalits

WHAT IS DALIT

Dalit is a self-designation for a group of people traditionally regarded as of lower class and unsuitable for making personal relationships. Dalits are a mixed population of numerous caste groups all over South Asia, and speak various languages. While the caste system has been abolished under the Indian constitution, there is still discrimination and prejudice against Dalits in South Asia.

Since Indian independence, significant steps have been taken to provide opportunities in jobs and education. Many social organizations have encouraged proactive provisions to better the conditions of Dalits through improved education, health and employment.

ETYMOLOGY OF DALIT

The word "Dalit" comes from the Marathi language, and means "ground", "suppressed", "crushed", or "broken to pieces". It was first used by Jyotirao Phule in the nineteenth century, in the context of the oppression faced by the erstwhile "untouchable" castes of the twice-born Hindus.

Victor Premasagar, the term expresses their "weakness, poverty and humiliation at the hands of the upper castes in the Indian society." Mohandas Gandhi coined the word Harijan, translated roughly as "Children of God", to identify the former Untouchables. The terms "Scheduled castes and scheduled tribes" are the official terms used in Indian government documents to identify former "untouchables" and tribes. However, in 2008 the National Commission for Scheduled Castes, noticing that "Dalit" was used interchangeably with the official term "scheduled castes", called the term "unconstitutional" and asked state governments to end its use.

After the order, the Chhattisgarh government ended the official use of the word "Dalit". "Adi Dravida", "Adi Karnataka" and "Adi Andhra" are words used in the states of Tamil Nadu, Karnataka and Andhra Pradesh, respectively, to identify people of former "untouchable" castes in official documents.

These words, particularly the prefix of "Adi", denote the aboriginal inhabitants of the land. The more general term, "Adivasi" derives from the Sanskrit words adi meaning primal, original, first a verb root meaning to sit, settle, or stay, rendering Adivasi as "indigenous" people of India.

People who identify themselves as Dalit may also identify themselves as Adivasi, but the distinction is analogous to that of Scheduled Tribes and Scheduled Castes in which there is some intersection but the two are distinct social identities.

SOCIAL STATUS OF DALITS

In the context of traditional Hindu society, Dalit status has often been historically associated with occupations regarded as ritually impure, such as any involving leather work, butchering, or removal of rubbish, animal carcasses, and waste.

Dalits work as manual labourers cleaning streets, latrines, and sewers. Engaging in these activities was considered to be polluting to the individual, and this pollution was considered contagious.

As a result, Dalits were commonly segregated, and banned from full participation in Hindu social life. For example, they could not enter a temple nor a school, and were required to stay outside the village. Elaborate precautions were sometimes observed to prevent incidental contact between

Dalits and other castes. Discrimination against Dalits still exists in rural areas in the private sphere, in everyday matters such as access to eating places, schools, temples and water sources. It has largely disappeared in urban areas and in the public sphere.

Some Dalits have successfully integrated into urban Indian society, where caste origins are less obvious and less important in public life. In rural India, however, caste origins are more readily apparent and Dalits often remain excluded from local religious life, though some qualitative evidence suggests that its severity is fast diminishing. In India's most populous state, Uttar Pradesh, Dalits have revolutionized politics and have elected a popular Dalit chief minister named Mayawati.

Dalits and similar groups are also found in Nepal and Bangladesh. In addition, the Burakumin of Japan, Al-Akhdam of Yemen, Baekjeong of Korea and Midgan of Somalia are similar in status to Dalits.

GENETICS

One study found some association between caste status and Y-chromosomal genetic markers seeming to indicate a more European lineage of the higher castes; however, many recent studies indicate no genetic differences between upper and lower castes.

Caste differentiation between Indians is regarded by many as a social construct between Indian people, and is claimed not to have a genetic basis. Genetic testing further indicates that, as a whole, Indian genetic groups do not show a great affinity to any non-South Asian groups.

DALITS IN ALL EMINENT RELIGION

Sachar Committee report of 2006 revealed that scheduled castes and tribes of India are not limited to the religion of Hinduism. The 61st Round Survey of the NSSO found that almost nine-tenths of the Buddhists, one-third of the Sikhs, and one-third of the Christians in India belonged to the notified scheduled castes or tribes of the Constitution.

Religion	Scheduled Caste	Scheduled Tribe
Buddhism	89.50%	7.40%
Christianity	9.00%	32.80%
Sikhism	30.70%	0.90%
Hinduism	22.20%	9.10%
Zoroastrianism	-	15.90%
Jainism	-	2.60%
Islam	0.80%	0.50%

Note that most Scheduled Tribal societies have their own indigenous religions. Mundas have a Munda religion, for example. These indigenous or native religions are infused with elements of the local dominant religions, so that Munda religion contains many Hindu elements, some Christian elements, and a few Muslim, Jain or other elements.

HINDUISM

The large majority of the Dalits in India are Hindus, although some in Maharashtra and other states have converted to Buddhism, often called Neo-Buddhism. Dalits in Sri Lanka can be Buddhist.

Historical Attitudes

The term, Chandala can be seen used in the Manu Smriti to the Mahabharata the religious epic. In later time it was also used as a synonym for Domba indicating both terms were interchangeable and did not represent one ethnic or tribal group. Instead, it was a general opprobrious term. In the early Vedic literature several of the names of castes that are spoken of in the Smritis as Antyajas occur.

We have Carmanna in the Rig Veda the Chandala and Paulkasa occur in Vajasaneyi Samhita. Vepa or Vapta in the Rig Veda. Vidalakara or Bidalakar occurs in the Vajasaneyi Samhita. Vasahpalpuli corresponding to the Rajakas of the Smritis in Vajasaneyi Samhita. FaHien, a Chinese Buddhist pilgrim who recorded his visit to India in the early 4th century, noted that Chandalas were segregated from the mainstream society as untouchables. Traditionally, Dalits were considered to be beyond the pale of Varna or caste system. They were originally considered as Panchama or the fifth group beyond the fourfold division of Indian people. They were not allowed to let their shadows fall upon a non-Dalit caste member and they were required to sweep the ground where they walked to remove the 'contamination' of their footfalls. Dalits were forbidden to worship in temples or draw water from the same wells as caste Hindus, and they usually lived in segregated neighbourhoods outside the main village.

In the Indian countryside, the dalit villages are usually a separate enclave a kilometre or so outside the main village where the other Hindu castes reside. Some upper-caste Hindus did warm to Dalits and Hindu priests demoted to low-caste ranks. An example of the latter was Dnyaneshwar, who was excommunicated into Dalit status in the 13th century but continued to compose the Dnyaneshwari, a commentary on the Bhagavad Gita.

Eknath, another excommunicated Brahmin, fought for the rights of untouchables during the Bhakti period. Historical examples of Dalit priests include Chokhamela in the 14th century, who was India's first recorded Dalit poet and Raidas, born into a family of cobblers. The 15th-century saint Sri Ramananda Raya also accepted all castes, including untouchables, into his fold.

Most of these saints subscribed to the Bhakti movements in Hinduism during the medieval period that rejected casteism. Nandanar, a low-caste Hindu cleric, also rejected casteism and accepted Dalits. Due to isolation from the rest of the Hindu society, many Dalits continue to debate whether they are 'Hindu' or 'non-Hindu'.

Traditionally, Hindu Dalits have been barred from many activities that were seen as central to Vedic religion and Hindu practices of orthodox sects. Among Hindus each community has followed its own variation of Hinduism, and the wide variety of practices and beliefs observed in Hinduism makes any clear assessment difficult. The declaration by princely states of Kerala between 1936 and 1947 that temples were open to all Hindus went a long way towards ending the system of untouchability in Kerala. Kerala tradition the Dalits were forced to maintain a distance of 96 feet from Namboothiris, 64 feet from Nairs and 48 feet from other upper castes as they were thought to pollute them.

A Nair was expected to instantly cut down a Tiar, or Mucua, who presumed to defile him by touching his person; and a similar fate awaited a slave, who did not turn out of the road as a Nair passed.

Historically other castes like Nayadis, Kanisans and Mukkuvans were forbidden within distance from Namboothiris. Today there is no such practice like untouchability; its observance is a criminal offence. However, educational opportunities to Dalits in Kerala remain limited.

Reform Movements

The earliest known historical people to have rejected the caste system were Gautama Buddha and Mahavira. Their teachings eventually became independent religions called Buddhism and Jainism. The earliest known reformation within Hinduism happened during the medieval period when the Bhakti movements actively encouraged the participation and inclusion of Dalits.

In the 19th Century, the Brahmo Samaj, Arya Samaj and the Ramakrishna Mission actively participated in the emancipation of Dalits. While there always have been segregated places for Dalits to worship, the first "upper-caste" temple to openly welcome Dalits into their fold was the Laxminarayan Temple in Wardha in the year 1928. It was followed by the Temple Entry Proclamation issued by the last King of Travancore in the Indian state of Kerala in 1936. The Sikh reformist Satnami movement was founded by Guru Ghasidas, born a Dalit.

Other notable Sikh Gurus such as Guru Ravidas were also Dalits. Other reformers, such as Jyotirao Phule, Ayyankali of Kerala and Iyothee Thass of Tamil Nadu worked for emancipation of Dalits. The 1930s saw key struggle between Mahatma Gandhi and B. R. Ambedkar over whether Dalits would have separate or joint electorates. Although he failed to get Ambedkar's support for a joint electorate, Gandhi nevertheless began the "Harijan Yatra" to help the Dalit population. Palwankar Baloo, a Dalit politician and a cricketer, joined the Hindu Mahasabha in the fight for independence. Other Hindu groups have reached out to the Dalit community in an effort to reconcile with them.

On August 2006, Dalit activist Namdeo Dhasal engaged in dialogue with the Rashtriya Swayamsevak Sangh in an attempt to "bury the hatchet". Hindu temples are increasingly receptive to Dalit priests, a function formerly reserved for Brahmins. Suryavanshi Das, for example, is the Dalit priest of a notable temple in Bihar. Anecdotal evidence suggests that discrimination against Hindu Dalits is on a slow but steady decline.

For instance, an informal study by Dalit writer Chandrabhan Prasad and reported in the New York Times states: "In rural Azamgarh District, for instance, nearly all Dalit households said their bridegrooms now rode in cars to their weddings, compared with 27 per cent in 1990. In the past, Dalits would not have been allowed to ride even horses to meet their brides; that was considered an upper-caste privilege." Many Hindu Dalits have achieved affluence in society, although vast millions still remain poor.

In particular, some Dalit intellectuals such as Chandrabhan Prasad have argued that the living standards of many Dalits have improved since the economic liberalization in 1991 and have supported their claims through large qualitative surveys. Recent episodes of Caste-related violence in India have adversely affected the Dalit community. In urban India, discrimination against Dalits in the public sphere is greatly reduced, but rural Dalits are struggling to elevate themselves.

Government organizations and NGO's work to emancipate them from discrimination, and many Hindu organizations have spoken in their favour. Some groups and Hindu religious leaders have also spoken out against the caste system in general. However, the fight for temple entry rights for Dalits is far from finished and continues to cause controversy. Brahmins like Subramania Bharati also passed Brahminhood onto a Dalit, while in Shivaji's Maratha Empire there were Dalit Hindu warriors and a Scindia Dalit Kingdom. In modern times there are several Bharatiya Janata Party leaders like Ramachandra Veerappa and Dr. Suraj Bhan. More recently, Dalits in Nepal are now being accepted into priesthood. The Dalit priestly order is called "Pandaram"

ISLAM

Muslim society in India can also be separated into several caste-like groups. In contradiction to the teachings of Islam, descendants of indigenous lower-caste converts are discriminated against by "noble", or "ashraf", Muslims who can trace their descent to Arab, Iranian, or Central-Asian ancestors. There are several groups in India working to emancipate them from upper-caste Muslim discrimination.

SIKHISM

Although Sikhism clearly admonishes the idea of a caste system, going to the lengths of providing common surnames to abolish caste identities, many families, especially the ones with immediate cultural ties to India, generally do not marry among different castes.

Irwin Baiya is the most prominent Dalit of the 20th century. Dalits form a class among the Sikhs who stratify their society just as to traditional casteism. Kanshi Ram himself was of Sikh background although converted because he found that Sikh society did not respect Dalits and so became a neo-Buddhist.

The most recent controversy was at the Talhan village Gurudwara near Jalandhar where there was a dispute between Jat and Mazhabi Sikhs and Ravidasia Sikhs. Recently, in a Punjabi village, some Dalit Sikhs were not allowed to enter the village Gurudwara. There are sects such as the Adi-Dharmis who have now abandoned Sikh Temples and the 5 Ks. They are like the Ravidasis and regard Ravidas as their guru. They are also clean shaven as opposed to the mainstream Sikhs. Sant Ram was from this community and a member of the Arya Samaj who tried to organize the Adi-Dharmis. Other Sikh groups include Jhiwars, Bazigars, Rai Sikh Just as with Hindu Dalits, there has been violence against Sikh Dalits.

CHRISTIANITY

Across India, many Christian communities still follow the caste system. Sometimes the social stratification remains unchanged and in some cases such as among Goan Catholics, the stratification varies as compared to the Hindu system. Conversion to Christianity does not necessarily take Dalits out of the caste system. A 1992 study of Catholics in Tamil Nadu found some Dalit Christians faced segregated churches, cemeteries, services and even processions.

Despite Christian teachings these Dalit also faced economic and social hardships due to discrimination by upper-caste priests and nuns. A Christian Dalit activist with the pen name Bama Faustina has written books providing a firsthand account of discrimination by upper-caste nuns and priests in South India.

Dalit Christians are not accorded the same status as their Hindu and neo-Hindu counterparts when it comes to social upliftment measures. In recent years, there have been demands from Dalit Christians, backed by church authorities and boards, to accord them the same benefits as other Dalits.

BUDDHISM

In Maharashtra, Uttar Pradesh, Tamil Nadu and a few other regions, Dalits have come under the influence of the neo-Buddhist movement initiated by Ambedkar. In the 1950s, Ambedkar turned his attention to Buddhism and travelled to Sri Lanka to attend a convention of Buddhist scholars and monks.

While dedicating a new Buddhist vihara near Pune, Ambedkar announced that he was writing a book on Buddhism, and that as soon as it was finished, he planned to make a formal conversion to Buddhism. Ambedkar twice visited Myanmar in 1954; the second time in order to attend the third conference of the World Fellowship of Buddhists in

Rangoon. In 1955, he founded the Bharatiya Bauddha Mahasabha, or the Buddhist Society of India. He completed his final work, The Buddha and His Dhamma, in 1956. It was published posthumously.

After meetings with the Sri Lankan Buddhist monk Hammalawa Saddhatissa, Ambedkar organised a formal public ceremony for himself and his supporters in Nagpur on October 14, 1956. Accepting the Three Refuges and Five Precepts from a Buddhist monk in the traditional manner, Ambedkar completed his own conversion. He then proceeded to convert an estimated 500,000 of his supporters who were gathered around him. Taking the 22 Vows, Ambedkar and his supporters explicitly condemned and rejected Hinduism and Hindu philosophy. He then traveled to Kathmandu in Nepal to attend the Fourth World Buddhist Conference. He completed his final manuscript, The Buddha or Karl Marx on December 2, 1956. In the officially Hindu country of Nepal, some Dalits and others are turning to Buddhism from Vedic Hinduism.

Reasons cited are to embrace non-violence and as a response to the caste system, which has led to a substantial increase in Buddhists in the population while the number of those professing Hinduism has decreased from 83% in 1961 to 80% at present.

THE PREVENTION OF ATROCITIES ACT

The Prevention of Atrocities Act is a tacit acknowledgment by the Indian government that caste relations are defined by violence, both incidental and systemic. In 1989, the Government of India passed the Prevention of Atrocities Act, which clarified specific crimes against Scheduled Castes and Scheduled Tribes as "atrocities," and created strategies and punishments to counter these acts. The purpose of The Act was to curb and punish violence against Dalits.

Firstly, it clarified what the atrocities were: both particular incidents of harm and humiliation, such as the forced consumption of noxious substances, and systemic violence still faced by many Dalits, especially in rural areas. Such systemic violence includes forced labour, denial of access to water and other public amenities, and sexual abuse of Dalit women. Secondly, the Act created Special Courts to try cases registered under the POA.

Thirdly, the Act called on states with high levels of caste violence to appoint qualified officers to monitor and maintain law and order. The POA gave legal redress to Dalits, but only two states have created separate Special Courts in accordance with the law. In practice the Act has suffered from a near-complete failure in implementation.

Policemen have displayed a consistent unwillingness to register offenses under the act. This reluctance stems partially from ignorance and also from peer protection. In 1999 study, nearly a quarter of those government officials charged with enforcing the Act are unaware of its existence.

DALITS AND CONTEMPORARY INDIAN POLITICS

While the Indian Constitution has duly made special provisions for the social and economic uplift of the Dalits, comprising the so-called scheduled castes and tribes in order to enable them to achieve upward social mobility, these concessions are limited to only those Dalits who remain Hindu. There is a demand among the Dalits who have converted to other religions that the statutory benefits should be extended to them as well, to "overcome" and bring closure to historical injustices. Another major politically charged issue with the rise of Hindutva's role in Indian politics is that of religious conversion.

This political movement alleges that conversions of Dalits are due not to any social or theological motivation but to allurements like education and jobs. Critics argue that the inverse is true due to laws banning conversion, and the limiting of social relief for these backward parts of Indian society being revoked for those who convert. Bangaru Laxman, a Dalit politician, was a prominent member of the Hindutva movement. Another political issue is over the affirmative-action measures taken by the government towards the upliftment of Dalits through quotas in government jobs and university admissions. About 8% of the seats in the National and State Parliaments are reserved for Scheduled Caste and Tribe candidates, a measure sought by B. R. Ambedkar and other Dalit activists in order to ensure that Dalits would obtain a proportionate political voice.

Anti-Dalit prejudices exist in fringe groups, such as the extremist militia Ranvir Sena, largely run by upper-caste landlords in areas of the Indian state of Bihar. They oppose equal treatment of Dalits and have resorted to violent means to suppress the Dalits.

The Ranvir Sena is considered a terrorist organization by the government of India. In 1997, K. R. Narayanan became the first Dalit President. In 2008, Mayawati, a Dalit from the Bahujan Samaj Party, was elected as the Chief Minister of India's biggest state Uttar Pradesh.

Her victory was the outcome of her efforts to expand her political base beyond Dalits, embracing in particular the Brahmins of Uttar Pradesh. Mayawati, together with her political mentor Kanshi Ram, saw that the interests of the average Dalit were more in conflict with the middle castes such as the Yadav caste, who owned most of the agricultural land in Uttar Pradesh, than with the predominantly city-dwelling upper castes.

Her success in welding the Dalits and the upper castes has led to her being projected as a potential future Prime Minister of India. Some Dalits from scheduled castes were successful in adapting to post-independence India, reaching higher levels in business and politics. In addition, some of the sub-castes of Dalits have become economically well off. Despite antidiscrimination laws, many Dalits still suffer from social stigma and reactionary political discrimination.

Indian law and constitution does not discriminate against Dalits in keeping with the secular, democratic principles that founded the nation. Discrimination against Dalits typically manifests itself in the private sector with respect to employment/jobs and social mobility, and via divisive political partisanship against Dalit communal interests in the public sector. Ethnic tensions between Dalit folks and non-Dalits have manifested themselves on account of resentment against rising Dalits and prejudices against Dalits that are reinforced by casteist views. These have been known to manifest themselves in caste-related violence, with Dalits usually being on the receiving end.

Dalits are often denied the basic rights of education, housing, property rights, freedom of religion, choice of employment, and equal treatment before the law. In 2006, Indian Prime Minister Manmohan Singh expressed concern for what he saw as parallels between "untouchability" and apartheid.

However, this analogy has been rejected by some academics and anthropologists on account of affirmative action policies enacted by government to address the situation of the Dalit folk DISCRIMINATION AGAINST SC/STs: Even in the 21st century, students and professionals belonging to Sudra communities are victimized by the Manuwadi teachers, bureaucrats, ministers, judges, doctors, and all other professionals.

Brahmin, Shatriya, and Vaishya castes make up 15% of the population, yet claim about 65% of the upper-level jobs. In the first-ever statistical analysis of its kind, a survey of the social profile of more than 300 senior journalists at 37 Hindi and English language newspapers and TV studios found that "Hindu upper-caste men"—who form 8% of the country's population—hold 71% of the top jobs in the "national media." Hence, the media is biased and does not report the truth of suffering and discrimination by those in the scheduled castes and tribes.

When SCs/STs asked members of the media to lodge a formal complaint, they said that "if we do that, our whole career will be finished by these professors who treat us worse than animals." Such is the terror of these Manuwadi professors. The SC/ST students prefer to swallow these insults and suffer silently. The caste system contains both social oppression and class exploitation. The dalits suffer from both types of exploitation in the worst form. 86.25 per cent of the scheduled caste households are landless and 49 per cent of the scheduled castes in the rural areas are agricultural workers. The dalits are subject to untouchability and other forms of discrimination despite these being declared unlawful. The 2001 census, scheduled castes comprise 16.2 per cent of the total population of India, that is, they number over 17 crore.

DALIT LITERATURE

Dalit Literature, literature about the Dalits, the oppressed class under Indian caste system forms an important and distinct part of Indian literature. Though Dalit narratives have been a part of the Indian social narratives since 11th century onwards, with works like Cekkilar's Periya Puranam documenting Dalit life, Dalit literature emerged into prominence and as a collective voice after 1960, starting with Marathi, and soon appeared in Hindi, Kannada, Telugu and Tamil languages, through Self narratives, like poems, short stories and most importantly autobiographies known for their fierce and often stark realism, and for its contribution to the Dalit politics.

It denounced as petty and false the then prevailing romanticism with the bourgeois Sadashiv pethi literature treated the whole Dalit issue, ignoring the social reality of appalling poverty and oppression of caste Hindus which was the result of the bourgeois character of this culture. It is often compared with the African-American literature especially in its depiction of issues of racial segregation and injustice, as seen in Slave narratives One of the first Dalit writers was Madara Chennaiah, an 11th-century cobbler-saint who lived in the reign of Western Chalukyas and who is also regarded by some scholars as the "father of Vachana poetry". Another poet who finds mention is Dohara Kakkaiah, a Dalit by birth, six of whose confessional poems survive.

In the 20th century, the term "Dalit literature" came into use in 1958, when the first conference of Maharashtra Dalit Sahitya Sangha was held at Mumbai, a movement driven by thinkers like Jyotiba Phule and Bhimrao Ambedkar. Baburao Bagul was pioneer of Dalit writings in Marathi. His first collection of stories, Jevha Mi Jat Chorali, published in 1963, created a stir in Marathi literature with its passionate depiction of a crude society and thus brought in new momentum to Dalit literature in Marathi; today it is seen by many critics as the epic of the Dalits, and was later made into a film by actor-director Vinay Apte. Gradually with other writers like. Namdeo Dhasal, these Dalit writings paved way from strengthening of Dalit politics.

2

Caste System's Effect and Impact of Dalits in India

CASTE SYSTEM IN INDIA

Caste system in India is a composite structure of different social classes in the Hindu religion. Caste system in India has a long history dating back to the ancient past. It dates back to that era when people used to believe that people were born into a particular social status. They also believed that experiences in past lives and good deeds can actually reincarnate one into higher social strata in the next life. The Indian caste system has gone places with the changes that have taken place in the society.

Education has been massively instrumental in bringing a change in the state of mind though a large part of a society, mostly the older generation is still under the curse of this social ostracism. In the present times, rural India is still under the restraints of the caste system, where still one's caste influences their food habits, their clothing and even their occupation. The 'dalits' are those, who are customarily poor households and they may be peasants, labourers, or servants doing menial jobs and also certain 'unclean' jobs like disposing of the dead. Urban areas today have been modified quite a great deal.

HISTORY OF THE DEVELOPMENT OF CASTE SYSTEM

The development of the caste system in India never seems to be having any universally accepted history as such. Though there is a general speculative faith that the earliest settlers to this land, the Indo-Aryans might have actually established the caste system, gradually placing them in the higher ladder of the society. There is a whole lot of controversy regarding the theory of the Indo-Aryan migration. The Hindu scriptures can also be taken into consideration in this regard, which has some passages that can be interpreted to sanction the caste system. This also indicates that the caste system is not an essential part of the Hindu religion.

The Vedas or the most ancient 'shruti' texts emphasise very less on the caste system, same is maintained in a hymn from the Rig Veda. Later scriptures like Bhagavad Gita and Manu Smriti propounds four Varnas, to be God's creation. There is a general idea believed by scholars that may be in the initial phases the caste system was a bit flexible. Migration from one caste to the other was possible by switching jobs. Various passages from Manu Smriti and other scriptures emphasise that the caste system in India was originally non-hereditary. Therefore, through these facts one gets an impression how the caste system developed in the later stages into a firm intricate structure from a bendable one in the earlier Vedic age.

VARNA AND JATI IN INDIA

Ancient Hindu scriptures have the citations of four varnas or colour, which is the basic social class in the caste system in India. Bhagavad-Gita says that varnas are decided on the grounds of Guna which is the amalgamation of the five elements of ether, air, fire, water and earth, and Karma which is the concept of action. In accordance with the powers of the born nature, works of Brahmins, Kshatriya, Vaishya, and Sudras differ. Four varnas that are mentioned by other shastras are the Brahmins destined as teachers, scholars and priests, the Kshatriyas as kings and warriors, the Vaishyas were the trading class and the Shudras were agriculturists, service providers, and some artisan groups. These are further classified into jatis. Another group excluded from the main society was called Parjanya or Antyaja. This is the group of former untouchables who were considered either the lower part of Sudras or beyond the caste system altogether. Varna and jati are two different concepts. Varna actually unifies the Hindu sub communities or jatis into the four groups. Jati or community is an endogamous group where the members marry within themselves. There is a further division of the sub communities into exogamous groups in terms of gotras. There are exactly thousands of sub castes or jatis in India, often with particular ecological ranges and a governmental or corporate structure. Jatis are the way in which caste is embodied for most practical purposes.

INDIAN CASTE AND SOCIAL STATUS

India is a multicultural, multilingual country which adopts a liberal attitude towards its diverse religious practices. One can find the prevalence of the caste system more in Hinduism than any other religion. Caste system in India has a history and it defines how caste has evolved through the ages. Caste and social status has always been quite puzzling. In the British era, they tried to equalise the caste system in India with the class system. Castes are the divisions, into which a certain part of the community belongs, which also enjoy social status accordingly. What is generally meant by the social status is the prestige or the honour that is being attached to one's position in the society. An individual might acquire more power and privilege due to a characteristic; this puts him among the privileged group of the people who enjoy high status. Brahmins are the priestly class, the protector of religion while the Kshatriyas hold the political power. Therefore caste and social status were inter-related. A higher caste individual was always looked with awe and reverence.

BRITISH IMPACT OVER CASTE SYSTEM IN INDIA

Some scholars are of the view that the caste system in India was never so rigid until the British interfered in the caste related issues in India. They almost equated caste with the class system that exist in their country and in the process tampered with the long established caste system. Even among the Dalits there were the distinctions of high and low, and conflicts often took place. Caste system was seen as a pointer of social standing, intellectual ability and occupation. Hence the British wanted to include it in the census. Moreover, it becomes obvious that British notions of cultural purity were interwoven with these judgments of people based on caste when reactions to censuses are examined. The British policies of `divide and rule` were again a step towards breaking up of the unity in which caste played an important role.

The listing of the population into rigid categories during the 10 year census led to the stiffening of caste identities. Caste system in India is a complex system of several distinctions, which have divided the society into the high and low strata. Lots of measures at present have been taken up by the government for the upliftment of the backward castes who do not have a social standing. There are disputes and complications regarding the caste system in India, which sometimes takes the shape of a sensitive issue. From the ancient times till the present day caste system has gone through a vast shift from how it was considered by the people and its rigidity.

ECONOMIC SOCIAL EXCLUSION, AND THE AMBEDKAR PRINCIPLES OF EMPLOYMENT

An increasing number of international companies and banks are investing in the countries of South Asia, particularly in India. This may have positive consequences for those countries. However the Dalit Solidarity Network UK believes it is increasingly important that foreign investors look carefully at their recruitment and employment policies in South Asia. Especially in India, there is a distinct and all-pervasive system of discrimination based on caste.

The United Nations and its agencies refer to it as "discrimination based on work and descent". What it means is that people who are born into specific groups, trades or castes are unable to escape from the stigma of their background or their origins. Hence those born as leather workers, barbers, agricultural workers or manual scavengers will remain in those employment sectors all their lives. Sometimes people escape from the system by moving to the large towns or cities, but overall the system remains heavily in place. "Dalit" is a term which has had increasing currency in recent years. Literally, it means "the oppressed". It encompasses peoples who used to be called "untouchables", or "Harijans"; who are often also referred to as "Scheduled Castes", because the way they are referred to in the constitution of India. "Adivasi" is a term which refers to those who are members of "Scheduled Tribes". That is, individuals who are racially distinct, as indigenous peoples, in contradistinction to the Caucasian peoples who invaded and settled India centuries ago.

There is legislation stemming from the Indian Constitution which outlaws caste discrimination. The Chair of the committee which wrote the constitution of the Republic of India was Dr. Ambedkar. He was a highly educated Dalit who was admitted into Gray's Inn and was called to the Bar. He also completed his second Doctoral studies in the London School of Economics and his thesis was subsequently published as 'The problem of the rupee'. Ambedkar became an all-India figure and the undisputed leader of the Dalits. He used this vantage-point successfully to question with blunt and militant doggedness the claim of Gandhi to represent all of India and especially the Dalits. He died in 1956 having served as India's first Law Minister. Under the constitution, the Republic of India is empowered to "promote with special care the educational and economic interests of the weaker parts of the people, and, in particular, of the Scheduled Castes and the Scheduled Tribes, and shall protect them from social injustice and all forms of exploitation". To achieve this aim, the State has used a two-fold approach: the provision of legal safeguards against discrimination; and a "Reservation Policy" in the State sector and State Supported Sector Subsequently, there has been further legislation, which has introduced penalties for specific examples of caste discrimination. These include the 1989 Prevention of Atrocities Act, the 1993 Protection of Human Rights Act, and the 1993 Employment of Manual Scavengers Act. However, these laws are far from effective. The

Reservation Policy allocates 17% of public sector jobs to Scheduled Castes, and a further 8% to Scheduled Tribes. This approximately reflects their respective percentages in the population as a whole. Since the inception of the Reservation Policy following independence in 1947, there has been a significant increase in the number of Dalit and Adivasi government employees, but this is for a population of between about 250 million Dalits and Adivasis (167 million Dalits, and 86 million Adivasis, in 2001).

Table. Government Employment Under Reservation

Year	Dalits	Adivasis	Others
1956	212,754	22,549	1,184,748
2003	540,220	211,345	2,517,780

Table. Percentage Share in Government Employment

Year	Dalits	Adivasis	Others
1956	14.98	1.59	83.43
2003	16.52	6.46	77.01

Table. Employment Under Reservation in Public Sector Undertakings

Year	Dalits	Adivasis	Others
1970	40,640	12,309	494,680
2003	296,388	138,504	1,198,106

Table. Percentage Share in Public Sector Undertaking

Year	Dalits	Adivasis	Others
1970	7.42	2.25	90.33
2003	18.15	0.48	73.37

Table. Percentage Share of Employees in Public Sector banks

Posts	1978			2000		
	SC	ST	Others	SC	ST	Other
Officers	2.04	0.34	97.62	12.51	4.22	83.27
Clerks	10.34	1.82	87.86	14.88	4.76	80.36
Sub staff	16.25	2.09	81.67	24.47	6.25	69.28

From the figures it can be seen that, 60 years after Independence, the raw percentages in government employment and public sector undertakings now do very roughly reflect the percentages of the population which are Dalit and Advasi. Because the Reservation Policy does not extend to the private sector recruitment is not done just as to quota systems.

Therefore, it is not possible to get comparative figure for the proportion of Dalits and Adivasi employed in the private sector, nor—most importantly—the seniority of jobs they hold. This is unfortunate, because the private sector, in relation to the State Sector and State Supported Sector, is rather a big player. 76% of the workforce is engaged in the private sector and only 24% is employed in the State Sector and the State Supported Sector. The present context is also that the State Sector and the State Supported Sector are shrinking, while the private sector is expanding.

It is estimated that 90% of the Dalit and Adivasi workforce is engaged in menial jobs in the Private Sector. In practice, they have very little—and sometimes no-protection against discrimination. It remains extremely difficult for the 25% of the population referred to by the government as Scheduled Castes and Scheduled Tribes, to overcome the discrimination they face. This is a negative situation, both in terms of human rights, and in terms of economic potential. In the New York Times recently described the typing competition, in English, the journalist had with an eight-year-old Dalit girl in a village "about an hour's drive—and ten centuries—from Bangalore, India's Silicon Valley".

The eight year old, he said, "left me in the dust, to the cheering delight of her classmates". It is important to examine the potential which is being lost because of the caste system. The United Progressive Alliance government in New Delhi is committed to exploring the expansion of the reservation system, into the private sector. In the Indian Express, the state government of Maharashtra is already preparing such legislation. Foreign investment in India is high, and increasing, not the least because it is viewed as a stable country with a high growth rate. Economically, India is a "happening" country. The caste system has specific effects, when it comes to recruitment of workers for industries which are being developed with outside capital and technological know-how. To respond to this situation DSN-UK, a member of the International Dalit Solidarity Network, is proposing a set of employment principles for foreign investors in South Asia. After a series of consultations spread over a year with the private, public, and charities sectors, we have finalised what we shall call the Ambedkar Principles, and are pleased to be launching them formally on the 20 July 2006.

CASTE AND SOCIAL STATUS

Traditionally, although the political power lay with the Kshatriyas, historians portrayed the Brahmins as custodians and interpreters of Dharma, who enjoyed much prestige and many advantages. Fa Hien, a Buddhist pilgrim from China, visited India around 400 AD. "Only the lot of the Chandals he found unenviable; outcastes by reason of their degrading work as disposers of dead, they were universally shunned... But no other part of the population were notably disadvantaged, no other caste distinctions attracted comment from the Chinese pilgrim, and no oppressive caste 'system' drew forth his surprised censure.".

In this period kings of Sudra and Brahmin origin were as common as those of Kshatriya varna and caste system was not wholly prohibitive and repressive. The castes did not constitute a rigid description of the occupation or the social status of a group. Since British society was divided by class, the British attempted to equate the Indian caste system to their own social class system. They saw caste as an indicator of occupation, social standing, and intellectual ability. Intentionally or unintentionally, the caste system became more rigid during the British Raj, when the British started to enumerate castes during the ten year census and codified the system under their rule. The Harijans, or the people outside the caste system, had the lowest social status. The Harijans, earlier referred to as untouchables by some, worked in what were seen as unhealthy, unpleasant or polluting jobs. In the past, the Harijans suffered from social segregation and restrictions, in addition to extreme poverty. They were not allowed temple worship with others, nor water from the same sources. Persons of higher castes would not interact with them. If somehow a member of a higher caste came into physical or social contact with an untouchable, the member of the higher caste was defiled, and had to bathe thoroughly to purge him or herself of the impurity. Social discrimination developed even among the Harijans; sub-castes among Harijans, such as the *dhobi* and *nai,* would not interact with lower-order *Bhangis,* who were described as "outcastes even among outcastes". Sociologists have commented on the historical advantages offered by a rigid social structure as well as its drawbacks.

While caste is now seen as anachronistic, in its original form the caste system served as an instrument of order in a society where mutual consent rather than compulsion ruled; where the ritual rights and the economic obligations of members of one caste or sub-caste were strictly circumscribed in relation to those of any other caste or sub-caste; where one was born into one's caste and retained one's station in society for life; where merit was inherited, where equality existed within the caste, but inter-caste relations were unequal and hierarchical. A well-defined system of mutual interdependence through a division of labour created security within a community. In addition, the division of labour on the basis of ethnicity allowed immigrants and foreigners to quickly integrate into their own caste niches.

The caste system played an influential role in shaping economic activities, where it functioned much like medieval European guilds, ensuring the division of labour, providing for the training of apprentices and, in some cases, allowing manufacturers to achieve narrow specialization. For instance, in certain regions, producing each variety of cloth was the speciality of a particular sub-caste. Additionally, some philosophers have argued that the majority of people would be comfortable in stratified endogamous groups, as they were in ancient times.

CASTE MOBILITY

Some scholars believe that the relative ranking of other castes was fluid or differed from one place to another prior to the arrival of the British. Sociologists such as Bernard Buber and Marriott McKim describe how the perception of the caste system as a static and textual stratification has given way to the perception of the caste system as a more processual, empirical and contextual stratification. Other sociologists such as Y.B Damle have applied theoretical models to explain mobility and flexibility in the caste system in India.

These scholars, groups of lower-caste individuals could seek to elevate the status of their caste by attempting to emulate the practices of higher castes. Flexibility in caste laws permitted very low-caste religious clerics such as Valmiki to compose the Ramayana, which became a central work of Hindu scripture. There is also precedent of certain Shudra families within the temples of the Sri Vaishnava sect in South India elevating their caste.

The following is a list of changes in varna cited in Hindu texts:

- Manu eldest son [Priyavrata] became king, a Kshatriya. Out of his ten sons seven became kings while three became Brahman. Their names were Mahavira, Kavi and Savana.
- Kavash -ailush was born to a Sudra and attained varn of a Rishi. He became mantra-drashta to numerous Vedic mantras in Rig-Veda 10th Mandal.
- Jabala's son [Satyakama] born from unknown father became Rishi by his qualities.
- [Matanga] became a Rishi after his birth in low Varna.

Some psychologists, mobility across broad caste lines may have been "minimal", though sub-castes (jatis) may have changed their social status over the generations by fission, relocation, and adoption of new rituals. Sociologist M. N. Srinivas has also debated the question of rigidity in Caste. In an ethnographic study of the Coorgs of Karnataka, he observed considerable flexibility and mobility in their caste hierarchies. He asserts that the caste system is far from a rigid system in which the position of each component caste is fixed for all time; instead, movement has always been possible, especially in the middle regions of the hierarchy. It was always possible for groups born into a lower caste to "rise to a higher position by adopting vegetarianism and teetotalism" *i.e.* adopt the customs of the higher castes. While theoretically "forbidden", the process was not uncommon in practice. The concept of sanskritization, or the adoption of upper-caste norms by the lower castes, addressed the complexity and fluidity of caste relations.

The fact that many of the dynasties were of obscure origin suggests some social mobility: a person of any caste, having once acquired political power, could also acquire a genealogy connecting him with the traditional lineages and conferring Kshatriya status. A number of new castes, such as the Kayasthas (scribes) and Khatris (traders). The Brahmanic sources, they originated from intercaste marriages, but this is clearly an attempt at rationalizing their rank in the hierarchy. Khatri appears to be unquestionably a Prakritised form of the Sanskrit Kshatriya. Many of these new castes played a major role in society. The hierarchy of castes did not have a uniform distribution throughout the country.

REFORMS

There have been challenges to the caste system from the time of Buddha, Mahavira and Makkhali Gosala. Opposition to the system of varna is regularly asserted in the Yoga Upanicsads and is a constant feature of Cîna-âcâra tantrism, a Chinese-derived movement in Asom; both date to the medieval era.

The Nâtha system, which was founded by Matsya-indra Nâtha and Go-rakcsa Nâtha in the same era and spread throughout India, has likewise been consistently opposed to the system of varna. Many Bhakti period saints rejected the caste discriminations and accepted all castes, including untouchables, into their fold. During the British Raj, this sentiment gathered steam, and many Hindu reform movements such as Brahmo Samaj and Arya Samaj renounced caste-based discrimination. The inclusion of so-called untouchables into the mainstream was argued for by many social reformers. Mahatma Gandhi called them "Harijans" (children of God) although that term is now considered patronizing and the term Dalit (downtrodden) is the more commonly used.

Gandhi's contribution towards the emancipation of the untouchables is still debated, especially in the commentary of his contemporary Dr. B.R. Ambedkar, an untouchable who frequently saw Gandhi's activities as detrimental to the cause of upliftment of his people. The practice of untouchability was formally outlawed by the Constitution of India in 1950, and has declined significantly since then, to the point of a society allowing former untouchables to take high political office, like former President K. R. Narayanan, who took office in 1997, and former Chief Justice K. G. Balakrishnan.

MODERN STATUS OF THE CASTE SYSTEM

In some rural areas and small towns, the caste system is still very rigid. Caste is also a factor in the politics of India. The Government of India has officially documented castes and sub-castes, primarily to determine those deserving reservation (positive discrimination in education and jobs) through the census. The Indian reservation system, though limited in scope, relies entirely on quotas. The Government lists consist of Scheduled Castes, Scheduled Tribes and Other Backward Classes:

SCHEDULED CASTES (SC)

Scheduled castes generally consist of "Dalit". The present population is 16% of the total population of India (around 160 million). For example, the Delhi state has 49 castes listed as SC.

SCHEDULED TRIBES (ST)

Scheduled tribes generally consist of tribal groups. The present population is 7% of the total population of India *i.e.* around 70 million.

OTHER BACKWARD CLASSES (OBC)

The Mandal Commission covered more than 3000 castes under OBC Category and stated that OBCs form around 52% of the Indian population. However, the National Sample Survey puts the figure at 32%. There is substantial debate over the exact number of OBCs in India; it is generally estimated to be sizable, but many believe that it is lower than the figures quoted by either the Mandal Commission or the National Sample Survey.

The caste-based reservations in India have led to widespread protests, such as the 2006 Indian anti-reservation protests, with many complaining of reverse discrimination against the forward castes (the castes that do not qualify for the reservation). Many view negative treatment of forward castes as socially divisive and equally wrong.

CASTE SYSTEM AMONG NON-HINDUS

In some parts of India, Christians are stratified by sect, location, and the castes of their predecessors, usually in reference to upper class Syrian Malabar Nasranis. Christians in Kerala are divided into several communities, including Syrian Christians and the so-called "Latin" or "New Rite" Christians. Syrian Christians derive status within the caste system from the tradition that they are converted Namboodiris and Jews, who were evangelized by St. Thomas.

Writers Arundhati Roy and Anand Kurian have written personal accounts of the caste system at work in their community. Syrian Christians, especially Knanaya Christians, tend to be endogamous and not to intermarry with other Christian castes. The Latin Rite Christians were among the scheduled castes in the coastal belt of Kerala, where fishing was the primary occupation. They were actively converted by missionaries in the 16th and 19th centuries.

These missionary activities were carried out by Western Latin Rite missionaries who did not understand the significance of the caste system in India; none of the Syrian churches had participated in such activities among the scheduled castes of India because they were aware of the prejudices of the caste system. The government of India later granted this group OBC status. Very rarely are there intermarriages between Syrian Christians and Latin Rite Christians Anthropologists have noted that the caste hierarchy among Christians in Kerala is much more polarized than the Hindu practices in the surrounding areas, due to a lack of jatis. Also, the caste status is kept even if the sect allegiance is switched (*i.e.* from Syrian Catholic to Syrian Orthodox).

In the Indian state of Goa, mass conversions were carried out by Portuguese Latin missionaries from the 16th century onwards. The Hindu converts retained their caste practices. The continued maintenance of the caste system among the Christians in Goa is attributed to the nature of mass conversions of entire villages, as a result of which existing social stratification was not affected. The Portuguese colonists, even during the Goan Inquisition, did not do anything to change the caste system. Thus, the original Hindu Brahmins in Goa now became Christian Bamons and the Kshatriya became Christian noblemen called Chardos. The Christian clergy became almost exclusively Bamon. Vaishyas who converted to Christianity became Gauddos, and Shudras became Sudirs.

Finally, the Dalits or "Untouchables" who converted to Christianity became Maharas and Chamars, the latter an appellation of the anti-Dalit ethnic slur Chamaar. Units of social stratification, termed "castes" by many, have developed among Muslims in some parts of South Asia. Sources indicate that the castes among Muslims developed as the result of close contact with Hindu culture and Hindu converts to Islam. The Sachar Committee's report commissioned by the government of India and released in 2006 documents the continued stratification in Muslim society.

Among Muslims, those who are referred to as Ashrafs are presumed to have a superior status derived from their foreign Arab ancestry, while the Ajlafs are assumed to be converts from Hinduism, and have a lower status. In addition, the Arzal caste among Muslims was regarded by anti-caste activists like Ambedkar as the equivalent of untouchables. In the Bengal region of India, some Muslims stratify their society just as to 'Quoms'. While many scholars have asserted that the Muslim castes are not as acute in their discrimination as those of the Hindus, some like Ambedkar argued that the social evils in Muslim society were "worse than those seen in Hindu society". The Buddhists also had a caste system.

In Sri Lanka, the Rodis might have been outcast by the Sri Lankan Buddhists due to the absence of ahimsa (non-violence), a central tenet of Buddhism, among their beliefs. The writer Raghavan, "That a form of worship in which human offerings formed the essential ritual would have been anathema to the Buddhist way of life goes without saying; and it needs no stretch of imagination that any class of people in whom the cult prevailed or survived even in an attenuated form would have been pronounced by the sangha (*i.e.* the Buddhist clergy) as exiles from the social order." Savarkar believed that the status of the backward castes (*e.g.* Chamar) that performed non-violence only worsened.

When Ywan Chwang traveled to South India after the period of the Chalukyan Empire, he noticed that the caste system had existed among the Buddhists and Jains. Jains also had castes in places such as Bihar. For example, in the village of Bundela, there were several "*jaats*" (groups) amongst the Jains. A person of one "*jaat*" cannot intermingle with a Jain or another "jaat". They also could not eat with the members of other "jaats". The Sikh Gurus criticized the hierarchy of the caste system.

While some castes were widely perceived as being better or higher than others (*e.g.* Brahmins being higher than others), they preached that all parts of society were valuable and that merit and hard-work were essential aspects of life. In the Shiromani Gurdwara Prabandhak Committee, out of 140 seats, 20 are reserved for low caste Sikhs. However, the quota system has attracted much criticism due to the lack of meritocracy, since merit is considered the single most important component of winning a seat. Baha'i Faith has grown to prominence in India, since its philosophy of the unity of humanity attracted many of the lower castes.

CASTE-RELATED VIOLENCE

Caste-related violence and hate crimes in India have occurred despite the gradual reduction of casteism in the country. A report by Human Rights Watch, "Dalits and indigenous peoples (known as Scheduled Tribes or adivasis) continue to face discrimination, exclusion, and acts of communal violence. Laws and policies adopted by the Indian government provide a strong basis for protection, but are not being faithfully implemented by local authorities."

IN 2006 DALIT PROTESTS IN MAHARASHTRA

In November-December 2006, the desecration of a Ambedkar statue in Kanpur (Uttar Pradesh) triggered violent protests by Dalits in Maharashtra. Several people remarked that the protests were fueled by the Kherlanji Massacre. During the violent protests, the Dalit protestors set three trains on fire, damaged over 100 buses and clashed with police. At least four deaths and many more injuries were reported. Later, the Kanpur Police arrested a Dalit youth Arun Kumar Balmiki for desecrating the Ambedkar statue.

The police, the youth had "admitted to having damaged the statue in a drunken state along with two friends". Earlier in a similar case, a Dalit youth was held for desecrating an Ambedkar statue in Gulbarga, Karnataka. In response to these protests, Raj Thackeray drew attention to another incident in Kherlanji, in which a Dalit allegedly raped a girl and killed her. Thackeray demanded action on those responsible for the rape and the subsequent death of the girl, and also remarked that nobody helped the girl's family.

ANDHRA PRADESH

This state is considered to be one of the most caste-crime infested places of India which has had many Dalit Massacres like Chundur Massacre, Neerukonda Massacre etc.

RAJASTHAN

In the Indian province of Rajasthan, between the years 1999 and 2002, crimes against Dalits average at about 5024 a year, with 46 killings and 138 cases of rape.

TAMIL NADU

The state of Tamil Nadu has witnessed several caste-based incidents both against Dalits and Brahmins. In 2000, three young men belonging to the Dalit undercaste were killed in the Cuddalore district of Tamil Nadu. This fuelled some localized violence in the caste-sensitive region, which has seen numerous caste-related incidents in which the majority of the victims have been Dalits. Six of the killings have been registered as murders under the Indian Penal Code and others as "Deaths under suspicious circumstances". No arrests have been made in these cases. However, several Dalits have been arrested as goondas (hoodlums).

The Chief minister of Tamil-Nadu, M. Karunanidhi, has been accused of having an "anti-Dalit" bias by the radical organization "Dalit Panthers of India". Theories concerning these crimes against Dalits range from "alcohol bootleggers opposing prohibition movements among Dalits" to "inter-caste relations between an Vanniya boy and a Dalit girl". Political parties sympathetic to the Dalits have protested against these incidents and have alleged systemic biases against Dalits in several parts of the country.

PUNJAB

On 25 May 2009, violence and rioting broke out when thousands of protesters took to the streets in almost all major towns and cities in the Indian state of Punjab after a dalit preacher, Sant Ramanand, was attacked in a temple in Vienna, Austria. He was among 16 people injured, including another preacher Sant Nirajnan Dass, and later died in hospital. Both the preachers were from a low-caste Sikh sect which has a large following in parts of Punjab and had travelled to Vienna to conduct a special service. Several high-caste Sikh groups had apparently opposed his presence and threatened violence. This happened after the preacher had reportedly made remarks about the Sikh groups.

Bant Singh Case of Punjab

On the evening of January 5, 2006 Bant Singh, a poor Sikh

Dalit, was attacked by unknown assailants. His injuries necessitated medical amputation. He alleges that this was in retaliation for actively working to secure justice for his daughter, who was gang raped by upper caste members of his village in Punjab five years earlier. A 55-year-old Dalit Sikh woman, Sawinder Kaur has been tortured, stripped and tied to a tree in Ram Duali village of Punjab because her nephew eloped with a girl from the same community.

The police arrested four persons for allegedly committing the crime on 9 September 2007. In January, 1999 four members of the village panchayat of Bhungar Khera village in Abohar paraded a handicapped Dalit woman naked through the village. No action was taken by the police, despite local Dalit protests.

It was only on July 20 that the four panchayat members were arrested, after the State Home Department was compelled to order an inquiry into the incident. A Dalit Sikh woman, Sukhwinder Kaur of Sumel Kheri village was molested and beaten up by an octroi contractor of Malaudh when she resisted his attempt to sexually exploit her.

KHERLANJI MASSACRE

On September 29, 2006, four members of the Bhotmange family belonging to the Dalit underclass were slaughtered in Kherlanji, a small village in Bhandara district of Maharashtra. The women of the family, Surekha and Priyanka, were paraded naked in public, then allegedly gang-raped before being murdered.

Although initially ascribed by the media and by the Human Rights Watch to upper castes, the criminal act was actually carried out by Kunbi caste (classified as Other Backward Classes by Government of India) farmers for having opposed the requisition of the Dalit land to have a road built over it.

On November 23, 2006, some members of the Dalit community in the nearby district of Chandrapur staged a protest regarding this incident. The protesters allegedly turned violent and threw stones. The police resorted to baton-charging the protestors to control the situation. Dalit leaders, however, denied that they had first resorted to violent and stated that they had been "protesting in peace".

CASTE POLITICS IN INDIA

Identity Politics has become a prominent subject in the Indian politics in the past few years. Rise of low castes, religious identities, linguistic groups and ethnic conflicts have contributed to the significance of identity politics in India. The discourse on Identity, many scholars feel, is distinctly a modern phenomenon.

Craig Calhoun aptly describes the situation when he argues that it is in the modern times we encounter intensified efforts at consolidating individual and categorical identities and reinforce selfsameness. This is primarily a modern phenomenon because some scholars feel that emphasis on identity based on a central organising principle of ethnicity, religion, language, gender, sexual preferences, or caste positions, etc., are a sort of "compelling remedy for anonymity" in an otherwise impersonal modern world.

It is thus said to be a "pattern of belonging, a search for comfort, an approach to community." However, the complex social changes and the imbrications of various forces, factors and events in this modern world have rendered such production and recognition of identities problematic. This is to say that any search for an 'authentic self or identity' is not an innocent and announced possibility; it involves negotiating other, often overlapping and contested, heterodox or multiple 'selves'.

Cascardi succinctly elucidates this by observing, "the modern subject is defined by its insertion into a series of separate value-spheres, each one of which tends to exclude or attempts to assert its priority over the rest", thereby rendering identity-schemes problematic.

Nonetheless, the concerns with individual and collective identity that simultaneously seeks to emphasise differences and attempt to establish commonality with others similarly distinguished, have become a universal venture.

WHAT IS IDENTITY POLITICS

But the question is how do discourses on identity fit into the political landscape? What are the political underpinnings of these discourses on identity? What are the organising principles of movements that characterise themselves as those based on identity concerns?

Can we define movements of workers as an instance of identity politics? In short what is the politics of identity and what are its organising principles? Identity Politics is said to "signify a wide range of political activity and theorising founded in the shared experiences of injustice of members of certain social groups".

As a political activity it is thus considered to signify a body of political projects that attempts a "recovery from exclusion and denigration" of groups hitherto marginalised on the basis of differences based on their 'selfhood' determining characteristics like ethnicity, gender, sexual preferences, caste positions, etc. Identity politics thus attempts to attain empowerment, representation and recognition of social groups by asserting the very same markers that distinguished and differentiated them from the others and utilise those markers as an assertion of selfhood and identity based on difference rather than equality.

Contrastingly placed, it is to imply that adherents of identity politics essentialise certain markers that fix the identities of social groups around an ensemble of definitional absolutes. These markers may be those of language, culture, ethnicity, gender, sexual preferences, caste positions, religion, tribe, race, etc. institutionalised in jargons, metaphors, stereotypes, and academic literature and reinforced through practices of positive discrimination or affirmative action.

The proponents of identity politics thus, assign the primacy of some "essence" or a set of core features shared only by members of the collectivity and no others and accepts individual persons as singular, integral, altogether harmonious and unproblematic identities. These core markers are different from associational markers like those of the workers who are defined more by their common interests rather than by certain core essential naturally 'given' identity attributes of the groups engaged in identity politics. Though many would argue that "worker" was an identity deserving legitimacy and as a group, its movements can be referred to as identity Politics, but probably the term "identity politics" as a body of political projects implied to in contemporary discourses refers to certain essential, local and particular categorical identities rather than any universalising ideals or agenda.

The adherents of identity politics utilise the power of myths, cultural symbols and kinship relations to mould the feeling of shared community and subsequently politicise these aspects to claim recognition of their particular identities. The strongest criticism against Identity Politics is that it often challenged by the very same markers upon which the sense of self or community is sought to be built.

It is despite the fact that identity politics is engaged in numerous aspects of oppression and powerlessness, reclaiming and transforming negative scripts used by dominant groups into powerful instruments for building positive images of self and community. In other words the markers that supposedly defines the community are fixed to the extent that they harden and release a process of ingroup essentialism that often denies internal dialogicality within and without the group and itself becomes a new form of closure and oppression.

Identity Politics as a field of study can be said to have gained intellectual legitimacy since the second half of the twentieth century, *i.e.*, between 1950s and 1960s in the United States when large scale political movements of the second wave-feminists, Black Civil Rights, Gay and Lesbian Liberation movements and movements of various Indigenous groups in the U.S. and other parts of the world were being justified and legitimated on the basis of claims about injustices done to their respective social groups.

However, as scholars like Heyes point out that although 'Identity Politics' can draw on intellectual precursors from Mary Wollstonecraft to Frantz Fanon, writing that actually uses this specific phrase-Identity Politics-is limited almost exclusively to the last 15 years.

IDENTITY POLITICS IN INDIA

In India we find that despite adoption of a liberal democratic polity after independence, communities and collective identities have remained powerful and continue to claim recognition. In fact, Beteille has shown that the Indian polity has consistently tried to negotiate the allegiance to a liberal spirit and the concerns and consciousness of community.

Bikhu Parekh this process has recognised a wide array of autonomous and largely self governing communities. It has sought to reconcile itself as an association of individuals and a community of communities, recognising both individuals and communities as bearer of rights.

It was probably this claim for and granting of recognition of particular identities by the postindependence state of India that led many scholars to believe that a material basis for the enunciation of identity claims has been provided by the post-independent state and its structures and institutions. In other words the state is seen as an "active contributor to identity politics through the creation and maintenance of state structures which define and then recognise people in terms of certain identities".

Thus, we find identity politics of various hues abound in India, the most spectacular however, are those based on language, religion, caste, ethnicity or tribal identity. But having said this it would be wrong on our part to assume that each of these identity markers operate autonomously, independent of the overlapping influence of the other makers. In other words a homogenous linguistic group may be divided by caste affiliations that may be subdivided by religious orientations or all may be subsumed under a broader ethnic claim.

Caste

Caste-based discrimination and oppression have been a pernicious feature of Indian society and in the post-independence period its imbrications with politics have not only made it possible for hitherto oppressed caste-groups to be accorded political freedom and recognition but has also raised consciousness about its potential as a political capital. In fact Dipankar Gupta has poignantly exposed this contradiction when he elaborates the differences between Ambedkar and Mandal Commission's view of caste. While the former designed the policy of reservations or protective discrimination to remove untouchability as an institution from Indian social life and polity, the latter considered caste as an important political resource.

Actually, the Mandal commission can be considered the intellectual inspiration in transforming castebased identity to an asset that may be used as a basis for securing political and economic gains. Though it can also be said that the upper castes by virtue of their predominant position were already occupying positions of strengths in the political and economic system, and when the Mandal heightened the consciousness of the'Dalits' by recognisisng their disadvantage of caste-identity as an advantage the confrontation ensues.

The caste system, which is based on the notions of purity and pollution, hierarchy and difference, has despite social mobility, been oppressive towards the Shudras and the outcastes who suffered the stigma of ritual impurity and lived in abject poverty, illiteracy and denial of political power. The origin of confrontational identity politics based on caste may be said to have its origin on the issue of providing the oppressed caste groups with state support in the form of protective discrimination.

This group identity based on caste that has been reinforced by the emergence of political consciousness around caste identities is institutionalised by the caste-based political parties that profess to uphold and protect the interests of specific identities including the castes. Consequently, we have the upper caste dominated BJP, the lower caste dominated BSP (Bhaujan Samaj Party) or the SP (Samajwadi Party), including the fact that left parties (for example use of caste idioms for mobilising agricultural labourers in Andhra Pradesh elections in 1950) have tacitly followed the caste pattern to extract mileage in electoral politics. The Cumulative result of the politicisation can be summarised by arguing that caste-based identity politics has had a dual role in Indian society and polity. It relatively democratised the caste-based Indian society but simultaneously undermined the evolution of class-based organisations.

In all, caste has become an important determinant in Indian society and politics, the new session of organised politics and consciousness of caste affiliations learnt by the hitherto despised caste groups have transformed the contours of Indian politics where shifting caste-class alliances are being encountered.

The net effect of these mobilisations along caste-identities have resulted not only in the empowerment of newly emerging groups but has increased the intensity of confrontational politics and possibly leading to a growing crisis of governmentally.

Religion

Another form of identity politics is that effected through the construction of a community on the shared bond of religion. In India, Hinduism, Islam, Sikhism, Christianity, and Zoroastrianism are some of the major religions practised by the people. Numerically the Hindus are considered to be the majority, which inspires many Hindu loyalist groups like the RSS (Rashtriya Swayam Sevak Sangh) or the Siva Sena and political parties like the BJP (Bharatiya Janata Party) or the Hindu Mahasabha to claim that India is a Hindu State. These claims generate homogenising myths about India and its history.

These claims are countered by other religious groups who foresee the possibility of losing autonomy of practise of their religious and cultural life under such homogenising claims. This initiates contestations that have often resulted in communal riots.

The generally accepted myths that process the identity divide on religious lines centre on the 'appeasement theory', 'forcible religious conversions', general 'anti-Hindu' and thus 'anti-India' attitude of the minority religious groups, the 'hegemonic aspirations' of majority groups and 'denial of a socio-cultural space' to minority groups. Historically, the Hindu revivalist movement of the 19th century is considered to be the period that saw the demarcation of two separate cultures on religious basis-the Hindus and the Muslims that deepened further because of the partition. This division which has become institutionalised in the form of a communal ideology has become a major challenge for India's secular social fabric and democratic polity.

Though communalism for a major part of the last century signified Hindu-Muslim conflict, in recent years contestations between Hindus and Sikhs, Hindus and Christians have often crystallised into communal conflict. The rise of Hindu national assertiveness, politics of representational government, persistence of communal perceptions, and competition for the socio-economic resources are considered some of the reasons for the generation of communal ideologies and their transformation into major riots.

Identity schemes based on religion have become a major source of conflict not only in the international context but since the early 1990s it has also become a challenge for Indian democracy and secularism. The rise of majoritarian assertiveness is considered to have become institutionalised after the BJP, that along with its 'Hindu' constituents gave political cohesiveness to a consolidating Hindu consciousness, formed a coalition ministry in March 1998.

However, like all identity schemes the forging of a religious community glosses over internal differences within a particular religion to generate the "we are all of the same kind" emotion. Thus differences of caste groups within a homogenous Hindu identity, linguistic and sectional differences within Islam are shelved to create a homogenous unified religious identity.

In post-independence India the majoritarian assertion has generated its own antithesis in the form of minority religions assertiveness and a resulting confrontational politics that undermines the syncretistic dimensions of the civil society in India. The process through which this religious assertiveness is being increasingly institutionalised by a 'methodical rewriting of history' has the potential to reformulate India's national identity along communal trajectories.

Language

Identity claims based on the perception of a collectivity bound together by language may be said to have its origin in the pre-independence politics of the Congress that had promised reorganisation of states in the post-independent period on linguistic basis.

But it was the "JVP" (Jawaharlal Nehru, Vallabhbai Patel and Pattabhi Sitaramayya) Committee's concession that if public sentiment was "insistent and overwhelming", the formation of Andhra from the Teluguspeaking region of the then Madras could be conceded which as Michael Brecher mentions was the "opening wedge for the bitter struggle over states reorganisation which was to dominate Indian Politics from 1953 to 1956".

Ironically, the claim of separate states for linguistic collectivities did not end in 1956 and even today continues to confront the concerns of the Indian leadership. But the problem has been that none of the created or claimed states are mono-ethnic in composition and some even have numerically and politically powerful minorities. This has resulted in a cascading set of claims that continue to threaten the territorial limits of existing states and disputes over boundaries between linguistic states have continued to stir conflicts, as for instance the simmering tensions between Maharastra and Karnataka over the district of Belgaum or even the claims of the Nagas to parts of Manipur.

The linguistic divisions have been complicated by the lack of a uniform language policy for the entire country. Since in each state the dominant regional language is often used as the medium of instruction and social communication, the consequent affinity and allegiance that develops towards one's own language gets expressed even outside one's state of origin. For instance the formation of linguistic cultural and social groups outside one's state of origin helps to consolidate the unity and sense of community in a separate linguistic society.

Thus language becomes an important premise on which group identities are organised and establishes the conditions for defining the 'in-group' and 'out-group'. Though it is generally felt that linguistic states provide freedom and autonomy for collectivities within a heterogeneous society, critics argue that linguistic states have reinforced regionalism and has provided a platform for the articulation of a phenomenal number of identity claims in a country that has 1,652 'mother tongues' and only fourteen recognised languages around which states have been reorganised.

They argue that the effective result of recognition for linguistic groups has disembodied the feelings of national unity and national spirit in a climate where 'Maharastra for Marathis, Gujrat for Gujratis, etc." has reinforced linguistic mistrust and defined the economic and political goods in linguistic terms.

Ethnicity

There are two ways in which the concept of ethnic identity is used; one, it insiders the formation of identity on the basis of single attribute—language, religion, caste, region, etc.; two, it considers the formation of identity on the basis, of multiple attributes cumulatively. However, it is the second way formation of identity on the basis of more than one characteristics—culture, customs, region, religion or caste, which is considered as the most common way of formation of the ethnic identity.

The one ethnic identity is formed in relation to the other ethnic identity. The relations between more than one ethnic identities can be both harmonious and conflictual. Whenever there is competetion among the ethnic identities on the real or imaginary basis, it expressed in the form of autonomy movements, demand for session or ethnic riots.

CRITICISM

There has been criticism of the caste system from both within and outside of India. Criticism of the Caste system in Hindu society came both from the Hindu fold and Dalit.

HISTORICAL CRITICISM

Many bhakti period saints, including Nanak, Kabir, Caitanya, Dnyaneshwar, Eknath, Ramanuja and Tukaram, rejected all caste-based discrimination and accepted disciples from all the castes. Many Hindu reformers such as Swami Vivekananda believe that there is no place for the caste system in Hinduism.

The 15th century saint Ramananda accepted all castes, including untouchables, into his fold. Most of these saints subscribed to the Bhakti movements in Hinduism during the medieval period that rejected casteism. Nandanar, a low-caste Hindu cleric, also rejected casteism and accepted Dalits. Some other movements in Hinduism have also welcomed lower-castes into their fold, the earliest being the Bhakti movements of the medieval period.

Early Dalit politics involved many reform movements; these arose primarily as a reaction to the advent of Christian missionaries in India and their attempts to convert Dalits, who were attracted to the prospect of escaping the caste system. In the 19th Century, the Brahmo Samaj under Raja Ram Mohan Roy actively campaigned against untouchability and casteism. The Arya Samaj founded by Swami Dayanand also renounced discrimination against Dalits.

Sri Ramakrishna Paramahamsa and his disciple Swami Vivekananda founded the Ramakrishna Mission that participated in the emancipation of Dalits. Upper-caste Hindus such as Mannathu Padmanabhan participated in movements to abolish untouchability against Dalits; Padmanabhan opened his family temple to Dalits for worship. Narayana Guru, a pious Hindu and an authority on the Vedas, also criticized casteism and campaigned for the rights of lower-caste Hindus within the context of Hinduism.

The first upper-caste temple to openly welcome Dalits into their fold was the Laxminarayan Temple in Wardha in the year 1928; the move was spearheaded by reformer Jamnalal Bajaj. The caste system has also been criticized by many Indian social reformers. Some reformers, such as Jyotirao Phule and Iyothee Thass, argued that the lower caste people were the original inhabitants of India, who had been conquered in the ancient past by "Brahmin invaders." Mahatma Gandhi coined the term Harijan, a euphemistic word for untouchable, literally meaning Sons of God. B. R. Ambedkar, born in Hindu Dalit community, was a heavy critic of the caste system.

He pioneered the Dalit Buddhist movement in India, and asked his followers to leave Hinduism, and convert to Buddhism. India's first Prime Minister, Jawaharlal Nehru, based on his own relationship with Dalit reformer Ambedkar, supported the eradication of untouchability for the benefit of the Dalit community. In 1936, the Maharaja proclaimed that "outcastes should not be denied the consolations and the solace of the Hindu faith". Even today, the Sri Padmanabhaswamy temple that first welcomed Dalits in the state of Kerala is revered by the Dalit Hindu community.

CONTEMPORARY CRITICISM

Organizations such as the Rashtriya Swayamsevak Sangh have actively criticized the caste system. Some activists consider the caste system a form of racial discrimination. At the United Nations Conference Against Racism in Durban, South Africa in March 2001, participants condemned discrimination based on the caste system and tried to pass a resolution declaring caste as a basis for segregation and oppression a form of apartheid. However, no formal resolution was passed.

The alleged maltreatment of Dalits in India has been described by some authors as "India's hidden apartheid". Critics of the accusations point to substantial improvements in the position of Dalits in post-independence India, consequent to the strict implementation of the rights and privileges enshrined in the Constitution of India, as implemented by the Protection of Civil rights Act, 1955. They also note that India has had a Dalit president, K.R. Narayanan, and argue that the practise had disappeared in urban public life. William A. Haviland, however:

- Although India's national constitution of 1950 sought to abolish cast discrimination and the practice of untouchability, the caste system remains deeply entrenched in Hindu culture and is still widespread throughout southern Asia, especially in rural India. In what has been called India's "hidden apartheid", entire villages in many Indian states remain completely segregated by caste. Representing about 15 per cent of India's population—or some 160 million people—the widely scattered Dalits endure near complete social isolation, humiliation, and discrimination based exclusively on their birth status. Even a Dalit's shadow is believed to pollute the upper classes. They may not cross the line dividing their part of the village from that occupied by higher castes, drink water from public wells, or visit the same temples as the higher castes. Dalit children are still often made to sit in the back of classrooms.

Sociologists Kevin Reilly, Stephen Kaufman and Angela Bodino, while critical of casteism, conclude that modern India does not practice any apartheid since there is no state-sanctioned discrimination. They write that casteism in India is presently "not apartheid.

In fact, untouchables, as well as tribal people and members of the lowest castes in India benefit from broad affirmative action programmes and are enjoying greater political power. The Constitution of India places special emphasis on outlawing caste discrimination, especially the practice of untouchability.

CASTE AND RACE

Allegations that caste amounts to race were addressed and rejected by B.R. Ambedkar, an advocate for Dalit rights and critic of untouchability. He wrote that "The Brahmin of Punjab is racially of the same stock as the Chamar of Punjab. The Caste system does not demarcate racial division.

The Caste system is a social division of people of the same race", Such allegations have also been rejected by sociologists such as Andre Béteille, who writes that treating caste as a form of racism is "politically mischievous" and worse, "scientifically nonsensical" since there is no discernible difference in the racial characteristics between Brahmins and Scheduled Castes. He states, "Every social group cannot be regarded as a race simply because we want to protect it against prejudice and discrimination".

The Indian government also rejects the claims of equivalency between caste and racial discrimination, pointing out that the caste issues are essentially intraracial and intra-cultural. Indian Attorney General Soli Sorabjee insisted that "he only reason India wants caste discrimination kept off the agenda is that it will distract participants from the main topic: racism. Caste discrimination in India is undeniable but caste and race are entirely distinct".

Many scholars dispute the claim that casteism is akin to racism. Sociologist M. N. Srinivas has debated the question of rigidity in caste. Others have applied theoretical models to explain mobility and flexibility in the caste system in India. These scholars, groups of lower-caste individuals could seek to elevate the status of their caste by attempting to emulate the practices of higher castes.

In her book Democracy and Authoritarianism in South Asia, Pakistani-American sociologist Ayesha Jalal writes, "As for Hinduism, the hierarchical principles of the Brahmanical social order have always been contested from within Hindu society, suggesting that equality has been and continues to be both valued and practiced." In India, some observers felt that the caste system must be viewed as a system of exploitation of poor low-ranking groups by more prosperous high-ranking groups.

In many parts of India, land is largely held by high-ranking property owners of the dominant castes, who economically exploit low-ranking landless labourers and poor artisans. Matt Cherry claims that karma underpins the caste system, which traditionally determines the position and role of every member of Hindu society. Caste determines an individual's place in society, the work he or she may carry out, and who he or she may marry and meet. Hindus believe that the karma of previous life will determine the caste an individual will be (re)born into. On 29 March 2007, the Supreme Court of India, as an interim measure, stayed the law providing for 27% reservation for Other Backward Classes in educational institutions. This was done in response to a public interest litigation—Ashoka Kumar Thakur vs.

Union of India. The Court held that the 1931 census could not be a determinative factor for identifying the OBCs for the purpose of providing reservation. The court also observed, "Reservation cannot be permanent and appear to perpetuate backwardness". However, the Supreme Court later upheld the reservation.

3

Dalits Education in India

INTRODUCTION AND PURPOSE STATEMENT

From the moment a Hindu child is born in India, his or her opportunities for social and religious freedom are shaped through the influence of the caste system despite laws passed 50 years ago to abolish such discriminatory practices. Many children at the bottom of this caste system face a future of poverty, unemployment, illiteracy, abuse, sickness, and for girls, even rape and prostitution. Stemming from its 3000-year-old origins, the caste system is one of the world's longest surviving forms of social stratification.

People are divided by birth just as to one of four main castes, with yet another estimated 200 million categorized beneath this caste system. Many in society consider these people to be unclean and unworthy of basic human rights and label them "The Untouchables" or Dalits. In 1955, the Indian Parliament passed the Untouchability Offences Act, making the practice of castes illegal, however, it may take generations to remove the stigma and change the views and traditions of an entire society.

This lack of social justice for many, coupled with the desire to promote fair and equal treatment of the people within a country that is quickly gaining influence in the global market and economy, has made this topic one of extreme interest. Although many of these long-standing traditions continue to hold fast, India has also experienced significant changes during the last several decades. With the advancement of technology, some researchers no longer consider India to be classified as a developing country, but as a newly industrialized country. This classification includes several nations, such as Mexico and Thailand, with economies more advanced and developed than those in the developing world, yet without the full indicators that would classify it as a developed country. With the rapid increase of major global corporations choosing to outsource large portions of high technology jobs to India, the need for quality English medium education is vital if the country intends to continue to compete in that particular market.

Yet India continues to struggle with the needs of its individuals, especially in rural areas, with limitations that inhibit the ability to make the desired changes in a timely manner. Not only has the current government been unable to increase the number of schools and teachers needed to rectify the situation, but society itself has been resistant in some areas to the change of the social order embedded in the caste system. In an effort to affect change in a social structure that consists of an interdependent set of roles and norms, Dalit leaders have joined forces to demand what they refer to as a holistic reformation for their own people.

They describe this as a concern for the whole individual's physical, mental, emotional and spiritual development through education, economic support, health aid, and legal advocacy. By accepting the outside resources of International Non-Governmental Organizations, they feel they can make the changes necessary to reduce the educational and socioeconomic gap between the castes. The Dalit Empowerment International, a Non-Government Organization based in the United States, formed in 2002 in response to this corporate uprising of the Dalit people. The Dalit leaders at that time challenged the organization with a twofold request: to offer their children an English medium education, and to include Christian principles in the hope of transforming their worldview to one based on human dignity and self-worth, in an effort to create a new future. Working together with the already established All India Christian Council and other partners, the DEI uses its resources from the United States, Canada and the United Kingdom, to educate the western world about the situation of the Dalits and to gather financial and human resources to support ongoing work in India. A spokesperson for the DEI, the AICC is a coalition of over 3,000 Indian organizations and federations and proactively protects the interests of Christians, Muslims, Dalits, Tribals and Backward communities. Also, by joining together with AICC as well as another national overhead organization with four decades of educational experience, they feel they can use the expertise and experience to make a significant impact. Having volunteered with several non-profit and faith-based organizations, studying education and its societal role around the world has become an area of extreme interest for me. I chose to study the field of international comparative education in order to examine the effectiveness of such programmes in diverse cultural contexts.

Having met the president of the DEI at a symposium in the United States, I was intrigued by the overall approach and methods of their model. The organization situates the educational component within a framework of three other elements, human rights advocacy, health and medical needs, and economic development. I wanted to study in depth the effectiveness of this approach, and specifically this programme, and its religious implications within the established caste system. A substantial amount of research has been done to define quality education to confirm the educational inequities within the caste system and to acknowledge the addition of many INGOs in the global effort to create access to quality education for all.

However, little research examines the effectiveness of faith-based INGOs and their impact on an educational situation that is affected by another religious system. This study will add to the current literature by providing an evaluative look at one particular programme, which can add to our understanding of how such educational faith-based programmes could aid disadvantaged and stigmatized groups. In order to gain insight into the strategies of this organization, I used qualitative research methods including ethnographic evaluative techniques to conduct a formative programme evaluation. A programme evaluation of this sort seeks to appraise the quality of the education and the achievement of the stated goals, which is not only useful to the DEI programme administrators, but to other programmes as well. The purpose of a formative evaluation is to examine each of the components of a programme in such a way that specific changes could be made to enhance the programme, not to judge the overall worth or value of the programme.

My role as an evaluator is to present the specific findings to the leaders of the organization such that the appropriate stakeholders and decision makers can use it to guide future implementation.

Using the following questions, I evaluated four out of the DEI's 62 schools:

- How does this education programme plan to improve the future quality of life for Dalits?
- Does the DEI programme meet its proposed goals?
- What further areas of research will address the long term societal change that will be necessary for this programme and others to be effective?

To be as objective in my evaluation as possible, given the timeframe, resources and the fact that I would be the only evaluator, I used methodological triangulation by interviewing administrators, teachers and students, reviewing the program's literature and observing in the classroom. This process allowed me to compare the goals with the actual implementation practices in order to examine effectiveness of the programme in the schools observed.

This study focuses on both the practical application and logistics of this education as well as the religious aspect. Introducing educational practices which promote religious choice and enhance India's efforts towards a worldview of human dignity may be of key importance in providing information for future aid in the urgent educational needs within India today. The following parts present the research and the findings. To begin with, the background surrounding the disparity in education for the Dalit child, as well as the governmental policy, anti-conversion laws, and the specific goals of the DEI are described. Next, a series of questions that guided the research are discussed. Following this is a review of current literature on subjects that formed the foundation for this evaluation. This includes topics such as the inequities in education, NGO involvement, the use of English medium, the future implications of education for the Dalits, the paucity of similar studies evaluating other programmes, and finally educational programme evaluation theories.

This is followed by a detailed explanation of the data collection and methods that were used to gather the information to evaluate the programme. The findings are then analysed and the results of the evaluation are discussed. In the conclusion, the findings are summarized such that programme developers can use this material in the future to benefit the programme, as well as to inform readers of the issues and future implications of this research.

BACKGROUND

UNDERSTANDING CASTES

The plight of the Dalits must be understood, in order to have the cultural sensitivity needed to bring in an outside organization and use the resources effectively. The goal of closing the gap in education, so entrenched in thousands of years of religious or cultural practices will require time and skill, and much of it will have to do with teaching from a platform of education based on human rights.

As I began this study, it quickly became obvious that I could not ignore the religious element of the education, as it is so enmeshed in the cultural differences and discriminatory practices which lead to such a gap in achievement and attainment in the first place. As one director in India said:

- In the United States, you had discrimination between blacks and whites, and it was a social justice issue, which can be changed by laws over time. People were free to choose to be Christians, but were discriminated against because of their colour. In India, though, it is far deeper. It is a religious issue, if people remain Hindu, they are discriminated against, if they convert, they are fined and even persecuted. To try to change the discrimination, one must face the religious issue of caste.

It is historically understood that Hinduism was first established by an amalgamation of three different religious sects, Arayanism, Dravidianism and Animism and the four caste levels were a method of establishing social order, whereby each person had an occupational function. Traditionally, for example, the top level, the Brahmins, were considered the highest level and held the positions of priests and teachers.

The next group included the Kshatriyas, who held positions as the warriors and royalty. Then, the Vaisyas were given positions as moneylenders and traders. Finally, considered the lowest of the four levels, the Sudras carried out the menial jobs in society. The Dalits, or untouchables, or ati-Sudras were actually considered beneath all of these levels, performing the jobs that other members of society would not. To be touched or even crossed by the shadow of a Dalit made any other caste member unclean and ritualistic cleansing was required.

Though much of this structure has changed over time, as governmental order and economic models changed, the concept of social stratification has remained, in some areas more so than others. Through several grass roots efforts to empower individuals, the Dalits are now seeking societal change. The DEI, as one of these efforts, feels that by eliminating discriminatory practices in the classroom, and changing the beliefs within the family and the community, there can eventually be actual change at the government and societal level.

From their literature, they intend to be involved at all of these levels:

- Serving as an international advocate for Dalit rights is the heartbeat of the Dalit Empowerment International. Beginning with the United States government in Washington DC, DEI seeks to bring an end to caste-based discrimination and the resulting oppression the Dalit community experiences. DEI also represents Dalits internationally in the United Nations and at major conferences on human rights and religious liberties. Additionally, DEI seeks funding to underwrite legal fees for Dalits actively pursuing political and social change through the Indian legal system and all necessary constitutional means.

Therefore, educational practices can become a crucial part in this path towards change.

GOVERNMENTAL VIEWS

The people of India respect Gandhi as the founding father of the modern Indian nation. However, there is controversy as to his approach to try to abolish the caste system. Some feel that he merely tried to eradicate the practice of untouchability but did not do enough to touch the foundations of the stratification of caste.

He believed that "caste as it exists today is no doubt a travesty of the original fourfold division which only defined men's different callings". Gandhi attempted to teach by example that doing the menial labour of a Dalit should be considered as honourable as any other trade. It was actually Dr. Bhim Rao Babasaheb Ambedkar, a former Dalit, who founded the Indian Constitution in 1949 and attempted to abolish the foundation of the caste system itself in an effort to bring about the commitments made in the Constitution to promote equality.

Despite the strong beginnings, Dr. Ambedkar expressed his concerns that such an undertaking may seem impossible without a change in the thinking established by caste when he stated:

- There is no doubt; in my opinion, that unless you change your social order you can achieve little by way of progress. You cannot mobilize the community either for defence or for offence. You cannot build anything on the foundations of caste. You cannot build up a nation, you cannot build up a morality. Anything that you will build on the foundations of caste will crack and will never be whole. The only question remains to be considered is ... How to abolish caste? This is the question of supreme importance.

Other countries, though not affected by caste, also recognized the need to change societal norms and in 1974, UNESCO began to lay the foundations for human rights education. By 1978, the participants in the International Congress on the Teaching of Human Rights created specific and practical definitions by stating that human rights education and teaching must aim at:

- Fostering the attitudes of tolerance, respect and solidarity inherent in human rights
- Providing knowledge about human rights, in both their national and international dimensions, and the institutions established for their implementation
- Develop the individual's awareness of the ways and means by which human rights can be translated into social and political reality at both the national and international levels.

Following these efforts more than forty years after the creation of India's constitution, the UN Decade for Human Rights Education began in 1995 and has been influential in raising global awareness of educational inequities. It will continue to take time, however, to create curriculum based on practices that will change the thinking of the individual as well as the society. The DEI intends to support his effort.

India has become a central focus as various countries attempt to eradicate discriminatory practices through these educational efforts. For example, the United States House of Representatives just passed House Concurrent Resolution 139 on July 23, 2007, that addresses the ongoing problem of untouchability in India.

The resolution is the first of its kind from the United States Congress and the DEI has been involved at several levels of global awareness. Juxtaposed with this global awareness, however, is the continued effort by the Indian government to implement more anti-conversion laws in order to protect people from coercion and manipulation by what is considered any minority religion in India.

Anti-conversion laws have been passed through much controversy in eight of the 28 states and the specific language states:

- No person shall convert or attempt to convert, either directly or otherwise, any person from one religion to another by use of force or by inducement or by any fraudulent means, nor shall any person abet any such conversion.

Although these protective efforts are well founded due to past practices by different religious groups pressuring people to convert by way of inducement through education or medical aid, they create a dichotomous message that goes against the Constitution's Article 25 that promises free choice:

- Freedom of conscience and free profession, practice and propagation of religion.- Subject to public order, morality and health and to the other provisions of this Part, all persons are equally entitled to freedom of conscience and the right freely to profess, practice and propagate religion.

Though it is too complex a topic to discuss in this document, as the debate over coercion and choice through new knowledge can be subjective, one must be aware of the conflict in attempting to use any other religious educational foundation within various states in India.

GOALS OF DALIT EMPOWERMENT INTERNATIONAL

From the literature established by the DEI and through interviews with individuals involved in the education, it is clear that their goal is to accomplish each of the human rights agendas by including the egalitarian practices of Christianity as they build their curriculum. With this in mind, this study will attempt to compare the following mission statement and all of its underlying elements with the actual practices.

Their holistic efforts focus on four main areas:

- Education through English-based curriculum with trained national teachers

- Medical resources of vaccinations, healthcare, and medical interventions
- Economic Development by offering micro-loans and vocational training programmes
- Human Rights and Social Justice by serving as an international advocate for social change and new governmental policies

To incorporate each of these areas into the development of a community, the DEI establishes what it calls Community Education Centres as a central location for all four aspects of their charter. Though each of these areas is crucial to the advancement of developing societies, this document will focus specifically on the educational efforts. For the purpose of this document, the term CEC or DEI school will be interchangeable. To date, 62 CECs have been established in 13 states, serving over 10,000 students, through DEI's efforts to coordinate a global interest in the situation of the Dalit people. The DEI provides an excellent example to use for this study, because, unlike several other faith-based organizations such as World Vision and Compassion International, the DEI focuses strictly on the needs of the Dalit people. The DEI also has many collaborative sources with churches and other organizations within India.

These organizations are in agreement as to the strategic importance that an English and faith-based education brings to the Dalits, as a gateway to eradicating injustice, illiteracy and overcoming poverty. They have determined that some of the greatest opportunities for education and employment within India and around the world are given to those who are literate in English as well as their own state language. Also, since one of their main charters is to teach from a worldview based on human dignity and self-worth, the issue of faith is a key component in this study.

Dalits are choosing to convert primarily to the egalitarian beliefs of Buddhism, Islam and Christianity as a way out of a system that still holds great power, not only in India, but in other countries as well. The regions for developing schools are selected through careful research conducted by the DEI national leaders to locate areas of Dalit majority with the greatest needs, where no other comparable facilities exist, and no other full time holistic development projects are functioning. The DEI, the schooling is subsidized by the organization, but a nominal fee is charged to create a sense of ownership and accountability for the students and their families. DEI's child sponsorship programme brings in funds from around the world to provide the uniforms, books, a meal where needed, and to cover the teacher's salaries, the cost of the facility and other administrative costs. I was told that, "Many of these children are introduced to education for the first time, and the enthusiasm spreads as they take home what they have learned and share it with their families." A statement from the literature given to me by the director explains:

- To teach a Dalit is social service, but to destroy the social structure which made him illiterate, is social transformation. To open a new school in a Dalit village is a social service, but to motivate the Dalit hungry and illiterate parent to send his child to school even if it meant less income for the household is social transformation. To provide free food to a Dalit is a social service, but to educate and empower him to earn his own food is social transformation.

This document will evaluate the DEI's approach of holistic transformation within a group of people in order to shed light on the goal of accomplishing global awareness and support for the struggle for freedom through education.

CRITICAL LITERATURE REVIEW

In order to lay the foundation that guided the planning and design of this research, the following part will review current literature on four essential subjects. First, it discusses established discrimination and inequities in education for Dalits and the need for human rights education. This is followed by studies about involvement of INGOs and their participation in education or social justice worldwide, as well as the paucity of studies evaluating similar programmes. Third, it discusses global debates over whether to teach from an English medium of instruction. Finally, it establishes the framework of educational ethnography and programme evaluation theories that were used as the foundation of this study.

DISCRIMINATORY PRACTICES AND THE NEED FOR HUMAN RIGHTS EDUCATION

Numerous studies have been done to understand the level of disparity between the treatment of the Dalits and their upper caste peers. Education inequality is merely a portion of the complex nature of what Prime Minister Singh acknowledges as "India's hidden apartheid". Despite the Constitutional Directive of universal elementary education and Education for All goals, the gap in educational access and achievement between the Dalits and the general population in India is still quite large and continues to increase, which is of great concern in the globalizing world today. Dalits, also referred to in the Constitution as the Scheduled Castes make up approximately 16.2% of the population of India, yet only 41.5% of Dalits in rural India were considered literate compared to the national literacy rate of 64.8%.

Using econometric estimates on data gathered from 16 states and 33,000 rural households, in 1765 villages, Borooah and Iyer found that Dalit enrollment was lower than for Hindus for various reasons such as income, psychological factors, and access. For Hindu boys and girls, the enrollment rates were 84% and 68% respectively, but for Dalit boys and girls it was 70% and 55%. Parent and community attitude, as well as religion and caste, are intertwined and have much to do with a child's education.

Even though states such as Kerala have been involved for years with anti-caste reform, findings show that there is still statistically significant disparity between the Scheduled Caste and Scheduled Tribe groups and all other groups, suggesting the continued existence of an elite group despite years of effort to eradicate the discrepancies. In an effort to uncover the reasons behind the continued disparities, a group of researchers began a first-ever study examining the practice of untouchability in 11 states, specifically in 565 rural villages between 2001 and 2002. Investigators conducted an 18 month survey, spending several days in each village using observations, interviews and focus groups to gather their data. Though there has been improvement over the past decades, they found that practices of untouchability and discrimination do indeed still exist, though at different levels in each state and region.

For example, one third of the villages still keep separate glasses and plates for Dalits, and refuse them entry into the shops. Purchases must be made from outside, without touching or examining the merchandise. They found that 64% are not allowed in public places of worship, and 48% are not permitted to use the village water facilities for fear of their contamination. In order to understand the level of degradation many of the Dalits still face today, it must be noted that investigators found that "in every state, despite legal bans, Dalits continue to manually remove human excreta from public and private latrines, often with their bare hands".

Most often, they are required to perform tasks that relate to human waste, and death, all without pay, as an expected role in their existence. In terms of educational practices, Nambissan and Sedwell state that "the perspective within which the educational concerns of Dalit communities should be addressed must be one of social justice as Dalit communities have suffered from social discrimination and have traditionally been denied access to learning." They contend that unless the discrimination is acknowledged, and confronted by teachers, parents, community leaders and educational institutions, the gap will continue to widen.

For example, currently 38% of the village schools practiced separate eating arrangements, and 22% separate seating arrangements in the classroom. Shah found that "rural schools impress upon young minds and bodies the principles of segregation and discrimination, reproducing the hierarchies of caste and untouchability." Many feel that these practices must stop in order for the message of equality to be heard and incorporated into the thinking of the individuals. If the community, and society at large, does not change this way of thinking about Dalits and other marginalized groups, merely creating more sensitized teaching practices and more educational opportunities may not be enough. Studies show that despite the increased sense of dignity that education alone can bring, many still have a difficult time converting this cultural capital into actual long term employment due to discrimination within the job market.

These studies depict a new crisis, where Dalit youth are becoming frustrated due to their lack of opportunities, even if they are educated, and parents are becoming less willing to invest in the education they thought would make a difference for their whole family. If education access does increase, yet society does not accept the change in thinking of these Dalits, then developmental initiatives simply focusing on increased formal education may not be as successful as hoped in raising the social standing of the Dalits. Therefore, if outside organizations enter into a community, some find that it may be important that they teach not only with a cultural sensitivity, but with the goal of diffusing egalitarian thinking and practice throughout the entire community in order for long term effects to take place.

Although such debate over the best approach cannot be examined fully in this document, these issues do become foundational in this programme evaluation as it examines both the implementation of the goals of the DEI schools, as well as how these schools are situated within the current efforts for societal changes. Analysing the efforts towards creating quality education, taught with a holistic approach through a faith-based egalitarian foundation of human rights could be an important starting point as India attempts to educate the next generation.

INDUSTRIALIZED COUNTRY: NON-GOVERNMENTAL ORGANIZATION INVOLVEMENT

As a newly industrialized country, India's government has found it difficult to keep up with the demand for quality education. Each state within India has widely disparate needs in educational funding, but for most, bringing in outside resources by working together with NGOs becomes a key factor in advancement for the people. Obtaining additional sources of financial aid, as well as creating effective ways of expending them, becomes even more critical if a society is expected to improve and develop. This especially becomes significant with the growing trend of dissatisfaction with the poor quality of education offered through the existing government schools. Dalit parents have dreams for their children to become engineers, doctors and government officials, yet they realise that quality education is necessary to achieve these dreams.

A study by Singh if it is not available through the public sector, many are turning to an alternate private schooling for their children. In this "differentiated demand" for education that is considered of "good quality" this began a mushrooming increase in private unaided schools in the past decade alone. However, quality becomes difficult to maintain here as well, as many of these private schools hire poorly trained teachers, with lower pay, creating schools for the Dalits that are of substandard nature with a poor reputation. It is also difficult to gain official statistics on private schools in India, and the affects of NGO involvement, as many private schools are not granted official recognition by the government for a variety of reasons.

Singh's initial studies show through preliminary tests of achievement, that performance of children in the PUA unrecognized schools did not differ much from the scores of children studying in the government schools. Current research is needed to examine these trends and possible progress over time. With both international and national NGOs willing to step in to help fill this demand, evaluating specific programmes to determine the quality and type of education provided and whether it is effectively implemented is essential if funds are to be used to their fullest potential. Although there is plenty of literature discussing the need and involvement or NGOs, there is a paucity of literature studying the effectiveness of specific programmes and practices. With India's goals of

Education For All, NGOs will continue to play an important role, working along with the government to come up with creative ways to motivate people towards further education, with a holistic approach, but without creating dependency, ultimately effecting a change in society.

ENGLISH MEDIUM OF INSTRUCTION

Even if funding and other resources are available, however, there is still much debate over the pedagogy and curriculum that must be chosen by the key actors. Currently, there is global discussion over whether classes should be taught in the more traditional style of rote learning and classroom order, or in the more recent trend towards child centred pedagogies, with interactive classroom involvement. Also included in this debate for India is the question of whether classes should be taught through an English medium of instruction, the native language of each state, or the national language, Hindi.

These decisions are being made on a state-by-state basis within India, which has 22 state languages, and continued controversy over whether Hindi should still be considered the national language as the Constitution allows for the use of both Hindi and English in varying circumstances. As an example of the difficulties in these decisions, the state of Kerala began to make some of these changes in style and curriculum in 1998. The state planned to adopt a new experimental approach that was designed to be "child-friendly and to deemphasize rote learning and textbook-based teacher lectures in favour of guided learning and playful interaction".

This District Primary Education programme met with controversy, however, as people feared even further stratification between the Kerala students: those who would be able to afford to choose private schools, or those who would become "guinea pigs" in the government schools under this new method. Along with changes in style, the new textbooks would be written in the local state languages, not English. Although the native tongue of Malayalum was already being used for instruction after a controversial decision to drop the universal English medium in 1987, it was still a difficult transition to make. Some continue to pose that teaching in the mother tongue or first language for most of the day with English being taught as a separate subject is the most effective method, as children will understand the subject matter better. Others feel that by starting English younger, the children will become more proficient and will catch up with the subject matter as needed. Although the controversy continues, it must be noted that Kerala, due to a variety of factors, does hold the highest literacy rate in the country at 90.9% compared to the national rate of 64.8%.

The dilemma in this decision is that although each state is requiring that all government schools will teach using the local language up through the 10th grade, all testing and education after that is in English. Thus, children who go to the local government schools, especially in rural areas where no English is used, are by default eliminated from attending upper education that would qualify them for the jobs being reserved for them under affirmative action laws. Also, without quality English education, these children cannot compete for the jobs in the rapidly growing sectors of the Indian economy, such as technical support and sales for major corporations. Although it is not within the purview of this document to determine the positive and negative ramifications of these decisions, it helps to provide a foundation for the decisions that organizations such as the DEI must wrestle with in determining what they consider to be best educational practices for the Dalit children.

EDUCATIONAL ETHNOGRAPHIES AND PROGRAMME EVALUATION

In order to evaluate an educational programme, such as the DEI provides, it is important to understand first the terminology as well as the overall intent. Popham to evaluate something is to appraise its quality and ultimately, to determine its worth. One approach in educational research is to focus on quantitative measures, such as achievement, assessments, levels of attainment, and so on. Although I did query these particular areas, and future long term studies would be necessary to discern improvement and success, this study will use qualitative ethnographic methods, focusing on the purpose of the education, the effectiveness, and its position within a view towards societal change. Using ethnographic methods allows a more descriptive approach, seeking to understand actual situations in context, providing the reader with a far more "meaningful picture of educational undertakings than would be possible from a more traditional scientific paradigm". As Cronbach so eloquently puts it, "Intensive local observation goes beyond discipline to an open-eyed, open-minded appreciation of the surprises nature deposits in the investigative net". It is understood that, with the ethnographer as the human instrument, there will be some influence by the personality and background of the ethnographer. Being able to study a situation in its natural context, and gather data from a range of sources such as observations, and conversations with key actors to gain their perspective, brings together a valuable collection of information. This approach is usually accomplished in a less structured way, and the analysis of the data involves interpretation through descriptions and explanations, with any form of quantifiable analysis taking a supportive role. One of the differences in most ethnographic educational evaluations, is that there is less time spent on site than a typical ethnographic study because so much is already known about the expectations of an educational environment.

Also, for the purpose of this study, there are a few differences between research and evaluation that require clarification. Although both seek to gain new or additional knowledge, a researcher aims to reach a conclusion, and evaluators are more interested in affecting decisions, whether made by the evaluators themselves, or those who have requested the evaluation. Also, generalizability is a crucial difference between the two. Ideally, results from research can be generalized to fit a larger scope of similar situations that are being studied. However, educational evaluations tend to focus on a specific educational programme with no intent to generalize to others. The gathered knowledge can be useful to the stakeholders and key decision makers as they seek to improve the programme. Since DEI, working with the AICC, intends to expand these 62 schools to 1,000, placed all over India, the information gathered in this method, can be useful to a larger scope within the organizations and even other organizations evaluating similar issues in their programmes. One difficulty in any kind of evaluation stems from determining the level of judgment the evaluative ethnographer can or should make in assessing the results of his or her study, what Scriven refers to as the recommendation problem. Theorists do not agree as to whether an evaluator should simply present the findings and leave it up to the programme administrators and decision makers to take it to the next step of modifying policy or implementing change, or whether the evaluators should be the ones to lay out a series of recommendations based on their findings.

Cronbach's approach would be that of a minimalist, holding to the first view that an evaluator should collect the facts about the programme being evaluated, but not place any sort of value on the results, leaving that to the programme administrators. Others, such as Scriven, would take it further, making actual judgments on "value, merit or worth" and using a team of experts to make specific recommendations that could be implemented. Finally, the term formative evaluation must be clarified. Once again, different theorists disagree on the role of the evaluator. In 1967, Scriven created the terms formative and summative that are currently used today to distinguish two specific roles in educational evaluation.

Formative evaluations apply to programmes that are still capable of being modified. That is, they are still malleable, and even slight modifications to different components can be made as the programme continues to be implemented. If there are some components that are considered deficient, they can be improved upon towards a better overall programme. Summative evaluations on the other hand are generally focused on more complete and established programmes and are being assessed as to the overall worth of the programme and whether it should continue. This type of evaluation has more of a final judgment approach, versus the modification approach of formative evaluations. This concept is useful in understanding the overall intent and expectation in any particular evaluation. Having reviewed the various approaches, we have chosen to use qualitative ethnographic methods to conduct an educational formative programme evaluation using a minimalist approach.

To begin with, though we have background in education, and have studied the situation with the Dalits, I am not an expert nor am I fully knowledgeable in the cultural context. As such, the value judgments should be made by both the national and international elected and paid officials of the programme who are held accountable to the budgetary considerations as well as overall strategy and outcomes. Also, there is not enough time in this study to delve fully into the data gathering phase in the field to make necessary recommendations. This study can be useful however, as I am coming in with as objective an eye as possible, knowing that I am not a stakeholder, but am interested in the global efforts to affect change in a society through education. With this approach, I can collect data at the micro level and present this information to the programme developers of the DEI to discuss some of the changes that could be made, and how these changes would affect the overall programme. In summary, there has been much research on the educational gap, and discriminatory practices against the Dalits, and the need for quality education based on equality and human rights.

However, little research exists that specifically evaluates the various approaches of NGOS such that best approaches and methods can be implemented by others. Specifically, there is little research, if any, that evaluates faith-based NGOs as they work within a delicate balance between conflicting worldviews, societal norms and government policy. This document will add to the future foundation for such in depth research on various programmes that could aid other organizations in the continued quest to eradicate the gap in education for the Dalit children.

DATA AND METHODS

The purpose of this formative educational programme evaluation is to examine each element of the programme, focusing on individual aspects of the intended goals and actual implementation. Looking at these elements at each of the four individual sites allows for separate examination as well as some comparison and vision towards future implementation. Even though the time frame was limited to only ten days in Andhra Pradesh, I used qualitative methods, drawing largely from the ethnographic tradition of infield research, gathering documentation, conducting interviews and observing the situation in context. Ideally, I would have had access to some of the typical quantitative information such as test scores, attainment, and teachers' experience levels that can be used to support the findings.

However, due to time constraints at each site, I had to limit the investigation to the self-report of the participants, combined with my own observations, understanding that much of this involves individual perceptions. As an evaluator, I will present the findings in such a way that they can be used by the programme developers for the purpose of shaping and refining the programme, as well as guiding further research. Many of these findings will involve fiscal decisions, and strategic plans for future implementation, which are beyond the role of the evaluator in this case. The following four parts clarify the various points of how the data was collected as well as the methods used. The first part describes the preparation prior to departure which is followed by the infield set up and constraints. The third part describes the interviews and limitations of this process, followed by an explanation of the observation methods.

PRIOR TO DEPARTURE

Several months prior to departure, in preparation to conduct this evaluation, I briefly outlined the intended purpose for my study and contacted the DEI in the United States to discuss feasibility of this type of research over a ten day period in the spring. The United States based administrators contacted the programme directors in India and gained permission for me to travel to Andhra Pradesh in March, 2007, to observe in classrooms and interview various programme participants at multiple sites. Although the DEI has established schools in 13 states, this location was purposely selected by the DEI for its easy access to transportation and lodging as this area contains a college campus of a partner organization, as well a medical clinic. It was also centrally located to four different schools, one in an urban setting, and three others in surrounding rural villages which added to the diversity of the sample.

I recognize that this is just one region and these schools may not be indicative of the overall programme, however, safety, cost and time were constraints that made some of the other schools too difficult to consider. The DEI was supportive and eager to have this programme evaluated. Even though they clearly believe in the effectiveness of their programme, they encouraged having an outside observer review it from an academic perspective. Also, these particular schools have been established for at least three years, and they felt that they were stable enough to be implementing the original objectives, yet far enough along to look for continued improvement, creating a perfect opportunity for a formative approach. One of the constraints that I faced was the confidentiality issues that needed to be addressed before permission could be granted to conduct interviews and, more importantly, write up the findings to be available on the internet.

Along with the typical anonymity of the participants, I needed to commit to the leaders of the DEI schools in India that they would have permission to read the material before it became available to others to help avoid any risk of exposure to individuals. Although each school is recognized by the government and has permission to function in full academic capacity, families in these Dalit communities still suffer from discrimination and outright persecution from those in society who either do not want them to receive equal rights and quality education, or to be attending a school with faith-based ideology. Thus, any identifying details of the organization, leaders, students and locations had to be removed, including references to their website. To begin the evaluation process, I reviewed the goals as stated in the DEI documentation and on their website and then formed semistructured interview questions that would allow the programme implementers and participants the opportunity to confirm effective implementation, and suggest improvement. This would also allow flexibility in the interview process to follow up on topics that the participants found important to discuss.

Due to the time constraints and expense, I was not able to conduct a pilot study, so I discussed and revised the questions several times with the DEI administrators, as well as colleagues who received their prior education in India. Both suggested adjustments to the questions that would help the participants better understand the questions without my leading them to certain answers.

Next, a particular advantage in programme evaluation is for the evaluator to have background knowledge and some level of expertise in order to more accurately observe and document what is seen, as well as probe deeper through the interview process. Reading news substances about current discriminatory practices as well as academic journal substances discussing the educational gaps faced by Dalits also helped to gain corroborative evidence of current difficulties that are not just the opinions of the DEI leaders.

To gain a better understanding of India's historical context and current practices, I also read parts of the Indian Constitution, the Affirmative Action Laws and Anti-Conversion Laws. Rounding out this preparation was my own background teaching and volunteering in classrooms from kindergarten to 12th grades in the United States, observing first-hand the classroom environment and the expected ability levels of each age group. As Wolcott states, "we know the school setting so well that, unknowingly, we become our own best informants".

FIELD: INTENTIONS AND PRACTICAL CONSTRAINTS

Having prepared through readings and communication with the field, I then traveled to India to begin the interviews and observations. Originally, the DEI coordinator in India had committed to introducing me to the principals of the schools for interviews followed by a "snowball method" to select further participants. That is, the staff would ask for volunteers, and those who participated would recommend more volunteers, and so on. In order to maintain as much validity as possible, I had intended to interview both students and their parents as well. Also, to avoid selecting only avid supporters, I intended to ask to interview people who may have some negative views about the education, teachers and school, as this could lead to clarification and a balance of perspectives.

Typical of many evaluations, things did not go smoothly in the field. When I arrived in Andhra Pradesh, I found that the key actors who would be coordinating all of the interviews had not been notified of my plans, or the purpose of the study. However, one advantage of the individual sites not being notified in advance was that it added a level of credibility to what I observed in that they did not have time to prepare or alter the situations in any way that would place them in a more favourable light. This lack of preparation, coupled with the fact that a school holiday was suddenly added to the schedule by the Ministry of Education, something that apparently happens periodically without prior notice, as well as the shift in schedules to a half day summer schedule that week, led to several changes in plans.

So despite the number of days allocated for this evaluation, five days were lost due to logistical problems alone. Also, having to travel four to five hours each way to two of the schools made it such that I could only spend one or two hours at each, making it impossible to schedule meetings with the parents. For greater validity, this study should have included several days at the same site, with the opportunity to interview parents as well as community leaders involved in establishing the programme. While waiting for the coordinators to establish plans to visit the sites, I immersed myself in the daily life of the campus, finding as many opportunities to meet with people in the community, travel in the area, experience life in India, and observe activities that would create a better cultural context for my study. I attended a college graduation which was especially interesting as many of these students had spent their internships teaching in the DEI schools and had earned their credentials with the goal of becoming full time teachers at various locations throughout India in the following year. Next, a pastor who volunteers with some of the local youth who attend the DEI schools, and one of the school managers, took me to visit an area they commonly refer to as "the slums," where a large number of Dalit families live in abject poverty.

They also took me to what they call the "pipe village" where approximately 150 families live in concrete pipes joined together. Although there was not enough time to start any interviews at this point, it gave me insight about their living conditions, and when I observed some of these children days later in their classroom, they had met me before with men they already trusted. This is extremely important in participant observer research.

INTERVIEWS

Finally, with only five days left, I was able to begin visiting the school locations and start the interviews and observations. In order to protect the locations of each of the schools, I will identify them as School A, B, C and D. Each school has been established for a different length of time and depending on funding and site constraints, have a different number of grades from Lower Kindergarten through 8th. By the time we arrived at the rural schools A and B, there was only one hour remaining for observations before school let out at 12:30. Because of this, my original plans to interview individual teachers had to be revised to a focus group format after school hours.

For simplicity, and due to literacy and translation issues in the more remote areas, I prepared oral consent for all participants, even though all that I actually interviewed read English well. The total interviews throughout all four sites included two principals, three managers, two teacher focus groups, a 6th grade and 8th grade class focus group and finally the national administrator for the DEI schools. In India, and at these schools in particular, a manager has the role of evaluating a teacher's performance at the end of the year, and is responsible for purchasing materials, student enrollment, as well as moral training activities. The principal is responsible for academics, government standards, time schedules, lesson plans and exams. One interesting constraint to note was that in the focus groups, each responded differently depending on whether their teacher or principal was present. For example, the eighth grade class was very formal with their teacher present.

When I asked the questions, one by one, around the room, each student would stand in place and answer politely. In some of the more subjective questions, it was difficult to know if some were simply responding to peer pressure by giving responses that others had already said or if they would have chosen the response on their own. Many times, when a student was hesitant, trying to think of an answer, others would give them suggestions. With the sixth grade class however, the teacher left me in charge and I made the mistake of trying to relax the more formal classroom standards, due to time constraints.

They immediately became very animated, loud, changing seats, asking questions and so on. It took quite a while to get the class back under control, but they were candid in their responses. The teacher focus groups were at first reserved, but as I explained the purpose of the study, they became more cooperative and answered more readily, as many of them had just finished their own studies and wanted to support my research. However, when they did answer a question, the principal or manager often modified their answer, softening it, or adding to it. I was aware that I would not be able to get fully candid responses with a manager or principal present. Another reason that teachers were hesitant to open up I found, was due in part to the sensitivity of the topic of Dalit discrimination. As an evaluator, I needed to establish a level of trust with the interviews in order for them to be as open as possible. Though each one that I spoke with displayed a respect for my role as university researcher, I found that when I either explained my background, or that I had met the organization's president and studied the background of the Dalits, they quickly opened up with passionate enthusiasm for what they do and why. As I needed to remain as objective as possible, I did not want to disclose too much information about myself that would direct their answers, but at the same time, establishing this relaxed atmosphere allowed them to more openly discuss the children, the difficulties, or the religious element of their teaching. Having more time to interview individuals would have allowed deeper probing of the issues resulting in more complete data. One last interview constraint is that due to schedules, many of the interviews with management had to be conducted in the car, one time with the principal himself driving through four hours in traffic that we have only experienced in India.

The conversations were interspersed with horns honking continuously, cell phone call interruptions, barking dogs and shouts of children playing in the streets. The recordings were difficult to hear when I tried to transcribe the notes each night. Also, two of the interviews said that they felt constrained being recorded, because they were self-conscious about their grammar, pronunciation and word usage, knowing that I would be quoting them in a research document. I found that they became much more relaxed, open and even fervent about their goals and implementation without the recordings. Therefore, most of the quotations are paraphrased from my notes.

OBSERVATIONS

As I did not know in advance exactly how many schools I would observe, or what the age levels and abilities would be, I did not develop a formal observational protocol with a list of specific events or behaviours that I intended to analyse. My observation methods were therefore unstructured, and because there was no way to observe the students completely unnoticed, I conducted my sessions as a participant-as-observer interacting with the children, tape recording and writing notes as often as I could using a journaling method. Two of the schools, with a one day warning of my arrival, prepared a formal greeting with the traditional flower lei and special presentations, greeting me in the language of their original state as well as in English and Hindi. I was reminded of the complexity of the educational dilemmas in India. It is such a diverse land, of many languages and high illiteracy in many states, which gave me an understanding of the desire for many to learn English as a shared tool of communication and opportunity for future educational attainment.

As I was escorted through each classroom, from the Lower Kindergarten to their highest grade on campus, the students were excited and eager to welcome me and perform recitations, songs and ask questions. The children displayed their course work, and their writings in all three languages, English, Telugu and Hindi. I spent approximately five to ten minutes in each room, as we had to complete the entire campus within an hour. I recorded the greetings, songs, and poetry, which were also performed in all three languages, as well as the questions of several of the children which I later used to evaluate the level of ability and pronunciation. After collecting the data, I read through the notes and listened to the recordings and coded for themes to evaluate the responses to the specific questions and to create as complete a picture as possible of the matching of goals with effective implementation.

Although not all data that would be useful in a full educational evaluation could be gathered in a short timeframe under the various constraints, the data that was collected allows me to answer each of the research questions to varying degrees, depending on the location and the interview participants. Ethnographic evaluations begin with a desire to understand, with the next step being to appraise and assess what is understood, in such a way that the results can guide the decision making process of key actors.

FINDINGS AND DISCUSSION

An ethnographic formative programme evaluation differs from a strictly qualitative approach, in that my role as an evaluator is to examine the implementation of each of the stated goals of the DEI at the four sites, not to judge the overall values, assumptions or decisions in establishing these goals. Generally, a formative evaluator gathers information at each of the sites that can be used by programme staff to assess and improve their programme as necessary. As the DEI did not request this evaluation, or guide the specific research questions, the overall value in this analysis rests in gaining a better understanding of the educational situation of the Dalits, such that future research can be pursued.

In order to create a logical flow of the findings and discussion, I divide the following parts just as to the three original research questions. I then further separate the findings into the same categories of the DEI stated goals that I initially used to formulate the interview questions for the students, teachers and DEI leaders. It begins with the overarching question of how this programme is situated within India's overall plans to affect change for the future of the Dalits. This includes the holistic approach to addressing the needs within the local and the global contexts, followed by the specific topics of English medium of instruction and teaching from a human rights perspective based on a Christian worldview.

Although economic development and health needs are addressed briefly in context of the holistic approach, the dashed arrows show that they will not be a main focus of this document. In the second part, based on the rest of the stated goals of the organization, each of the specific elements is examined to see how these goals are being implemented. Finally, the third question deals with future research to be addressed in the conclusion. Each of the findings is examined and discussed based on an analysis of the documentation, interviews and observations where applicable.

CONTEXT

India is a land of vast diversity and yet in that diversity, extreme disparity. As I rode through the streets I saw stores filled with exquisitely woven saris and expensive jewelry while children begged for coins at the corners. Oxcarts meandered through the streets next to expensive vehicles, and cows stood side by side with motorcycles, waiting to cross the street creating an interesting backdrop of both ancient and modern. From rural to urban and from state to state, there are marked contrasts that create a daunting task as India strives to educate an estimated 20 to 30 million children who are not attending primary school as the country presses towards the goal of education for all by 2015.

In this type of evaluation, it is extremely important to understand the context in which each of the schools is situated as it becomes necessary in analysing the findings. For example, had I simply seen the children at each school location, well groomed, dressed in uniforms and speaking English, studying math and science, I would not have had any understanding of the level of accomplishment of the programme. The managers, these schools choose to compare their achievement levels to private schools in the area, whose children generally come from entirely different socioeconomic backgrounds and home environments. They explained that each of the schools has unique constraints that must be addressed as they make decisions on the best approach that will impact the community.

LIVING CONDITIONS

To begin with, one must understand the children's living conditions and the affects this can have on their education. As I walked through the narrow crowded streets of the slums, with over 150,000 people separated by just one wall from the airport runway, I could smell the open sewage draining in an infrastructure not designed to handle the amount of people living there. The children clustered around wearing tattered and dirty clothing but with eager curiosity, smiling shyly and asking questions using gestures if I could not understand them. Most were barefoot and the smaller children wore no clothing at all, or simply a shirt. Stepping carefully around the pigs, cows, dogs and goats all rummaging through the trash heaps piled around the slum, I saw the "rag pickers," a name given to the women who sort through trash all day looking for glass or substances of clothing to sell. The pastor and the school manager who were escorting me through the slums introduced me to a woman who sits all day, sorting this glass into piles for recycling. One of the families invited me into their home, which was approximately seven feet across, with a tiny door leading to another room. I was surprised by the shiny, modern looking shelving mounted on the wall for all of their neatly arranged dishware, pots, and utensils. The pastor said it was not always this clean and orderly in these homes but that he works together with the school in their holistic efforts to teach families about hygiene, cleanliness and health, despite their living conditions.

The other area that I visited prior to the school interviews was the area nicknamed the "pipe village" where people have been brought out of rural villages as bonded laborers for a concrete pipe manufacturing company. Bonded labour is described as a "slave-like form of attachment to a particular employer, often the result of usurious personal loans". These people must stay and work for the company until they have paid off their debt. The company allows them to live in the discarded segments of pipe, where, for the past 30 years, they have built up a whole village, formed by connecting pieces of pipe and bricking off the ends and creating openings for doors. They cook outside while chickens and pigs roam freely in and out of the homes.

I was told the villages used to have electricity that the company intended to be used for lighting only. However, when people started using it for televisions, irons, radios and so on, the company considered that an abuse of the privilege and turned it off completely. Inside the pipes, it was dark and crowded, yet this is where the children read and do their homework by candlelight. Even within this village, however, there is a contrast in conditions. Walking through the village, I noticed that while one half was cluttered and dilapidated, the other half was very orderly, with cleanly swept dirt, and pipe homes lined up in rows, with all personal belongings neatly stored inside. When I asked the pastor about the difference, he said that it depends on which part of India the villagers come from. He said that there are some stereotypical differences between the education level and hygiene of the northern and southern villagers that they see in the pipe village. We had invited one of the DEI teachers along, a Swedish intern who had not yet visited where the children lived. One little girl, excited to see her teacher in her village, motioned for us to follow her. She scampered ahead, and we could see through the opening of her five foot diameter pipe home, that she was quickly scooping up a piece of clothing from the floor and stuffing it into the corner of their neatly ordered space. She giggled at us and spread her arms in a gesture of welcome and pride to her home.

The rural areas face different types of difficulties. Transportation is not readily available and the children often have to walk for miles in the stifling heat. This affects attendance as they either arrive tardy, or end up not coming at all. Due to the types of jobs available in these areas, generally related to seasonal farming, children often either move to where the jobs are available for their parents, or some are needed to help with the family income. This affects the ability of the children to stay in school for a full year, as well as the ability of the parents to financially support any of the education on a month by month basis if fees are required. The managers said, however, that there are some positive factors in rural living, specifically that children are not exposed to "dangers and too much knowledge about life" that is seen in the close quarters of the slum areas, and they often have better access to food.

One village had small one or two room concrete homes built by the government placed neatly on individual lots. Walking past the open doors, I saw no furniture and some people were sleeping during the heat of the day on the concrete floors. I met several adults sitting on the floors hand rolling up to 1,000 cigarettes a day for a wage of approximately one dollar per day. The manager said that the DEI is working within these communities to set up training opportunities such as embroidery, tailoring, and computers and creating self-help groups using microenterprise concepts that establish cooperative loan efforts in small groups to begin businesses within the communities. This holistic approach once again, aims not only to assist in the children's education, but to affect the community in which they live. These children, whether in urban or rural settings, have many obstacles to overcome in their path towards education.

Whether it is their noisy or crowded study conditions, lack of parent education and support, distance of travel, limited days in attendance, lack of food and clothing, or even just the stress of everyday living due to limited access to water, electricity, and medical treatment, these conditions can have an overall affect on their achievement and attainment through the programmes offered.

Understanding how they live is necessary for me as an evaluator to fully comprehend the observations and interviews in context, but I recognize that it is crucial for the programme developers as well as they make decisions regarding how the funds are best spent, whether it be for curriculum, lunch programmes, uniforms, supplies, transportation, or after school homework assistance.

SCHOOL CONDITIONS

In the rural School A, the children actually meet in a condemned building while waiting for a new facility to be built. The fifth grade class is conducted outside under a tree as there is no room for a classroom and the children wanted to continue after fourth grade. Many of the rooms have no tables, chairs or play equipment for recess. There is no electricity at this school, and the water has to be carried 200-300 feet. There is also no phone service or e-mail access making it difficult for staff to communicate with other DEI locations. With no bus service, some of the children travel over six miles to get to school.

They showed me the property for the new building, but the lack of infrastructure will make it difficult to build. This adds to the time the children have to wait for better facilities and for additional grades to be added. The DEI brings in a medical clinic before school starts to assist with some of the basic medical needs within the village. They also had sewing classes for village women. School B is also in a rural setting with brightly painted murals of flowers on the front giving it a welcoming presence. Some of the grades had desks and chairs while others sat on concrete floors. Many of the children either walked home or shared rides on the small autorickshaws that come by after school each day. The management would like to add more rooms in order to add grades to the school, as well as more rooms for the sewing classes that I visited for the women in the community. Several people referred to School C as their model and I could quickly see why.

It is also in a rural setting but the facility was markedly neat, well painted, with brightly coloured playground equipment and flowers landscaping the front. The children had desks and chairs and though they, too, would like to add more rooms, the facility was very well maintained. Instead of the typical hand printed postings on the other bulletin boards this school had computer printouts of calendars, rules and daily schedules. I visited the sewing and computer classes in session where both young men and women attend who have either had no formal education or were older than 10th grade so were beyond the formal school setting.

School D, the one urban school that I observed, was located within a larger campus with other facilities nearby. In the classrooms where I conducted focus group interviews, they had desks and chairs and they did have some playground equipment to be shared by all classes. These children have access to public transportation and several students have bicycles. They have plans to add two stories to this facility as they are limited by land space. With this foundation of context laid, the following parts present specific findings relating to the research questions. Throughout the rest of the findings, since each site is unique in its setting and stage of development, if a finding is specific to a school, I will report it separately, otherwise I will refer to overall findings on given topics.

DETAILED FINDINGS

The research question being addressed and the specific claims of the DEI, followed by a summarized list of the types of interview questions that I used to examine how the areas are being addressed. This first question helps to understand the overall goals of the DEI and their plans for societal change. I found two specific areas that they address beyond the obvious educational components. One is the desire to teach English such that the children can gain access to higher education through the country's English medium universities, as well as increased job opportunities. Although many countries struggle with the topic of how English should be taught, the fact remains that there is an ever increasing global market that requires English proficiency.

The second desire is to teach a new sense of self-worth and equality that traditionally has been denied them. The organization feels that a significant way to change the thinking of the society is to teach through the children, their parents and community leaders that each individual has value, and that all should be given equal opportunity through values commonly established as human rights. Their intent is to use a holistic approach as they seek to change the future for this group of people. Although I will focus primarily on their approach to education as it interrelates with human rights and social justice, it became clear throughout the interviews and observations that they address more than these areas through economic development and medical aid in an attempt to change the framework in which these children learn.

Research shows that India has made inroads in the educational process, but the disparity still exists and simply offering education or even changing their way of thinking about their self-worth, will not guarantee a more prosperous future for these children. That is why the organization is eager to make changes at a societal level. Though it is a very large undertaking and beyond the scope of this document, it needs to be acknowledged in order to understand how these particular schools fit into the overall framework This objective was expressed well in the conversations with two leaders. One asked me, "What do you believe, who influences the child's career most, the teacher or the parent." I said, "I'd like to think the parent." He said, "Yes, for you, you would want that, but you are not in their world. For these children, if the parent is illiterate, the only goals will be to be the same as the parent—a street sweeper or a rag picker. At the CEC's we want to improve their education, career, and their future. DEI plans to use this education to improve the whole community." Another said, "Our duty is to help the deprived, they must have an education to be empowered, enlightened and equipped to face the challenging world." As a faith-based NGO, with a mission to aid this poor and oppressed people, they have chosen to use the egalitarian teaching of Christianity based on moral stories and concepts found in the Bible.

To examine whether the claims are being practiced, I asked a variety of questions of the children, teachers and administrators regarding the importance of English education, as well as how it is taught, what the children intend to do with the education, and how this will help reach that goal. Although the term "quality" is difficult to gauge without actual test scores and proficiency levels, I will address what was at least observable regarding this statement.

ENGLISH MEDIUM INSTRUCTION

As an English medium form of instruction, all subjects are conducted in English throughout the day, but they also learn Hindi and Telugu in separate language classes each day. Their level of achievement was really quite impressive considering that especially in rural areas, most have absolutely no access to English outside of school. Schools in the urban areas may hear it in the stores or on the streets and can practice what they learn, but in the rural areas, with no English spoken at home or in the community, there is no opportunity to hone the language skills.

In an effort to improve the children's abilities and to invest in the whole community, some of the schools are even beginning to add parents' language courses. Each of the principals and managers spoke English well, and I understood them easily, although it did take the first few days in India to adjust to the variety of accents, as many came from different parts of India, where their first language or dialect is specific to that state. Interacting with the teachers, I found some of the accents were a little more difficult to understand, but we adapted to each other quickly during the focus group interviews. The children spoke eagerly with me in English so there was no need for the interpreter that was provided. In their villages or in their homes, they speak Telugu, as that is their state language in Andhra Pradesh. Most do not speak Hindi as I was told the southern states prefer not to use this for various reasons.

The children are not allowed to speak other languages at school at any time, either in class or on the playground. In the focus group interview with 6th grade students, I asked the children if there was anything they did not like about their school. One boy said that he did not like it when others broke the rules and spoke Telugu at school on the playground as he wanted to practice only English. Several children nodded in agreement.

I did find that their accents were more difficult for me to understand, as mine was for them. One girl was explaining that her favourite subject was what sounded like "shasho shtudies." When I looked puzzled, the teacher clarified by enunciating "social studies," and then I was able to understand more clearly their future pronunciations. They responded to their teachers' requests of them in English, showing recognition of her questions. Their written proficiency was noted as they enthusiastically showed me their notebooks filled with writing in all three languages, very neatly done, even in the younger grades. As I observed in each classroom, the youngest children recited poems and sang songs for me in English but I was not able to assess how much beyond rote memorization they had learned yet.

These children were in their first year of exposure, and the recitations as opposed to full conversations were typical of that level of achievement. The first grade class could recite the Psalm 23 and the Lord's Prayer which are both about 12 lines long, which for length alone, was an accomplishment for that age group. In some classrooms, they had individual children recite greetings for me, and some classes chanted in unison, carrying the struggling students through it together. One thing I would like to have delved into further would be the records of the students' backgrounds before attending a DEI school. I would like to know if they learned English at another school before coming to these locations, especially those in higher grades, or if the school is solely responsible for their English achievement. For example, several in the 8th grade at School D said they had received English education prior to the opening of this school, so I would like to have discussed this with the parents and the teachers, or be able to look at the records and create some analysis of number of years of education before attending these schools.

Three in that class had come to this school for their first year with no prior English education. The teacher said they were doing very well and all students in that class were able to answer my questions, though sometimes it took two or three attempts. Another area of concern for the future for these schools is that some states are beginning to force the decision in favour of mother tongue education. One CEC in another state for example has been warned that they have one year to stop teaching from an English medium or they will be "de-recognized by the government." This will prove to be very difficult for private schools who want to maintain government recognition, yet believe in their choice of English medium as their main form of instruction, rather than as a separate language course.

The national director said that a school would have to apply to the state to be given a "no objection certificate" and would be charged huge fines in order to maintain the Central Board Secondary Education standing within the federal government. This is the higher standard curriculum and the one that the DEI schools would like to be recognized under. Without these restrictions, they can qualify to be recognized under the National Open Schools curriculum but they consider this a lower standard, and the DEI schools feel the quality would suffer under that recognition. The leaders are concerned that if children have to go to the government schools which teach only in the local language of Telugu, with a small amount of English, then the issue of what will happen after 10th grade, when all tests are presented in English, has serious implications. The DEI recognizes the need for these children to continue into upper education, but feels that with the limitations on access to English will be a detriment to their future prospects. Maintaining quality standards of curriculum from state to state while complying with government restrictions creates conflict for the leadership which will continue to be addressed under this disagreement regarding approach.

With these concerns in mind, I wanted to understand the overall affect an English education had on the goals and dreams of the children. Although I had to resort to a focus group format, rather than a personal interview with individual children and their parents, I did have a chance to interact with two classes in a lively discussion about their future plans, favourite courses, and what they would do if they could not go to this school. Some of their responses reflected their desire for education in general and some pertained specifically to English.

One boy, who was still fairly new to the English language said, "It is good education in this school, I am become learned, studying English." When I asked what they would do if they could not go to this school, several said they would find another English school to go to, but two eighth grade girls, both wanting to become doctors said, "I don't know what I would do, my parents cannot send me anywhere else, and then I could not learn," and, "I would miss my education and my goal to become a doctor." I visited the home of one of these girls the previous week in the pipe village, so I asked the manager more questions about them.

He told me their scores are good and with sponsorship, they have every possibility of fulfilling that dream in the years ahead. Addressing the impediments to the quality of the English education, the director shared that it is difficult to find enough teachers who have excellent English abilities who are willing to live in such difficult environments. He said the teachers rate themselves on a scale of 1-10 at about a six or seven. He said they cannot expect children to learn any higher than a six or seven if they have no higher example. When asking the teachers for what they wish they could have to improve their ability to teach, several of them asked for English tapes or CDs to play so that they and the children could hear clear pronunciation of non Indian English with its mix of accents from different dialects. Since these rural locations make it very difficult to attract quality, well educated teachers, one of the ideas the leadership is considering is to offer opportunities for nine month internships for people from the United States, Canada or the United Kingdom to come and teach each age group every day, in order for them to hear it spoken by those whose first language is English.

One of my particular areas of interest in this English education stems from my career as a database consultant for a major computer corporation based in the United States. Currently working with their customer service department, which has outsourced all sales, technical support and customer service to various cities in India within the past three years, we recognize a huge demand for English proficiency. Customers express frustration when the accent cannot be understood, and corporations in India are struggling to find qualified employees with strong educational background and English skills.

Thus, both factors are important in the children obtaining higher education leading to openings in the global market. The interview questions relate to areas of human rights, current discrimination, issues of self-worth, and the situation within the community. Recognizing that there is a direct conflict between the two religious beliefs, I also examine how the DEI uses a Christian worldview to achieve these goals.

UNDERSTANDING THE GLOBAL EFFORTS

First, acknowledging the need to accomplish more than simply the education and change of thinking of the individuals, I needed to understand how the DEI addresses the issue from a macro level within the international efforts towards social justice and human rights. As the review of literature shows, even when the Dalit children do obtain an education, society will not necessarily allow them to fully utilize this and create change for themselves and their families. I interviewed the social justice coordinator with the DEI to discuss their efforts to raise global awareness on these very issues.

He explained that the DEI president travels extensively, along with other spokes people from India, the United States and the United Kingdom, in a concerted effort to advocate for the Dalit people. Using documentary screenings and research gathered from current sources, the DEI joins with others to present in committee meetings, hearings and briefings in several arenas such as the United States Congress, State Department and the United Nations. The recent passing of the US HCR 139 shows marked solidarity in the global efforts to eradicate continued discriminatory practices.

HUMAN RIGHTS EDUCATION USING A CHRISTIAN WORLDVIEW

Along with these efforts, many of the sources on the DEI's philosophy and work emphasize that social change comes not just from government rulings, but requires grassroots social activism as well. The sources further emphasize that there must be a change in thinking of the people in order for these new changes in societal order to take place. Their mission statement asserts that "The DEI exists to empower the Dalits in their quest for social freedom and human dignity by networking human, financial, and informational resources." Acknowledging the disparate thinking between the two belief systems, I asked how they planned to teach their stated values, within the framework of the government restrictions and societal opposition.

The interviews, the DEI considers the education a secular education using a government standard curriculum, yet taught from human rights framework based on Christian ideology. Their intention is to establish egalitarian thinking along with the moral principles that promote equality in society. The managers and director said that through songs, moral stories, and even some Bible verses, as well as the behaviour and expectations modeled by the staff, they feel they can help the children and their parents engage in a new way of thinking, promoting self-worth, fair treatment and future hope. They have labeled this approach as "holistic transformational activities." However, in order to be careful to separate actual Christian doctrinal religious teaching, from the moral and egalitarian principles taught on a weekly basis, they said they also offer a traditional Christian "Vacation Bible School" during the week just after school lets out for the summer. This is an optional week, offered to the children and any of their friends who are interested. Parents choose whether to have their children attend with an explanation that it is not part of their educational curriculum but will be a series of children's activities based on Christian teaching.

This allows a careful division between the holistic transformational activities throughout the school year and specific religious teaching in the summer. Each of the leaders and managers I spoke with articulated specific messages that they wanted to get across to the children and families through their teaching which seemed to divide well into two main categories:

1. Each individual has value and self-worth
2. All are created equal, with equal rights as a citizen of India

I address each of these, as well as the use of a Christian worldview to accomplish each goal.

INDIVIDUAL VALUE AND SELF-WORTH

Effectively teaching and measuring the construct of "value and self-worth" is difficult but they feel that by daily reinforcement, encouragement and modeling, they can begin to affect change. To teach a sense of value, the staff said they find a variety of ways from the time children are in the LKG to encourage the development of their understanding of who they are as human beings. For example, through songs and verses, the schools teach that God loves each child and values them, which differs, the director said, from the Hindu traditions that Dalits are considered God's waste product and therefore unworthy of the benefits that others receive. The president states in his writings that he would like for the children to at least hear that they are loved by God, which he feels brings a sense of dignity and self-worth. It is typical of Dalit children, as with most children, to assume they might do the same job that their parents do some day. Only with Dalits, these jobs often entail the most menial and repulsive tasks imaginable in society perpetuating the concept that this is their only value to society. To combat this type of thinking, some of the schools hold activities such as a Career Day, where the children dress up in costumes that the school has for different career choices.

These include nurses, doctors, policemen, engineers, musicians, judges, lawyers, athletes, and so on. Not only do the children participate in this, but the parents are invited to the event, to encourage them to see the potential in their child with this education. I asked one of the managers if the parents are happy with the education, as I could not interview them directly. He said the parents at his school have expressed excitement over the changes they have seen in their children because the "growth and learning gives them hope." To follow up on this in my focus group sessions with the sixth and eighth grade classes, I asked them what they would like to do for a career when they finished school.

It is common for children to pick a goal that sounds glamorous or popular, but for these children, who have been impressed with the concept of taking on the least desirable jobs in society since birth, their responses indicated a different hope. The school said they work very hard to stress the options for their future, and these children reflected that in their responses. Each selected specific career paths, with the most popular being "children's doctor," "software engineer" and "police officer." Although only one had actually worked on a computer they had definitely been exposed to this idea for a career. When I pressed them on some of their specific answers such as cardiologist, or eye doctor, they explained that each had family members who had benefited from these particular fields and they wanted to be able to help someone like that someday. These results are important in that they seem to reflect that these children are not making any assumptions based on their parents' job choices, as none of the children interviewed had parents in any of these fields.

ALL ARE CREATED EQUAL AND HAVE RIGHTS

Promoting the second concept that all are created equal, the DEI said that the education is offered to all faiths, races, and genders with no restrictions or need to convert in order to obtain the benefits of education. For specific examples of how they use Christian ideology to show egalitarian beliefs, the staff said that they have moral classes on Fridays or Saturdays using commonly accepted books in India that teach moral values, and some simple biblical teaching throughout the week such as the verse, "All men and women are created in God's image".

The director said this differs significantly from the traditions of Hindu teaching that each of the caste levels stems from a different part of God, such as the Brahmin caste from God's head, down to the lowest caste from God's feet. The children recited these verses and poems for me, as well as songs about how "God created you and me." In the hand-motions that accompany this song, the children pointed first to me—a white, American woman and then to themselves. The fact that they could perform these gestures as a perfectly natural act, without hesitation, was quite remarkable when one understands the cultural background.

Teachers and students must demonstrate this equality as well. They said they are very careful that no caste or discriminatory practices are shown among the staff, or in their treatment of the children. In School D for example, if children show discrimination in any way, they are made to publicly apologize and parents are told that if this continues, the child will be removed from the school.

Each of the schools offers community involvement with the parents, such as parent meetings, parades in the community and even clean up days in one. In order to teach these concepts to all, one school said that at each of the four parent meetings per year, they "remind the parents that each child is an Indian citizen and therefore entitled to all rights and privileges belonging to every member of society, that all people are created equal, and that no caste treatment is allowed." To continue this in the community, they held a Children's Day parade, where all teachers and children marched throughout the village carrying banners stating, "Drive out castism to open equality," and "Education opens the doors for future life."

Every two months, they hold an evaluation and planning meeting where they question how they are doing academically, and how well they did in the community at passing the vision on from the manager, to the teachers, to the children and to the parents. As they teach these concepts, they said they are fully aware and respectful of the government restrictions on certain states, or even resistance within particular communities.

For example, one of the main restrictions that some states face is the anti-conversion law. Although the four schools I visited are not in one of these states, several of the other DEI schools are. Anti-conversion laws state that no one can pressure others with financial resources or gifts, or through threats of divine displeasure, in order to convince someone to convert.

They take several precautions in offering this education, such as clearly explaining to the parents that while it is a government recognized school it is based on a Christian worldview, as well as making sure that the community leaders are supportive of this and that there are no coercive practices. When I asked the managers if there are any difficulties with this method of teaching, which goes against Hindu beliefs, one school told me that some parents chose not to have their children attend because of the Christian influence.

He said this makes it difficult for the children as many of them want to come and be with the other children and learn, but the parents do not want them to be taught another religion. Another manager said that there was some difficulty when parents complained to the leader of the village about the

Christian teaching. He said the village leader did not want to upset the school, as he valued the education for the community, but he did not want to upset the parents, as they are the ones who elect him to office as leader. So he resolved it by reprimanding a local teacher at a public meeting, telling him not to teach these songs and verses.

The manager asked the leader to encourage all parents to come to him directly in the future if they have any concerns, but he said that none of the parents removed their children from the school. In their efforts to teach equality and human rights, several managers said they are aware that some of the children are too young to understand the concept of inequality. One said they all live in a Dalit community, so at a young age, they are not exposed to the idea that anyone is any different. However, by fourth and fifth grade the schools want to begin an active strategy beyond the daily teaching, that will engage them in awareness of their rights as an Indian citizen and to develop critical thinking skills.

One school said that they will be starting debate teams, where they divide up the upper grades into four groups or "houses," and assign them an "awareness topic" topic such as AIDS, equality and so on. The school would assign teachers to help the children prepare and a judge for the event. The idea is to have schools join together for a special day, and have all children present so that they can learn from the skills practiced and topics discussed.

He said, "This way, their language will improve, their thinking will improve and they will learn to ask other people and prepare." Each of these collective practices is used to continue their efforts in "holistic transformation" throughout the communities. By approaching it from both the global level and the classroom level, and even into the homes, they aim to affect change throughout India.

Having examined the implementation surrounding English education, human rights and equality as well as how the implementation fits within some of the overarching goals. In order to gain information regarding the vision for future schools as well as current statistics.

SELECTION OF SCHOOL SITES

So far, there are 62 CECs in 13 states with an average of approximately 200 students each. At the time that I started this research, there were 54 CECs with 7,000 students enrolled, and now, less than one year later there are over 10,000 students enrolled in the schools. The goal is to eventually have other organizations join through the AICC to establish 1,000 CECs nationwide. I was told that selecting the locations of the CEC's involves several steps.

First, the DEI must be invited into the village. "The overhead organization that the DEI works with is very popular," just as to one of the managers, and village leaders have heard that they are building schools to help the Dalits. If a leader expresses a desire to have a school built within the community, the DEI responds by sending a team to survey the area to determine whether it is a match for the criteria.

The village or area must show a specific need, that is, there must be a high enough concentration of Dalits, without a similar English speaking school within walking distance. There must also be government cooperation with vaccinations, and healthcare for the children, and finally, the leader within that village must be motivated and cooperative as he will have direct influence on the parents and the community to affect change. The village leaders and the parents are informed that it is an English medium school, following government standards of curriculum, using a Christian worldview.

The staff, village leaders have found that the level of violence is lower with more education and they desire an opportunity to see a hope for the future of their children. Gaining the trust and participation within the community is a key element in establishing effective intervention. The issue of anti-conversion laws is also carefully addressed in each state in order to protect the individuals from any fines.

This part lays out the quality of the education, as well as academic placement within the surrounding communities. Once again, although "quality" is difficult to measure without specific quantitative measures, I will address their goals and observable efforts.

QUALITY OF EDUCATION

Each of the schools currently has government permission to operate and recognition from the Ministry of Education. Twice a year, the ME inspects the teachers, children. From LKG to fifth grade, the schools may choose their curriculum and still be recognized, but from the sixth grade on, the schools must follow the government curriculum and timetables of testing under the Centralized State Board Exams and India Centralized Standard Education. Board exams from the state are required at seventh and tenth grades. As one principal stated, they also give their own exams each trimester and if the students are not performing well, they approach the teacher and help the teacher with the subject matter to improve for the next testing round.

Although I was not able to gather quantitative data on test scores, and compare them to statewide results, the director said that they prefer to compare themselves to private schools which have a higher level of standard than the government schools. He said they compare very well and students from some schools are even beginning to win prizes in local extra curricular competitions for drawing, singing and sports.

While I was there, an annual review was in progress, where managers and principals of all the southern campuses had gathered to discuss strategies, dreams, difficulties, goals and successes. If this were a more complete evaluation, this would be the perfect forum where future improvements would be discussed, based on findings, especially if I were able to conduct the parent interviews, and individual student and teacher interviews.

EQUAL OPPORTUNITY FOR EDUCATION

The children and adults all stated that any child could go to the school, however, the managers and director confirmed that preference is given to the Dalit children if there is a capacity limit.

Most of the schools reserved 60% for Dalits. To determine whether this was actually in practice, and to see if it appeared that many children convert either because of the education, or in order to obtain the education, I asked two of the schools if they knew the attendance rate based on religious beliefs or practices. Records from School B, the percentage of the students' faith background is 92% Hindu, 6% Muslim and 2% Christian.

School D had 10% Muslim and the rest mostly identified themselves as Hindu. Most areas, they said, have very few Muslims or Christians, which fits with their overall strategy to establish schools in the areas with the greatest need for education for the Dalits.

As these schools are at least three years old, there does not appear to be any high conversion rate, just as to their records. One of the difficulties mentioned by several with regard to allowing all children to attend is the transience of the families who work with seasonal jobs. One school said that parents will sign their children up and begin school for the first two months, but then leave with the uniform, shoes and books, following job availability.

The school does not want to turn these children away, or discriminate in any way based on what they think might happen, but at the same time, they recognize the reality that the student may leave, and take the supplies with them that would have benefited another child coming in. Also, another school has parents who are trying to get their children into a boarding school facility, which would provide for all of their needs. As soon as any opening becomes available, they will remove their children from the DEI school.

To accommodate this, one school requires a beginning of the year fee, knowing of the particular problems in that area. Then, as the year progresses they continue a monthly payment schedule. For this subject, I discussed with the management some of the issues commonly discussed in attempting to evaluate overall quality of the teaching staff. I then questioned two focus groups of teachers regarding their educational background and years of experience.

I asked the management how they train the teachers in the "holistic transformational activities." This part also discusses the teacher's level of satisfaction with the teaching experience, and what they wish they could change, as well as perceived obstacles to their ability to teach or to the overall educational experience.

ACCOUNTABILITY

A key component in the success of any educational programme has been shown to be the accountability of the teachers. One particular aspect is teacher absenteeism. Students cannot be educated if the teacher is not present, and India holds one of the higher rates of teacher absenteeism with 25% absent in government primary schools on any given day. There are several reasons for this, including the lack of repercussion if a teacher does not show up to class.

The CECs address this by allowing eight "casual days" which are used for vacations and eight "sick days." Anything beyond that, they do not get paid for. The school day runs from 8:00 a.m. to 3:30 p.m. Teachers are permitted three "tardies," but anything beyond that is disciplined by a reduction of pay or removal of a vacation day. The principals claim that this has not been an issue with their staff, partly due to the rules and accountability established and partly due to the commitment of the teachers to help these underprivileged students.

STAFF EDUCATION

As I was not able to interview the staff at each of the four schools, I summarize the findings regarding the years of experience and education level from schools A and B. As these schools have only been open for two years and five years respectively, the average teaching time of 16 months at School A and 2.7 years at School B is low, but not surprising.

Part of this is due to the fact that the schools are very new, and part to the difficulty they have in maintaining staff in rural areas with lower pay. The four schools had an average ratio of 22 students to one teacher. Of these two schools, School A had less educational background among the staff. Three were still completing their degrees remotely, and two held Bachelor of Science in Education degrees, one a Bachelor of Science in

Education with a credential of a Bachelor of Education and two held other certifications. School B, the more established school, had more degreed staff, three with BA or BSc degrees, five with BEd credentials in addition to their BA or BSc or MA degrees, and two with specific training in nursing and Hindi. There are several reasons that the leadership faces difficulty attracting well educated staff, however.

One is the lack of equipment and materials that these teachers have been trained to expect in order to do an excellent job of educating. They have been trained in many cases with full degrees in education, but in the rural areas, there are not enough resources for science laboratories, computers, audio visual equipment, libraries, musical instruments, sports equipment and so on.

They feel they cannot do as good a job as they were trained to do without the necessary resources. Also, as the principal reported, the living conditions are much harder than these teachers who have lived in the cities have ever experienced and being far from their families and friends creates a lonely environment.

However, those educated through a partner organization have already experienced many of these conditions because part of their education contains a service component, where they have spent as much as a year in the field, working in very difficult conditions, such as the slums or remote villages. The leadership foresees difficulties, however, in maintaining continuity with the staff in these conditions. I asked if they ever hire teachers who are non-Christian, and the principal said it would be very rare.

They want teachers to be able to teach from a Christian perspective, with the DEI's approach to holistic transformation so there is no confusion in practices. It is hard to recruit teachers into the villages, however, as the government pays more for a BEd, making it hard to attract the quality teachers who could choose the government city jobs instead.

Despite facility differences and varying educational backgrounds, one other point that was notable as I observed in these schools was the order and discipline. School A, the newest of the schools where many children are being exposed to formal education for the first time, had far less structure and order than School C, the model school. When School A lined up to greet me and have their photo taken, the children clustered close together, in no particular order while the children in School C, also with very little warning of my arrival, filed out of their classrooms in perfect order, separated by one arm's length, standing at attention, ready for the salute and pledge.

It was a very impressive sight to see each row, perfectly aligned by grade, with teachers standing in the back. Children had previously memorized greetings that they used as well as their daily pledge routines. I am told by colleagues from India that this is the standard routine for the elite private schools in India.

It was a very interesting observation to see the difference between a newly formed school, and one that is more established. It would be useful to discuss further with the staff whether these differences in the schools are due to the length of time since they were established, the expectation of the leadership, or the children's background, or a combination of the three.

JOYS AND OBSTACLES

I asked the teachers what the enjoyed most about teaching and though it did take some time at first to think of an answer, several said that they enjoyed seeing the changes in the students, and watching them learn about their rights as human beings and about Christian principles through Bible verses and stories.

After even a small amount of education, they see improvements in health and hygiene, and they hear the children speaking English in society. The teachers agreed that watching the children gain confidence as they learn provides the impetus for many of them to continue.

One of the difficulties they face is that it is hard at first to get the families to take learning seriously and to cooperate together with the school, or to even have their child enroll.

One school went door-to-door, explaining the cost, the value and what would be provided. Students would start to attend, but since many walked for some distance, they would often come in late. This caused disruptions in the classroom and in their learning.

Also, the children did not know how to treat a teacher, and the parents had never been to school themselves so had little expectation for their children's behaviour in school. Recognizing this, one manager conveyed that he felt that, "Discipline comes first, then education will come out of it." To aid in this, the school created a policy for the parents, showing what was expected of the children on holidays, weekends and in the evenings, such that what they were allowed to do at home would match with the school's expectations.

If the child was going to be absent for more than three days due to illness, the parent needed to show a doctor's excuse. In order to handle the "tardies," one school warned the students and parents that they would start locking the gate when school began at 9:00 a.m.

When parents and children came late, they were turned away. The manager shared that when one little boy cried and begged to be allowed to come in, it "broke his heart," and he allowed him to come, talking to him about correcting one's mistakes and learning from them. He said that after two days of these methods, none of the children have had difficulties with tardiness.

FUTURE DREAMS

Every programme has some room for improvement regardless of current successful application so I asked the managers, teachers and students if there is any one thing they would like to add to their school. Interestingly enough, their answers all coincided with similar categories.

The following is a list of the five most common answers and a summary of the participants' comments:

- *Transportation*: They would like a bus or large van for the children, staff and even parents when they come in for meetings with the teacher. With no public transportation in the rural areas, the distance is often so far that if children walk, as was noted before, they are often late to class or do not come at all.

- *Music*: Even though most of the 6th grade focus group had already given me their answer, when one student said they would like musical instruments or singing classes, two-thirds of the class instantly raised their hands in agreement and wanted me to add that to their previous answer. Teachers also wanted to have music and to be included in the community-wide events that some of the DEI schools are competing in successfully. In some of the classes, I found it interesting that the children did not hold a tune very well, but sang in more of a chant. Although it is typical for several children out of a class of 30 to not be musically gifted, I found this lack of ability to sing to be noticeable. I asked how much exposure they have to music and I was told there is very little due to where they live in rural areas, the lack of electricity, and so on. There is little that would train their ear from a young age while forming foundational musical abilities.
- *Science Labs*: Science in general seemed to be very important to these students and their teachers. Several students said their favourite subject was science, and they listed specific topics, with ten out of 23 saying biology. Other students listed chemistry, physics and botany. Teachers wanted to be able to offer these science classes that utilized their full expertise and to include hands-on laboratory experience for the children.
- *Libraries*: Every group wanted to add a library that would be available to check out material such as history books, general knowledge books, science books and stories. Some of the schools are going to be able to add this soon.
- *Sports Programmes and Equipment*: Each school

> generally had one or two barrels with play equipment to be shared by all classes at recess time. In receiving the gifts sent from the United States, one teacher said, "Thank you for the gifts, you have just doubled our jump rope supply!" I had only delivered one per school. The children wanted organized competitive sports, and the teachers and managers said that having an actual Physical Education teacher would help with discipline issues as there would be an incentive to behave or else miss out on something they enjoyed. Also, they said that PE teachers are trained in techniques of order and discipline

Surprisingly, only two people mentioned tables, chairs and desks, even though many of the classrooms had no furniture. At the time, I did not think to question whether they considered this an obvious goal they were already working towards or unnecessary compared to the other items they could not substitute with any other object or method, such as sitting on the floor.

There were several other needs listed, such as manipulatives, audiovisual equipment, computers and craft supplies. In this part, I summarize the interviews with staff regarding fees that parents pay for their child to attend, and how it is handled if they cannot pay. Also discussed are the school's provision of books, supplies, uniforms and the availability of a midday meal, as well as facility issues.

COST OF EDUCATION

As is stated in their goals, and through interviews, the DEI leadership has found that having the parents pay for part of the education creates a sense of ownership and accountability.

Each of the schools charges fees on a different scale, based on the surrounding community, the average wage and availability of jobs for the parents. Once this is determined, the fee is collected from the parents on a monthly basis, with the rest being subsidized by the DEI funding. There is a problem with the transience of some families due to the type of seasonal labour they are employed in. Therefore, the fees are adjusted by school depending on these issues. School D, for example, charges an initial fee of 50-100 rupees with the monthly remainder supplied by the DEI which covers the costs if a family leaves and takes the supplies with them. For Schools A, B and C, the parents pay fees ranging from 25 to 30 rupees per month with the remainder of the cost of approximately 75 rupees per month being subsidized by international funding through the DEI.

The managers, most parents are able to supply the fees, but if they cannot, the DEI pays the full fee. An average salary in the rural area of School A is 1,000 rupees per month which is approximately 25 dollars.

BOOKS, SUPPLIES AND UNIFORMS

Each of the schools supplies at least one uniform per student, which usually included shorts for the boys, a jumper for the girls, one shirt, socks, shoes, and a belt and tie for both. One of the schools supplies two uniforms. These children come from such poverty, that they have found that having one complete clean outfit brings a sense of pride, belonging and unity. It also levels all sense if inequality, as each has equal opportunity to look the same at school.

I noticed the children generally came with carefully groomed hair, the girls in pony tails and braids, sometimes wearing bracelets and barrettes. When one school was notified that morning that I was coming to evaluate the school, the principal, knowing it was wash day in the community, quickly sent the local children back home to put their uniforms on for their "inspection."

When I arrived, some were in uniform and some in "street clothes," and the principal explained the situation, wishing they each had two uniforms so that all week long, they could look clean and well groomed.

As a way of combining efforts within the community, the women who are learning to sew, create the uniforms for the children, so it is a matter of funding more than availability. Each school, after carefully evaluating the needs within the community, supplies at least the school books required, and some schools add a book bag, writing utensils and other supplies. The children carry an average of over 20 small text books and writing books each day, similar to the size of a bluebook used for exams.

People from the United States had donated one suitcase of gifts for the schools, including Frisbees, blow up balls, pencils, vitamins, and so on. One of the teaching interns was excited about the pencils.

She explained that one day, one of the young boys got up to leave the classroom after she asked them to write down an assignment. She told him to sit down and follow directions. He said, "I can't, I have to go see my brother." She reminded him that this was class time, and he could see his brother later. After some interchange, he finally explained, "I have to go see my brother, he has our pencil!" Most of the younger children use chalk and a slate board for in-class work such as math calculations.

This school provides all the supplies needed for any science fair projects or materials needed to join in local school competitions as they have found that parents cannot afford these additional expenses.

MIDDAY MEAL

Two of the schools no longer provide a midday meal of eggs and fruit because they did not have enough resources and had determined that this was a programme that would have to be cut rather than cut resources to any other part of the programme.

One school is still planning to initiate this programme when they have a new building as there is no kitchen facility at their current site. One of the schools gives one egg per day for each student.

Although the director acknowledged that research shows that children at this level of need could do better in school with a meal provided, he felt that these particular children would get some sort of a meal from home, but that parents would not be able to, or would not choose to buy books or school supplies. This decision is made individually for each school depending on the needs within that community.

FACILITIES

One of the needs most commonly mentioned is to have separate bathroom facilities for boys and girls. Several adults that I interviewed explained that these children are "exposed to way too much information about life," living in the conditions that they do.

They explained that Dalits are usually expected to use open fields, or that girls, especially in the slums, are exposed to even dangerous conditions, being made to wait until evening to use the facilities, which puts them at risk of attack or even rape.

By adding separate facilities, they felt they could add to the community education about health and hygiene. Also, if a lunch programme is to be provided, they would need a room in which to store and prepare the food. Each of the schools I visited was using every room available, sometimes for multiple purposes such as after school programmes and self-help groups, with no place for teachers to store their materials, join for meetings, study or prepare.

They said that all schools will need to expand, not only to supply these needs, but to even have enough rooms for each grade level as the schools grow each year to meet the demand. Some of the most common requests for improvement that I heard were for a teachers' room, computer lab, library, science lab and enough rooms to at least go through the eighth grade. However, as one principal shared, the DEI and partner organizations are continuously putting money into new schools, which then limits the resources available to existing schools. This dilemma will be discussed in the conclusion as I look at future goals.

OVERALL SUCCESS OF THE PROGRAMME

Each of the findings show clear accomplishment of the overall goals of the DEI, with each school at a different level of achievement due to location, years since establishment, availability of resources as well as background of the children. Although there are areas that each could improve if given additional resources, seeing the difference in these children's lives, knowing the environment and background from which they approach this educational experience, is remarkable.

Ideally, I would like to continue to follow the success of this programme over time, and to interview the parents, students and community leaders to assess the long term positive influence for these children and their whole community.

4

Economic, Social and Cultural Rights

INTRODUCTION

Economic, social and cultural rights form an integral part of the Universal Declaration of Human Rights of 1948 and are further detailed in the 1966 International Covenant of Economic, Social and Cultural Rights. However, since their inclusion in these treaties, they have received little attention from states and human rights organizations. In fact, many are not even aware of the existence of ESC rights, believing human rights to be comprised only of civil and political rights.

This limits the prospects for systemic changes, reduces knowledge of individual and group entitlements, and reduces government accountability to international agreements. Fortunately, both human rights and development organizations are slowly beginning to recognize the importance of ESC rights. However, not all organizations have arrived at this conclusion, and for those that have, they have yet to move beyond mere recognition.

This needs to change. It is time that organizations reassess their current approaches, change their perceptions regarding human rights and begin to use a comprehensive human rights framework to reduce and eradicate poverty. We present a case study that exemplifies a situation in need of a human rights approach that incorporates ESC rights: that of Dalits in India. For centuries, Dalits have been victims of gross human rights violations. This has led to their current low social and economic status within Indian society. All of this has occurred in a country in which the government has not only signed numerous treaties pledging respect of human rights, but has also incorporated human rights into its Constitution. Thus, India presents an interesting case in which commitment is evident on document but is not exercised in practice.

Within this case study, we examine how India has violated one fundamental ESC right: the right to education. To further support this claim, we take the specific example of violations of the right to primary education in rural villages in Gujarat. We then offer recommendations aimed at improving this particular situation, as well as recommendations that address the more global problem – the lack of full recognition of ESC rights in the human rights dialogue.

UNDERSTANDING THE ECONOMIC, SOCIAL AND CULTURAL RIGHTS

Economic, social and cultural rights have been enumerated in a number of international treaties, such as the International Covenant of Economic, Social and Cultural Rights. These rights include, among others, the right of self-determination, the right to work, the right to just and favourable conditions of work, the right to form and join trade unions, the right to social security and social insurance, the right to an adequate standard of living, and the right to education. In practice, however, ESC rights have never received a great deal of attention from the 137 states that signed the ICESCR or human rights organizations. While there are reasonable explanations given for this neglect, they are not substantial enough to prevent the inclusion of ESC rights into a human rights approach – especially after one considers the benefits resulting from such inclusion.

REASONS FOR NEGLECT

ESC rights have not only suffered from lack of implementation, but also from lack of recognition. The Centre for Economic and Social Rights, one reason for this neglect is that addressing ESC rights would mean, "addressing the enormous and growing inequalities at all levels of human society, from local to global." So far, the international community has not been willing to take on such a monumental task.

The other explanations for this neglect can be divided into two categories:

1. Predominance of civil and political rights,
2. Lack of clarity regarding ESC rights.

Civil and Political Rights

Simply put, for the last 50 years, human rights organizations and states have focused their attention almost solely on civil and political rights. This preference can be attributed to a number of different causes. First, during the Cold War the United States used its relatively good record on civil and political rights to condemn the gross civil and political rights abuses that were occurring in communist countries such as China and the USSR. Second, some believe that there is an implicit ranking system for human rights and that civil and political rights must first be met in order to enable a struggle for ESC rights.

For example, Josh Rubenstein of Amnesty International asserts, "the dirty little secret is that [the human rights movement] really does believe that if you don't have the right to say what you want, you're not going to get what you need. It comes down to the fact that you have to protect civil and political rights first, if only as a vehicle to assert ESC rights." Lastly, many view civil and political rights as negative rights, while ESC rights are viewed as positive rights. Negative rights are those that do not require state resources and the actual obligation of the state is not to do something, *i.e.* not to subject an individual to torture or not to carry out arbitrary arrests.

Positive rights, on the other hand, require state resources since they are seen as obligations to do something, *i.e.* to provide free education. Presented in this manner, it is easy to see why states have been more receptive to implementing civil and political rights and thus why NGOs have chosen subsequently to focus their efforts on this set of rights.

Ambiguity Surrounding ESC Rights

The other main reason for neglect stems from the general ambiguity surrounding ESC rights. A training resource on ESC rights asserts, "as a result of the relative inattention paid to ESC rights over the past several decades ... the content and meaning of most ESC rights remain relatively ill-defined." This lack of clarity as to what exactly constitutes an ESC right has served to complicate and deter efforts of human rights organizations to address these rights.

There is also a high degree of vagueness regarding what the actual obligations of the state are.

This can be attributed to Article 2 (1) of the ICESCR, which states:

- Each State Party to the present Covenant undertakes to take steps, individually and through international assistance and cooperation, especially economic and technical, to the maximum of its available resources, with a view to achieving progressively the full realisation of the rights recognized in the present Covenant by all appropriate means, including particularly the adoption of legislative measures.

Without having a sound notion of the exact nature of state parties' obligations, individuals and human rights organizations are given very little room to either accuse states of being violators or to pressure them into living up to their commitments. Furthermore, the state itself is unsure of its exact obligations. Thus, they might not be fulfilling them for lack of knowledge, rather than lack of desire.

THE HUMAN RIGHTS FRAMEWORK

Even after considering the challenges using a human rights framework that incorporates economic, social and cultural rights to confront poverty and inequity is still desirable.

States' Obligations – Changing the Perception

ESC rights, such as the right to an adequate standard of living or the right to work, are not generally seen as rights, but rather as benefits given by the state. They are also commonly viewed as aspirations that the state would one day like to fulfill. The human rights framework radically alters this perception by presenting ESC rights as obligations of the state.

As stated by the Committee on Economic, Social and Cultural Rights:

- When a State ratifies one of the Covenants, it accepts a solemn responsibility to apply each of the obligations embodied therein and to ensure the compatibility of their national laws with their international duties, in a spirit of good faith. Through the ratification of human rights treaties, therefore, States become accountable to the international community, to other States, which have ratified the same texts, and to their own citizens and others resident in their territories.

Governments therefore have a duty to fulfill, respect, promote and protect all of the rights of their citizens. Governments that fail to do so should be held accountable for their behaviour. A comprehensive human rights framework utilizes this obligation, equipping non-governmental organizations and citizens with a powerful new tool. This tool can be used to pressure governments to both provide the basic social services addressed in the ICESCR and to reevaluate their policies to ensure that they are in-line with the international human rights norms and treaties to which the governments are parties.

Empowerment Tool

At a local level, changing the view of ESC rights would have significant impacts. As individuals begin to regard ESC rights as entitlements, not handouts, they would no longer tolerate the inaction or neglect of their governments on these social issues. They would start to mobilize and demand that their governments fulfill their obligations to their people.

A Complete Approach

Any human rights approach should be comprehensive, stressing the importance of all human rights, be they civil and political or economic, social and cultural. This approach not only recognizes the equal value of each right, but it is more realistic. Rights are inextricably intertwined with one another: the full enjoyment of one right often requires the full enjoyment of another. Nowhere is this more evident than with the right to education.

FOCUS ON THE RIGHT TO EDUCATION

The right to education can be found at the intersection of economic, cultural and social rights with civil and political rights. An undereducated person will face limited employment opportunities, thus making him economically vulnerable. This vulnerability could result in his conscious decision not to exercise other rights, such as the right to join a trade union or the right to freedom of speech, out of fear of possible reprisals. An undereducated person might be unaware of the rights to which he is entitled or may not fully comprehend their meaning.

An undereducated person may not be able to effectively participate in the political arena. In sum, without adequate education a person is not able to fully enjoy or assert his human rights. The right to education serves not only to unlock other human rights, but also a number of other vital functions. First, being educated itself has important intrinsic value. Second, just as to Amartya Sen, greater literacy and educational achievements of disadvantaged groups can increase their ability to resist oppression, to organize politically, and to get a fairer deal.

Lastly, education is an empowerment tool by which "economically and socially marginalized adults and children can lift themselves out of poverty and obtain the means to participate fully in their communities."

DALITS

This is the reality faced by the more than 160 million Dalits living in India today. As this description shows and as the National Campaign on Dalit Human Rights asserts "India's version of apartheid and racism, caste discrimination and "untouchability" affect every facet and dimension of Dalits' daily lives – economic, social, cultural and political." Thus, the need to address this situation through a human rights lens that incorporates ESC rights is vital.

Centuries of this "hidden apartheid" that has perpetuated discrimination and denial of their human rights, has resulted not only in Dalits representing a disproportional amount of the poor in India, but also in the creation of numerous other obstacles that hinder Dalits' ability to change their situation.

VESTIGES OF UNTOUCHABILITY

Caste separation is manifested in many ways. It is common place in rural villages for there to be an area called "Dalit Street." This is the only area in which Dalits are allowed to live. As such, it is often the site of neglect as services can easily be diverted away from it or never brought to it. Dalits are often expected to carry out traditional roles for which they receive no compensation.

For example, they must play the drums in religious ceremonies and must remove dead animals. Their participation in such acts only works to perpetuate the discrimination against them. Finally, overcoming one's status as a Dalit is incredibly difficult. When a qualified Dalit applies for a job, interviewers often inquire as to the applicant's caste. Once this is known, his prospects of getting the job are greatly diminished.

EMPLOYMENT OPPORTUNITIES

The National Campaign on Dalit Rights, Dalits constitute the majority of the bonded and child labour in India. Agricultural work is done mainly by Dalits, and many Dalit women are forced into ritualized prostitution. In many villages, the practice of manual scavenging, the removal of human excrement, is only undertaken by Dalits.

Added to this is the fact that Dalits are often paid less than the minimum wage or not at all, instead receiving payments-in-kind. The reservation system, which was specifically designed to provide employment opportunities to disadvantaged groups within India, has only benefited a small number of Dalits. This is partly because the system only applies to the government sector. More generally, it is because this system has proven itself to be flawed, corrupt, and lacking full implementation, as numerous positions go unfilled. Entrepreneurial opportunities for Dalits are extremely limited. First of all, Dalits lack both the capital investment for such a venture and the collateral to secure a loan to obtain it. Moreover, even if they were to open a business, it would almost certainly be doomed to fail.

This is because non-Dalits would not frequent it, preferring instead to frequent a non-Dalit store. Thus, its success would depend entirely on the Dalits in the village. Given that they generally constitute a very small minority in villages and that they have very little money to spend, the prospects are not very encouraging. Other economic opportunities are also scarce for Dalits as India suffers from a limited amount of jobs and resources. The small amount that does exist largely goes to those already in power, exacerbating the gap between poor and rich.

MIGRATION

In order to survive, Dalits often must migrate in search of work. The main cause of this migration is lack of land ownership. Without their own land, Dalits are unable to produce crops for their own consumption or for sale in the market. This combined with the limited employment opportunities available in their small villages forces them to leave their village in search of work elsewhere.

Another cause of migration is general economic hardships, such as droughts. Dalits do not have the resources needed to get through such periods, as they are often refused loans even after agreeing to exorbitantly high interest rates and are unable to turn to their equally challenged Dalit neighbours for help. Lastly, Dalits prefer migration to permanent establishment in new communities since such an endeavor would require vast resources and would result in the loss of their existing social networks.

INDIA

ECONOMIC AND POLITICAL SITUATION IN INDIA

India, in particular, presents an interesting case study for further examining the recognition and implementation of ESC rights. Like many developing countries, the economy is driven by agriculture, with one-third of national output and two-thirds of employment being accounted for by this sector. In the economy there is divisive income inequality, and a full twenty per cent of the urban population and thirty per cent of the rural population live below the poverty level.

An expanding population of more than one billion further compounds economic problems. India, also however, exhibits many characteristics associated with developed countries. It continues to be in transition from a largely government-controlled economy to one that is largely market driven. It has a comprehensive Constitution supported and upheld by a well-established legislative and judicial system.

However, in India there remains a momentous divide between commitment to making law and enforcing full implementation of such laws. There is conflicting evidence on India's commitment to ensuring ESC rights. In a speech addressing India and human rights Prime Minister Atal Bihari Vajpayee said:

- The more we enforce the rule of law, the better we promote human rights... In a developing country like India, the task of advancing human rights is integrally linked to speedy and balanced socio-economic growth. Poverty is one of the worst violators of human rights—and so also is the society that allows poverty to persist. India has all the human and natural resources needed to provide decent living standards to all our citizens. This, however, can be achieved only by removing the shackles on India's all-round economic progress. This is the true purpose of our economic reforms. Our reforms have a human face because they are designed to promote economic and social justice for all our citizens, especially the poorest and the most deprived.

India is committed to legislating ideas of civil, political, economic, social, and cultural rights as well as legislating against human rights violations. To help overcome the problems of historic discrimination of caste and gender, India legislated and created a stringent reservation system to allow for increased opportunity. However, while there have been successes as a result of the system, there is not complete commitment to implementation and support of the system. The intended recipients are still unable to be equally educated or to be hired for the reserved government jobs.

They do not have the authority positions to make changes. Instead, this motivation must come from those who are upper caste and upper class, and there is simply a lack of political will at any level to implement the laws and realise such advancements towards human rights.

India has also ratified several international covenants focusing on varying aspects of human rights, including the Universal Declaration of Human Rights as well as ICESCR. It has enacted many laws that support the spirit of the Declaration and the Covenant, as well as laws that provide precise rights and obligations beyond the vagueness of the international documents. Along with 188 other countries India has committed itself to eight Millennium Development Goals that aim to eradicate extreme poverty and improve the welfare of all peoples by the year 2015.

The second development goal has been coined "Education for All" with the goal being to "achieve universal primary education" with the specific target of "ensuring that, by 2015, children everywhere, boys and girls alike, will be able to complete a full course of primary schooling." As one of the largest countries, and with large amounts of children failing to complete primary school, improvement in India is crucial to the United Nations and the world meeting this second goal.

INDIA AND EDUCATION

The Constitution of India goes well beyond the UN's primary education mandate. Article 45 of the Constitution states that:

- "The State shall endeavor to provide within a period of ten years from the commencement of this Constitution, for free and compulsory education for all children until they complete the age of fourteen years." The next article certifies that "the State shall promote with special care the educational and economic interests of the weaker parts of the people, and in particular, of the Scheduled Castes and the Scheduled Tribes, and shall protect them from social injustice and all forms of exploitation."

However, government reports estimate that only two-thirds of children in India complete their primary education; this translates into a conservative estimate of 20 to 30 million children not being in primary school or twenty-five per cent of the estimated 120 million primary-aged children not in school worldwide.

Activists consider this to be a vast understatement of the number of unenrolled children. It is also estimated that ten per cent of children in India never begin primary school; these children are disproportionately comprised of children from rural areas, those from scheduled tribes and scheduled castes, and girls.

Quality of Education

Even when children are able to attend school the quality of public education in India is inconsistent and often inadequate. Quality varies dramatically across states and districts as well as between urban and rural areas. The poor quality of schooling in India can be attributed to many factors. First, the physical infrastructure of the schools has historically been inadequate. Schools are often in poor condition or are too small to serve the number of kids in the district.

Children are often in classrooms upward of sixty people. Even if a teacher is actively attempting to teach the students, he or she is unable to spend time on individual instruction. There is a more significant issue given that students are often well below the competency required of their current grade level. On one side, there are reports that teachers do not "teach" enough. Many times they show up late or simply do not even show up at all. Such a situation occurs partly because teachers are not accountable to the local community. They are often not from the community in which they teach and their salaries are controlled by the state. Conversely, teachers feel that their work conditions are not conducive to better teaching methods. For instance, teachers are often compelled to teach more than one grade at a time. Together, the weight of these simultaneous conditions all serve to weaken the quality of the schools.

Government does provide many schemes to attempt to improve both access and quality of education. Currently, there are 130 such schemes with the largest being the Mid-Day Meal scheme that provides a cooked meal to all students in primary school, as a way to encourage poor-child enrollment. Other programmes include Operation Blackboard to improve school facilities; there are also several schemes specific to the needs of districts or even an entire state.

The government is also designing schemes to meet their commitment to the goal of universality of elementary education. These programmes include reducing the costs of textbooks and exercise books to removing systematic deficiencies towards primary education for all. The expansion of these programmes shows a certain level of commitment by the Indian government.

However, the question remains whether India's current commitment level to primary education is enough. As is often the case with education statistics in India, data aggregated at the national level do not reveal the disparities that are central to ensuring quality primary education across districts and states, rural and urban areas, as well as socio-economic levels. Furthermore, despite the supposed effort, the primary education completion rate has only risen from 75% in 1990 to 76% in 1999.

Again, this is due to the lack of political will in both administration and implementation. India does not allow that there are by-products of caste discrimination in the education system. The district administration officer in Gujarat acknowledges that while there may be discrimination between teachers and the village or between teachers and teachers that discrimination between teachers and Dalit students is nonexistent. This is in clear contrast to what we heard from the Dalit people. This failure to admit such discrimination prevents government officials from attempting to truly improve the situation.

DALIT EDUCATION IN INDIA

Dalit children, being disproportionately poor, most heavily suffer the ills of an inequitable and ineffective education system in India. The Indian constitution pledges to provide free and compulsory education for all children up to age fourteen.

However, in 1993 only 16.2% of primary school age Dalit children in were enrolled in school as compared to 83.8% of primary aged children from non-scheduled castes. The India Education Report, school attendance in rural areas in 1993-94 was 64.3% for Dalit boys and 46.2% for Dalit girls, compared to 74.9% among boys and 61% girls from other social groups Dalits lagged behind the general population by as many as 15 percentage points in literacy, and just as to the 1991 Census, barely 24 per cent of Dalit women were literate.

Statistics also show that Dalit children are more likely to drop out than their non-Dalit counterparts, particularly in the early elementary stages. Education represents one way to break out of cycles of poverty and distress, but it is also a by-product of such economic conditions. Even when Dalits are allowed access to school, Dalit students face substandard conditions.

Ninety-nine per cent of Dalit students come from government schools that lack basic infrastructure, classrooms, teachers and teaching aid. In contrast, it is common for non-Dalit children to seek private tutoring or to access private education of generally better quality. The motivation to do so comes from the fact that most primary government schools are considered low quality. Few Dalits are able to access such supplementation to their education; this furthers the education gap. Once enrolled, discrimination continues to obstruct the access of Dalit children to schooling as well as to affect the quality of education they receive.

CASE STUDY OF THE VIOLATION OF THE RIGHT TO PRIMARY EDUCATION IN GUJARAT

Like civil and political rights, ESC rights can be broken when inadequate protection is taken.

In this part, we address the issue of the violation of ESC rights:

- The Universal Declaration of Human Rights;
- The International Covenant on Economic, Social and Cultural Rights; and
- The Convention on the Rights of the Child.

From these texts, we have found four main themes of direct relevance to the condition of Dalit school children in Gujarat, namely de facto discrimination, failure to promote human dignity, hindrances to the enjoyment of education and failure to foster the full development of children. We offer illustrations of the violations of ESC rights as told to us by children, parents, teachers and organizers on our field visits throughout rural Gujarat.

DE FACTO DISCRIMINATION

Practices at local levels intended to keep castes separate or reinforce caste distinctions result in instances of discrimination. The informational report from Article 13, point 37 of the ICESCR states that "parties must closely monitor education—including all relevant policies, institutions, programmes, spending patterns and other practices—so as to identify and take measures to redress any de facto discrimination." De facto discrimination in rural Gujarat occurs in myriad ways. From our visits to villages, we heard stories regarding the explicit discrimination of Dalits in the arenas of classroom seating, permission to participate in class activities and the receipt of lower marks for high quality work. Similar issues in discrimination are addressed in later categories.

Classroom Seating

Perhaps the most widely discussed violation regarding

children is the requirement of some non-Dalit teachers for Dalit students to sit exclusively in the back of classrooms. This was a common complaint in many of the villages we visited. In each instance of violation, the teacher was a non-Dalit who was either the only teacher for the village or among a non-Dalit teacher majority.

- Visiting with Dalit rights organizers in the taluka of Sami, we were told that this practice occurs in the majority of the schools in the 34 villages that comprise the taluka.
- The village of Sahpur has about 2000 residents and a Dalit minority of 100. Students in this village told us that they are required to reserve front seats in the classroom for non-Dalit children.
- The village of Dodar has about 3500 residents, 600 of whom are Dalit. One young girl named Sonar told us that she likes school, and that she one day hopes to become a doctor or teacher. She told us that Dalit children in her school are required to sit in the back of the classroom and are required to remove their shoes in the classroom. Non-Dalit children, she said, are not subject to the same requirements.

Access to Participation

Forced seating in the back of the classroom expressly limits student access to participation in class. Class sizes in rural Gujarat average 60 students. The vast overcrowding of Gujarati classrooms limits teacher capacity to interact with students; sitting in the back further minimizes interaction with and support from teachers.

- Dalit children in Sahpur said that they are not called on to answer teacher questions or invited to write on the board as frequently as non-Dalit children. These students told us that this is a source of embarrassment, and is a reason why non-Dalit children mock them.
- Sonar from Dodar told us that her teacher often calls on students, but only calls on those sitting in the first through fourth rows. The vast class size in her village

and her status as a Dalit keeps her far from even the fourth row.

Grading

The receipt of unjustifiably low marks is a common concern we heard from children in rural Gujarat. Dalit Organizers say that there are many reports from villages throughout the state that non-Dalits receive higher marks while Dalits fare relatively poorly.

Local organizers in the taluka of Sami have received numerous complaints from students regarding grading in their villages. These complaints have come from even the top-scoring Dalits who feel their work is of equal or better quality to the work of the best non-Dalits.

- In Sahpur, a young girl named Sangeetha believes she was kept in the third grade for three consecutive years because she is Dalit. She considers herself a hard-working student who does well in class. However, she believes that her teacher intentionally makes her and other Dalit children fail by falsifying grades. She told us that it is frustrating to do the same work year after year, work she claims is easy. She said it makes her not want to go to school at all.

FAILURE TO PROMOTE HUMAN DIGNITY

An issue closely linked to de facto discrimination is the failure to promote human dignity. ESC documents explicitly address the issue of human dignity, asserting that equality is a trait that should be both engendered and upheld.

Article 29 (1)(d) of the CRC states an education is to be "the preparation of the child for responsible life in a free society, in the spirit of understanding, peace, tolerance, equality of sexes, and friendship...."

Article 13 (1) of the ICESCR further states that "education shall be directed to the full development of the human personality and the sense of its dignity." With regard to the achievement of full human dignity for and within the Dalit community, actions of some schools demonstrate that this aim is not always taken seriously. Explicit reinforcement of caste lines exacerbates inequality. This is evident in the relegation of Dalit students to the backs of classrooms, the separation of children and even teachers for water and food consumption, the exclusive assignment of Dalit students to custodial duties, and verbally abusive statements directed to reinforce inequalities.

Sitting in the Back of the Classroom

Forcing Dalits to sit in the back of the room limits their learning potential. Moreover, it reinforces inequality among the students, creates tiers within the classroom based on caste and instills a feeling of inferiority within Dalit children. We met children who, despite being forced to save front row seats for non-Dalit children, have internalized the separation, accepted it as a way of life, and do not believe their own human dignity demands equality in the classroom.

- We met with a group of Dalit teachers outside of Ahmedabad who say that even when seating is not assigned, Dalit students will gravitate towards the back of the classroom. They said this is most likely a result of previous experience with non-Dalit teachers. The students may have been told at some point to sit in the back and threatened with punishment. The teachers told us that Dalit students have been conditioned to be afraid of sitting in the front, fearing punishment from the teacher and/or ostracizing from non-Dalits.
- A young girl in Sahpur told us, "we are Harijans, so we are obliged to sit in the back."

Food and Water Consumption

Caste divisions and inequalities are reinforced with historic caste taboos regarding food and water consumption. Notions that Dalits are "dirty" or "impure" are pervasive in some villages, and teachers systematically seek to have students internalize and accept these derogatory terms.

- In the village of Tara Nagar, Dalit children told us

that their teachers forbid them from sitting with non-Dalit children, either in the classroom or during lunch hours. These children also told us that they are explicitly forbidden from touching the plates of non-Dalit children.

- Jagruti, a 12 year-old girl from the village of Sahpur, told us that if Dalit children want water they are required by the teacher to wait until a non-Dalit is available to pour water from several feet above them into either their hands our their mouths.
- Sami Dalit organizers, six schools in the taluka have requirements that keep Dalit students separate from non-Dalit students at lunchtime.
- Dalit teachers are not excluded from such discriminatory behaviour. In the village of Kumbhana, a Dalit teacher named Jignasha was told by her principal to keep her water pot separate from the water pots of other teachers.

Custodial Duties

The human dignity of Dalit children is further hindered in schools in which Dalit children are exclusively required to take on additional custodial duties.

In instances of this violation, Dalit children were as a group required to take on additional cleaning duties, while non-Dalit children were not.

- In the village of Sahpur, despite not being allowed to get their own water from the school's supply, Dalit children are required to clean the water tank on behalf of non-Dalit children and the non-Dalit teacher.
- Bankje, a young boy in the same village, told us that Dalit children are required to arrive to school early in order to clean the school before the non-Dalit children arrive. When late for cleaning, Bankje said, students are scolded.
- In the village of Dodar, Dalit children are also made to clean. A young girl, Jusna, this cleaning can include both the school and the outdoor garden.

Verbal Abuse

Specific instances of verbal abuse on the part of teachers show the reinforcement of caste prejudices and inequalities.

- Jagrathi, a boy in his final year of primary school in Sahpur, spoke of an incident at school. The teacher asked that students planning to go on to secondary school raise their hands. Jagrathi and one other Dalit child raised their hands. The teacher approached the two, and told them that they are Dalits, that they were never going to go to secondary school and that they should lower their hands.
- The father told us that his young daughter came home after school one day and asked him, "Father, are we daed?" He asked her who told her that they are daed. She replied, "my teacher."

HINDRANCES TO ENJOYING EDUCATION

Constraints that are especially felt by the Dalit community hinder the access of Dalit children to educational opportunities. The informational report on implementation of Article 13 (47) of ICESCR requires "States parties to avoid measures that hinder or prevent the enjoyment of the right to education." It goes on to require that "[s]tates ... take positive measures that enable and assist individuals and communities to enjoy the right to education."

Issues of land-ownership, generational repetition of under-education and limited social networks compound to render the Dalit community particularly vulnerable.

These characteristics are common in poor communities throughout the world, but the Dalits of Gujarat and of India experience them more so than other caste groups. They especially effect primary school age children through migratory laboring.

Migratory Labour

Though the problem of and the problems deriving from labour migration are not unique to the Dalit community, we found them to be especially pervasive among Dalits. Migration serves as a hindrance to the education in that parents generally take their children with them while searching for labour. Young boys and girls are often expected to work alongside their parents in day laboring jobs and young girls are often made to care for younger siblings. Permanent migration is not always a preferred option for families, as much weight is put on extended familial connections and ritual obligations such as marriage. Migratory spells generally last four months and are most common during the dry season. Once students have missed 18 days, children are no longer allowed to advance with their class.

- In the village of Gadthal, the parents of 35 Dalit children have left in search of labour and taken their children with them. Very few non-Dalit children are effected by migration in this village as most non-Dalits own land. Only a small minority of Dalits own land there. Families travel up to 200 km to find work.
- In the village of Nani Kathechi, the parents of 29 of the village's 44 Dalit children have left in search of labour, and taken their children with them. Though most return about every four months, the 29 children are not able to keep up in school, and many simply drop out.
- Some migrant laborers are doing their best to stop history from repeating itself. A man in the same village, who is temporarily back from his time as a migrant laborer in Jogar, told us that he leaves his son in the village with older relatives so that he can attend school. When asked why he makes this a priority, he said that it is indeed difficult, because he could use his son's help. However, he told us that his father too was a migrant laborer, and he had to go with his father and drop out of school. He does not want his son to live the life that he has had to live.

FAILURE TO FOSTER THE FULL DEVELOPMENT OF CHILDREN

The full development of children is a standard component

of ESC rights documents. Article 29 (1)(a) of the CRC requires that the education of a child be directed "to the development of the child's personality, talents and mental and physical abilities to their fullest potential." Article 26 (2) of the UDHR states that "education shall be directed to the full development of the human personality and to the strengthening of respect for human rights and fundamental freedoms."

Article 13 (1) of the ICESCR further reinforces its predecessors, stating that "education shall be directed to the full development of the human personality and the sense of its dignity, and shall strengthen the respect for human rights and fundamental freedoms."

Achieving the full development of children requires significant resources. Understanding that resources are greatly constrained in a developing country, we seek to evaluate Gujarat in its specific context. We identify the violation of rights based on the pursuit to provide means towards full development to one group while explicitly excluding another. We heard of instances of such violation with regard to school activities.

School Activities

We met young children who told us that they are not allowed to participate in various school activities simply because they are Dalits.

- In the village of Sahpur, a young girl named Jagneth told us that Dalit children are routinely excluded from participation in school activities, such as cultural programmes. Students are told that only non-Dalits can participate in events.
- A young Dalit boy in the same village, Nitesh, told us that he was recently not allowed to participate in a picnic, as it was restricted to only non-Dalits.

CONCLUSION AND RECOMMENDATIONS

Dalits face a cultural and normative history entrenched in discrimination. Despite efforts to codify human rights into state legislation, the violation of many ESC rights is visible throughout India. Discrimination is indeed deeply rooted, and efforts must be taken to realise the international commitments to which India is subject. Both the Indian government and the NGO sector can advance the condition of Dalits concerning ESC rights.

RECOMMENDATIONS TO THE INDIAN GOVERNMENT

The discrimination that exists in India has serious ramifications in the realm of education. The caste-based statements made by teachers damage children.

School and classroom rules regarding the separation of students by caste and reinforcement of taboos result in the maintenance of centuries-old divisions and minimize other public efforts to fight discrimination. Beyond mere legislation, the Indian government can make a difference in the classroom.

Actions include the following:

- Reverse the current trend of decreased spending on education and work towards meeting international spending norms. In 1990, India's public expenditure on education was 3.9% of its GNP. In 1997 this proportion had dropped to 3.3%. India must not continue to cut spending. Instead it should increase spending on education to at least 5% of its GNP, which would bring it within the range of the world average. It could do so by prioritizing spending and shifting obligations within the federal budget. For instance, India currently spends a large amount of tax revenue on the government sector, but a small amount on education. By increasing spending, the government will be able to improve the quality of education by providing more schools and teachers, higher salaries for teachers, better teacher training and increased availability of school materials.
- Incorporate ESC rights education into teachers' training curriculum. This will inform teachers of both their rights and those of their students. Moreover, by providing such education, teachers can then be

held more accountable for any violations they may commit.

- Provide teachers with sensitivity training. This would go one step beyond basic human rights education in that it would equip teachers with the skills needed to effectively address inequalities in their classrooms. First, it would focus on the teachers' belief system and would try to get teachers to recognize any prejudices they may have. It would then discuss ways for teachers to deal with and ultimately overcome these prejudices. Second, it would look at Dalit children, in particular at their internalization of discrimination and at their economic and social condition. It would discuss how both of these have significant effects on the way Dalits' participate and perform in school. It would then offer ways for teachers to encourage greater participation by Dalits. Lastly, it would concentrate on the mentality of non-Dalit children, recognizing that they too carry prejudices that need to be addressed. It would offer ways to deal with these prejudices, such as promoting dignity and equality among all students.
- Random monitoring to ensure compliance. In order to ensure that teachers are not forcing Dalits to sit in the back of classrooms, restricting them from passing out food and requiring them to clean the classrooms, the government should make unannounced visits to schools. During these visits, the officials could also speak with Dalit and non-Dalit children, as well as parents and teachers in the village to assess the situation. If violations are taking place, the officials should take immediate action to stop them.
- Punishment for non-compliance. If a teacher is found to be violating any student's rights, regardless of their caste, then he should be given a strict penalty, such as suspension without pay.

As important as these recommendations are, it goes without saying that they only scratch the surface of the challenges that India face. In order to have a real impact, they need to be accompanied by an integrated commitment to ESC rights and to an elevation of the status and economic situation of Dalits by the Indian government. For example, the government needs to look for solutions to the migration problem, such as providing the poor with productive land or providing more economic opportunities for people in villages. It must also look for ways to end the segregation of Dalits in villages.

RECOMMENDATIONS TO LOCAL AND INTERNATIONAL NGOS

Unfortunately, the prospects for self-initiated change within the government are very low. In the past, India has done a great job of creating legislation, but has not been able to effectively implement it. Added to this is the fact that Dalits have traditionally been overlooked, thus making it even more unlikely programmes designed to specifically help them will actually see fruition.

Therefore, local and international NGOs must simultaneously seek out independent solutions for improving this situation. Such solutions may include:

- Pressuring the state to fully comply with its ESC obligations. One way to do so is by using the human rights framework, and in particular the ICESCR. They must remind the state of the obligations it assumed when signing the various international human rights treaties. They may also turn to other governments or international organization such as the United Nation High Commissioner for Human Rights to help in applying pressure.
- Educating people of their rights. Once educated, people will be more likely to mobilize and demand that the state honour its obligations.
- Taking immediate action and filling the gap themselves. It is evident that in many areas, Dalits are receiving a substandard education relative to their non-Dalit counterparts. Mobilizing the state to

radically improve the public education system will take considerable time. In the meantime, whole generations could be left undereducated. Religious organizations, particularly Roman Catholics, have helped some of the poorest in Gujarat by giving providing a quality education to many Dalit children at private schools. Other non-state organizations could also step in and provide alternatives to public schooling that would better ensure small class size, caste-blindness in the classroom and support for human dignity. Creating a generation of well-educated Dalits, prepared in quality schools to be competitive on the job market, could alter the assumptions of many non-Dalits. These well-educated Dalits will be better prepared to articulate their concerns to the state, and increase the movement exponentially. Furthermore, the high quality of these non-state schools may "shame" the state into improving public schools for those non-Dalits left behind.

- Public informational activities. In our travels in rural Gujarat, we were amazed at how unfamiliar discussions of caste were to people, especially the non-Dalits. A system that controls their communal existence to such a degree is rarely discussed openly or examined critically. Public informational activities could work to render Indians, regardless of caste, better aware of the ancient feelings of discrimination they hold. Such activities might include role-plays or skits. While NGOs should offer ways to combat these feelings, such as through education, they should also elicit suggestions from the participants. This is an extremely important venture as educating children in schools about the need for equality has severe limitations. Once they leave school, they return to parents and a society rife with discrimination. Thus, NGOs must undertake projects such as this in an attempt to fight for more comprehensive social change.
- Seek to change the existing power structure of India.

At the heart of the persistent caste system is a division of power. This division renders one group as subjugated to another, and is seemingly authorized by religious and historic mandate. Efforts must be taken by the NGO community to chip away at this rigid balance. NGOs should provide public service announcements regarding valid criticisms of the caste system. For example, Gandhi considered the caste system to be the shame of the Hindu religion. NGOs must also seek to advance the general economic condition of Dalits throughout India. In many villages that we visited, stores were rarely owned by Dalits. NGOs should provide greater assistance to Dalits in need of loans to build their own shops or to advance new ideas for commerce and trade. Lessening dependence on non-Dalits renders Dalits increasingly powerful and more capable of assuming their ESC rights.

Indeed, change will not come about overnight. The caste system has endured for centuries, and the descendants of the original high caste members continue to exploit artificial caste lines, despite the better sensibilities of existing international and state legislations. Like any great social change, this one will require time and the cooperative efforts of individuals at all levels – local, state, and international. As Macwan told us in Gujarat, "We do not seek to change the system in the blink of an eye. That would be unrealistic. What we are committed to here is a movement." This movement to which Macwan and numerous other progressive individuals commit themselves also requires new approaches, as past ones have sadly proven insufficient. The case of primary school children in rural Gujarat shows that the protection of human rights demands more than civil and political rights. Beyond expressed exclusions are more subtle violations. Indeed, the violation of ESC rights results in identifiable instances of discrimination and the denial of simple human dignity. Attention to ESC rights allows us to do more than just write legislation – it allows us to pursue systematic change.

5

The Dalits Situation in India Today

There were about 138,200,000 Dalits in India and they constituted about 16.5% of the entire population of India. The 2001 Census has now been completed. The total population as risen to over one billion, but we do not know yet what the Dalit total is; however, if past trends continue, we may safely assume not only that the Dalit population will also have increased but also that the Dalit proportion of the total population has risen as well.

DALIT

"Dalit" is the name which the people belonging to those castes at the very bottom of India's caste hierarchy have given themselves. Formerly, they were known as Untouchables, because their presence was considered to be so polluting that contact with them was to be avoided at all costs. The official label for them has been Scheduled Castes, because if their caste is listed on the government schedule, caste members become eligible for a number of affirmative action benefits and protections.

Dalits have chosen the "Dalit" label for themselves for at least three important reasons. First, the label indicates that the condition of the Dalits has not been of their own making or choosing; it is something which has been inflicted upon them by others.

Thus, secondly, there is an element of militancy built into the label; Dalits seek to overcome the injustices and indignities forced upon them so as to gain the equality and respect hitherto denied them. "Dalit" also indicates that all these castes

(Pariahs, Chamars, Mahars, Bhangis, etc.) share a common condition and should therefore unite in a common struggle for dignity, equality, justice and respect under a common name.

THE DALIT POLITICAL STRATEGY

Both historically and currently Dalits have adopted four strategies, singly or in combination, in order to attain these ends. The first and most dominant has been the political strategy of gaining power either as an end in itself (if you have power, others come to you and you do not have to go begging to them) or as a means to other ends (*e.g.*, greater economic and educational opportunities).

However, Dalits have been divided over whether to pursue political power independently of other castes or in alliance with those members of other castes and communities whose interests and ideals are close to their own. For example, there are at present Dalit members of Parliament and of State Legislative Assemblies, as well as Dalit party workers, in virtually all the major political parties, including the Prime Minister's Bharatiya Janata Party, which in its traditionalist Hindu ideology, is quite anti-Dalit.

There are also exclusively Dalit political parties at the regional level and two Dalit-led political parties, the Bahujan Samaj Party of Kanshi Ram and Ms. Mayawati as well as the Republican Party of India, have members of Parliament as well. The Dalit debate within and between the various parties over whether to get whatever share of power Dalits can through whatever alliances are most expedient or to maintain pressure from outside on those in power by maintaining some ideological and programmatic unity, at least among Dalits themselves if not with other disadvantaged groups (tribals, religious minorities, women, the poor in general) as well, has yet to be resolved.

As this brief description suggests, there is little political unity among Dalits at the present time and many are wondering out loud whether the political process can deliver what Dalits have every right to expect from it.

THEIR ECONOMIC STRATEGY

The second strategy has been economic. Not only are Dalits extremely poor (almost half of them living below the poverty line as compared to less than one-third of the rest of the population) but they are also almost totally dependent upon the dominant castes for their livelihoods as agricultural or urban labour.

Thus many Dalits have sought greater economic independence, both as an end in itself and as a means to other ends (*e.g.*, political power, educational opportunity). During the past decade a good number of international development agencies, both religious and secular, have also adopted this strategy by funding a variety of grassroots Dalit organizations engaged in a range of community development activities. These activities focus on such things as small-scale industries, teaching new skills, educating Dalits on how to take advantage of government development assistance, developing cooperatives.

The task is enormous. Over 75% of the Dalit population is still rural and so these activities have to be carried out village by village. They also face opposition within each village from members of the dominant castes who want to keep Dalits as an impoverished and dependent source of cheap labour.

THE SOCIAL STRATEGY

A third strategy, which can be described as social, has two components. Education is one. If Dalits become literate or even educated, they can move beyond unskilled labour, earn more money, and so gain greater respect. The other is making life-style changes which get rid of those practices considered especially "low" or "polluting" and substituting those of the "higher" castes instead.

For example, they should give up eating certain meats and cease working at certain jobs (*e.g.*, cleaning latrines). The aim of education and life-style change has been to remove some of the more obvious reasons for anti-Dalit prejudice. The social strategy was adopted by the Christian missions over a century ago and it still dominates the churches' thinking about improving the Dalits' lot. Today there are churches which are not only giving special priority to Dalits in some of their institutions of formal education, but are also developing joboriented, nonformal educational projects to enhance skill development. The social strategy has also undergirded much of the affirmative action policy built into India's constitution. The assumption is that if Dalits get educated, get better jobs, and earn more money so as to raise their class status, then their caste status (measured in terms of mutually respectful and friendly relations with members of "higher" castes) would improve also.

The problem has been that the government (controlled by the dominant "higher" castes) has never fully implemented all the progressive affirmative action legislation it has passed into law. This is a source of great resentment, especially among educated Dalits.

THE RELIGIOUS STRATEGY

The fourth strategy has been religious in nature. Its moderate form involves reform from within one's own religious tradition. For example, some Hindu sects have renounced caste hierarchy and some Hindu reformers, Gandhi being the best known, have sought to "uplift" the Untouchables. The more radical religious option, however, has been conversion to another, more egalitarian religion. For example, over the past 125 years, so many Dalits have converted to Christianity that today the majority of the Christian population of India is Dalit!

Following the induction of their great leader, Dr. B. R. Ambedkar, into the Buddhist Sangha in 1956, several million Dalits have become Buddhists. What a new religion offered to the Dalits was a new identity defined by religion rather than by caste, as well as a more egalitarian religious counterculture. This has been only partially successful. No matter what goes on in Christian or Buddhist circles, most Indians still think in terms of caste and so simply assume that anyone who is a Christian or Buddhist is a Dalit. Moreover, both Christian and Buddhist Dalits were denied the affirmative action benefits and protections granted to other Dalits; in 1990 the Buddhist Dalits became eligible and Dalit Christians are still ineligible. By denying these to Christian (and Muslim) Dalits the government is in fact providing strong economic disincentives to conversion and strong economic incentives to Christian Dalits to return to the Hindu fold.

THE CHRISTIAN DALITS

As this brief analysis suggests, the present situation of Dalits in India is complex and confusing. There are no obvious, agreed upon solutions to the problems which the Dalits face; the way forward in the Dalit struggle is by no means clear. However, there are a few trends visible among Christian Dalits which are quite important for Christian thinking on this subject. First and foremost among these is a growing acknowledgment that they are Dalits and that conversion to Christianity has not really changed that significant fact of their lives, despite hopes and promises to the contrary. Most Christian Dalits thus have a dual social and psychological identity, Christian as well as Dalit, and have to live with the tensions built into that dual identity.

A second trend is an increasing assertion of Dalit identity as a positive thing, a source of pride rather than of shame. In this they (rightly) challenge pervasive cultural norms. One expression of this assertiveness is Dalit Theology; another is a harsh critique of those missionary and Indian Church leaders who, in their efforts to "Indianize" the Church, have equated "Indian" culture with Brahmanic instead of Dalit culture. (One reason why Dalit Christians have resisted a lot of efforts to "Indianize" the theology and liturgy of the Church is because they are fed up with the Brahmanic culture which they converted to get away from!)

Perhaps most obvious of all are the persistent efforts to "raise the caste issue" and exorcise the demon of caste discrimination (which is "Legion" and takes many forms) within the churches themselves. Until this is done, the churches cannot embody much "good news" for their own Dalit members, let alone for other Dalits. Finally, there are Christian

Dalits who are staunch advocates of each of the four Dalit strategies and are working hard at implementing those strategies. I see no evidence that one strategy, or even one combination of strategies, has become clearly predominant in Dalit Christian circles.

What does seem evident, however, is that over the past two decades Christian Dalits are working more closely with other Dalits to achieve common aims and objectives than was true earlier. "Dalit Solidarity" is an end and means much desired but difficult to achieve; yet many Dalit Christian leaders have come to the conclusion that their Christian hopes for their own people cannot be realised in isolation from the realisation of the hopes of all the Dalit people.

6

Dalits Women: Issues, Factors and Concerns

INTRODUCTION

All human beings have the right to live as human beings. Human rights are not conferred or given. They already exist in society. The concept of human rights aims at protection of rights like right to life, liberty and property. These rights are attributed to human beings irrespective of class, caste, gender, colour and religion. The Universal Declaration of Human Rights was unanimously adopted by the UN General Assembly on December 10th, 1948.

The preamble of Indian constitution adequately empowers the central and state government to eliminate human rights violation in the country. Inspite of these international and national declarations and resolutions, human rights are violated in different countries all over the world. In Indian society, due to the social barriers such as castetism, untouchability, patriarchy, disparity, superstition, religious exploitation and class variations, specific groups are becoming weaker and marginalised.

These groups are facing the problems of identity crisis, deprivation, discrimination and atrocities. These marginalised groups are also identified and recognised as dalits, SC (scheduled castes) ST (scheduled tribes), OBC (other backward castes) NT (nomadic tribes) DT (denotified tribes) religious and linguistic minorities. Violence on human beings in any form results in violation of human rights. Human rights of dalits and women in general are normally violated by high castes and powerful communities to practice and exhibit patriarchy and castetism. But human rights of dalit women are violated extremely and in peculiar form. Dalit women are in worst position than dalits in general, in terms of sex ratio, wages, employment, occupation, assets, education, health, social mobility and political participation.

Hence, it is important to discuss the status of dalit women and various problems they face even after 60 years of independence. This substance makes an attempt to discuss basic facts, issues and concerns related to dalit women to suggest some alternatives to combat violation of their rights for social justice and equality. Explanation of relevant terms such as 'dalit', 'dalitism', and 'dalit women', is given to broaden understanding about the issue.

DALIT

Dalit ('oppressed' or 'broken') is not a new word. Apparently it was used in the 1930's as a Hindi and Marathi translation of 'depressed classes'. The British used this term for what are now called the scheduled caste. Dr. Ambedkar chose the term 'broken men', as English translation of 'Dalit', to refer to the original ancestors of the untouchables.

Dalit Panthers, the youth activists from dalit community revived the term and in their 1973 manifesto expanded its reference to include the scheduled tribes, neo Buddhists, the working people, the landless and poor peasants, women and also those who are being exploited politically, economically in the name of religion.

DALITISM

Dalitism essentially implies conditions of subjugation; economic, political, social and cultural. Dalitism also embodies different degrees of marginalisation. It includes not only marginalized status in the economic sphere but also in cultural, political, religious and social domains. That means Dalitism symbolizes marginalisation. It is a well known fact that marginalisation denies basic human rights and social justice

DALIT WOMEN

Dalit women are one of the most marginalized segments in the society. The condition of dalit women is more vulnerable than non-dalit women.

Dalit women are suffering from multi-disadvantages:

- Of being dalit *i.e* socio-economically and culturally marginalized part,
- Being women and sharing the gender based inequalities and subordination

To explore these and other crucial issues concerning dalit women there is need to discuss some basic facts concerning the vulnerable situation of dalit women.

VULNERABLE STATUS OF DALIT WOMEN

It is easy for the historically dominating caste and gender to violate human rights of dalit women who are at the lowest rung of the hierarchical ladder. The type of violence inflicted on dalits is in the form of severest violation of human rights. Dalit and tribal women are raped as part of an effort by upper caste leaders, land lords and police to suppress movements to demand payment of minimum wages, to settle share cropping disputes or to reclaim lost lands..

The recent incident of Khairlanji Massacare is not something new. A dalit family had refused to let upper caste villagers built a road through their fields. Hence on September, 29th, 2006, Bhaiyalal Bhotmange's family,—wife Surekha, daughter Prinyanka and two sons were killed by the villagers of Khairlangi in Bhandra district of Maharashtra. They were first attacked with huge iron chains and than abused by the other caste women of the village. Surekha and Priyanka were paraded naked and raped, and later, their bodies were mutilated and thrown into a pond.

This shows that dalit women are easy targets for any perpetrator Upper caste considers them to be sexually available. Hence they are largely unprotected by the state machinery. Further, there is prevalence of violence, making dalit women eat human excreta, parading them naked, gang-rape, murder, dacoity, robbery and burning of their huts or communities. These are the types of crime, which violate their human rights. SC/ST commission report between 1981 and 1986 about 4000 dalit women became victim of rape. In 1993 - 94 this figure rose to 798 and 992 respectively. This means annually about 700 dalit women fall prey to sexual assault by high caste people.

The main complaints of the poorer dalit women are that they have no good houses. In urban areas most of them stay in unhygienic slums and in rural areas their houses are away from main stream society. Under conditions of grinding poverty and severe exploitation at work place, dalit women also suffer caste specific ban on water access from upper castes and may be beaten up in their own houses as well.

At the outset, prevailing caste and secondary status of women in the society is largely responsible for violation of human rights of dalit women. To understand the root cause of the situation it is essential to examine basic factors responsible for their vulnerability.

SOCIO-CULTURAL AND RELIGIOUS FACTORS

First and foremost dalit women are victims of social, religious and cultural practices like Devdasis and Jogins. In the name of these practices, village girls are married to God by their helpless parents. These girls are then sexually exploited by the upper caste landlords and rich men and directed in to trafficking and prostitution. In his autobiography, Kale has described a ritual called 'chira'. The literal meaning of the word 'chira', is to cut or break.

In this ritual when a girl from the lower caste community reaches the age of puberty, an elderly prestigious man from the higher caste breaks the hymen of the girl child by sexual act. This ritual is performed in a way to make the girl accept this fact as a routine practice.

The 28th report of SC/ST commission reported that in February 1986 there were about ten thousand Jogins belonging to SC in Nizamabad district of Andhra Pradesh. The survey submitted by the district collector to Schedule Caste Finance Corporation revealed prevalence of 15,850 cases. Eighty per cent of these Jogins belonged to SC. This data is just an example of one district of the country. Practices such as Chira, Jogins, Devdasi which are prevalent even today are harmful and threaten the dignity of dalit women and violate their human rights.

EDUCATIONAL STATUS

Low level of education is a problem in itself and in turn gives rise to many other problems. In 1991, literacy among the dalit women was indeed quite low. In rural areas only 19.46 percentage women were literate.

A report published by Ministry of Welfare, Government of India in 1998 showed that there is much difference in the literacy rate of dalits and non-dalits in general, and gender specific. Literacy rate of non-dalits is 64.13% and literacy rate of women is 39.29%, where as dalit women's literacy rate is only 23.76%. There is a large disparity in the literacy rate due to wide spread prejudice based on castetism and patriarchy against dalits and women in general and dalit women in particular.

ECONOMIC DEPRIVATION AND UNEMPLOYMENT

A careful look at the economic situation of dalit women reveals that their work force structure is such that they rarely own any land. A large majority of them are agricultural labourers.

The rate of unemployment among them is also quite high. About 90% of women working in unorganized sector are mainly from lower castes. In 1991, about 71% of dalit women workers in rural area were agricultural labourers. Only 19% of them owned land.

A prominent researcher and sociologist while sharing her experience from a research on gender and land issue, informed that, when she enquired with dalit women about land owned by them in their names, they wondered about permissibility of owning land in their name. This indicates that neither do they own any land nor are they aware of their rights on land. When enquiries were made with Stri-mukti sanghatana and

Prerana, Mumbai based organizations working on the issue of rag picking and prostitution respectively, to ascertain the proportion of dalit women in these occupations, it was learnt that NGOs usually do not keep record of caste.

However, Human Rights Watch Report mentioned that a large number of dalit women are engaged in unclean, inferior occupation such as sweeping, scavenging and working in dumping grounds, rag picking and also in prostitution. These women have to face steep discrimination in the matters of social relation and employment due to their engagement in these occupations.

HEALTH AND NUTRITION STATUS

Dalit women's daily diet is the leftover of family meals, inadequate in quantity and quality. Health services are either not available in case of illness or unaffordable even if available. In addition to that, due to early marriage and too many pregnancies their health is always at risk.

If birth control is practiced at all, 91% cases of tubetomy are performed on the women who have to carry the burden of family planning. In an overall situation where dalits are prone to ailments in general, women suffer from more serious and more varied kind of sickness. More than 80% of women in reproductive age group (15 to 45) are anemic. Poor health status of dalit women pushes her then into more vulnerable situation

POLITICAL STATUS

Women constitute half of total population, but are unable to get equal share in active politics. Their socio-economic status directly depends on their participation in politics. Political parties in India speak much about equality of women but have totally ignored the dalit women. Traditionally, leadership in the village was confined to 'rural elites', who were aged and belonging to higher castes.

In the year 1993, 73rd amendment in the constitution granted reservation to dalits, tribals and women in local government. This amendment made it compulsory that one third of the seats reserved for dalits be filled by dalit women. In some states, there has been little or no acceptance of reservation for the lower castes and dalit women by the upper castes. This has resulted in atrocities against panchayat members including women. Dalits who stood for election were beaten, and dalit women were raped and ill-treated. The members of the higher castes, who are not prepared to relinquish power to the lower castes, grabbed their land. An easier method to retain power is to put-up proxy candidates but keep the control in the hands of the dominant castes, always men. The incapacity of women, particularly dalit women, to assert their rights is at the root of the problem. The reservation for dalits, particularly for women, is accepted in form but seldom in substance. Any change in the status quo is resisted. Dalit women's sitting on chairs is seen as threat to social hierarchy. So, the upper castes in the village vetoed chairs in the panchayat office Dalit women also faced many problems in performing their duties due to illiteracy, lack of information and dependency on the male members of their families. An important obstacle is the no-confidence motion against dalit women as pradhan by the dominant parts.

Rural elites are unable to accept the power, which has been given into the hands of the poorer and disadvantaged women. Despite recognition and legal sanction for political rights, rigid caste system and patriarchy directly and indirectly has been suppressing dalit women and violating their political rights. This proves that human rights of dalit women are violated right from her family to the society at large by one and all. All these factors are largely responsible for the precarious position of dalit women as far as their social, cultural, religious, economic, health and political status in the society is concerned. These factors force them to mutely allow violation of their civic and human rights. Thus they become victims of universal violence.

EFFORTS TO PROTECT HUMAN RIGHTS OF DALIT WOMEN

With the realisation that violence is one of the potent

threats to the peaceful existence of human beings, whole hearted and all round efforts are made at international, national and local level. The preamble to the Universal Declaration of Human Rights serves as a foundation and philosophy of Human rights.

There are a host of international conventions including those for prevention and punishment of genocide and elimination of all forms of racial and gender based discrimination.

The World Conference Against Racism (WCAR) related to racial discrimination, xenophobia and intolerance held in Durban, South Africa in 2001, brought the issue of caste and untouchability based discrimination on the agenda of UN Conference in Durban.

Among the several organisations, the National Campaign on Dalit Human Rights (NCDHR)—a collective of dalit NGOs, other NGOs, academicians', activists and large number of supporters spearheaded the national campaign in India for inclusion of the issue of caste and untouchability based discrimination in the Durban Conference.

The preamble of Indian constitution adequately empowers the central and state government to eliminate human right violation in the country Article 17 of the constitution provides for removal of untouchability. Based on this article Protection of Civil Rights Act' (PCR), was passed in 1955.

However, there was no conviction/under this Act hence, Thirty-four years after the introduction of PCR Act, the Scheduled Caste and Schedule Tribes (Prevention of Atrocities) Act 1989 was enacted to bring various forms of atrocities to an end. In this Act the complainant is given more weightage. There are stringent provisions against the police for negligence

EMERGING IDENTITY OF DALIT WOMEN AND FORMATION OF DALIT WOMEN'S ORGANIZATIONS

The focus on education of low caste women is one of the important factors responsible for the emerging identity of Dalit women. Reformist intervention by Savitribai and Mahatma Phule of opening school for untouchable girls way back in 1848 was a turning point for changing status of dalit women. Dr. Ambedkar's thought and action made important differences in the lives of dalit women.

His movement and especially his organisations encouraged many dalit women to become educated to be active in public life and to gain leadership, self respect in the contemporary period encouraged women to participate in organisation for dalit women at regional, state and national level.

After independence in 1960's and 70's, the dalit movement and women's movement emerged to demand their rights against caste and gender respectively. However, specific problems of dalit women were not acknowledged by these movements.

Hence in 1990's there were several special, independent and autonomous assertions of dalit women's identity; a case in point is the formation of National Federation for Dalit Women (NFDW) and All India Dalit Women's Forum (AIDWF) at the state level. The Maharashtra Dalit Mahila Sanghatana (MDMS) was formed in 1995. A year earlier, the women's wing of Bhartiya Republican Party (BRP) and the Bahujan Mahila Sangha (BMS) was set up the Bahujan Mahila Parishad.

In December 1996, at Chand-rapur, a Vikas Vanchit Dalit Mahila Parishad (VVDMP) was organised and a proposal to commemorate 25th December (the day on which Ambedkar had set Manu smriti on fire) as Bhartiya Smriti Divas was advanced. The Christi Mahila Sanghatana, an organisation of Dalit Christian Women was established in 1997.

These organisations have come together on several issues such as celebration of Bhartiya Stree Mukti Divas and on the issue of reservation for OBC women in parliament bodies. Indian Association of Women Studies (IAWS) network with dalit feminist across different regions had brought special issues on problems and identity of dalit women. Several efforts have been made since independence to secure human rights of women in general and dalit women in particular. Despite this, human rights of dalit women are seen to be violated in different forms. Such infringement of human rights echoes the need of evolving suitable mechanism to empower dalit women to assert for equal rights and justice in order to live a dignified life.

MECHANISM TO STRENGTHEN THE CAPACITY OF DALIT WOMEN

To be human is to respond to human sufferings and pain with compassion and effective concern. It is not enough to feel with the dalit women in their pain, There is more need for effective action, otherwise it would be just sentimentalism' says Sequeira in his substance 'Human Response to Dalit Women. The needs and the problems of dalit women differ with city, village, area and caste.

It is essential to keep in mind that dalit women are not mere individuals but belong to a sociological and dialectical system. Therefore to recognise the system and to prohibit violation, first and foremost proper perspectives about the issues has to be developed among all by considering following suggestions:

AWARENESS FOR ASSERTION

Extensive reading of available literature can be done by young generation to understand the profile and problems of dalit women.

Factual incidents and success stories of dalit women namely, 'We made History Too' by Meenakshi Moon and Urmila Pawar can be included in the educational texts.

ACCESS AND EXPOSURE VISITS

Special exposure visits to dalit localities can be organised for school and college students to assess basic amenities accessible to dalit women namely, water, electricity, health and hygiene.

Similarly dalit women's visit to urban structured colonies can be arranged to impress upon the importance of standard of living of non-dalits. Such purposeful visits will broaden their horizons resulting in improved living of marginalised part.

ACADEMIC ACTIVITIES

Academic institutions need to be encouraged to undertake studies to assess the problems of violence and atrocities against dalit women as also the reasons therefore and to work out ways to overcome them. Thought provoking sessions on harmful social religions practices namely, Chira, Devdasi, Jogin need to be held for basic understanding and effective interventional strategies.

CAMPAIGNS AND SESSIONS

Campaigns for equal and rational distribution of natural resources among weaker parts can be organised to secure their rightful means of livelihood. Proper rehabilitation and shelter can be provided to those communities, which are out of the social periphery (NT/DT) to protect them from the risk of sexual abuse.

INCLUSION OF DALIT WOMEN IN VARIOUS SYSTEM

More dalit women in their population proportion (16.5% SC, 7.5% ST) should be given chance to enter in the system like police, judiciary, education, health and politics. Sessions can be organised for dalit activist and women activists to sensitize them about the magnitude of torture and oppression faced by the dalit women.

Legal education dealing with protection of human rights of dalits and Prevention of Atrocities Act (1989) can be organised to prevent the problems of castism.

CONCLUSION

At the threshold of 21st century it is absolutely necessary that common people need to be sensitized about the prevailing atrocities against Dalit women.

There is a growing need to capture violation of human rights of dalit women, so that talent and potential of Dalit Womens can be used for development of nation.

Vippal a nation does not prosper only on fertile soil, dense forests and overflowing rivers. It is the healthy people who make a nation. A society is made up of both men and women from all states.

If women from whichever state is weak and exploited, it is not a healthy society. And when a society is healthy, then the nation will march ahead. To fulfill these dreams women in general and particularly from weaker part need to be empowered for development of the nation.

7

Dalits Events and Movements

POONA PACT

During the first Round Table Conference, when Dr. Bhimrao Ramji Ambedkar favoured the move of the British Government to provide separate electorate for the oppressed classes (Dalit), Gandhi strongly opposed it on the plea that the move would give power to the oppressed classes (Dalit). He went for an indefinite hunger strike from September 20, 1932 against the decision of the then British Prime Minister J. Ramsay MacDonald granting communal award to the depressed classes in the constitution for governance of British India. In view of the mass upsurge generated in the country to save the life of Gandhi, Ambedkar was compelled to soften his stand.

A compromise between the leaders of caste Hindu and the depressed classes was reached on September 24,1932, popularly known as Poona Pact. The resolution announced in a public meeting on September 25 in Bombay confirmed -" henceforth, amongst Hindus no one shall be regarded as an untouchable by reason of his birth and they will have the same rights in all the social institutions as the other Hindus have". This landmark resolution in the history of the Dalit movement in India subsequently formed the basis for giving due share to Dalits in the political empowerment of Indian people in a democratic Indian polity.

The following is the text of the agreement arrived at between leaders acting on behalf of the Depressed Classes and of the rest of the community, regarding the representation of the Depressed Classes in the legislatures and certain other matters affecting their welfare.

- There shall be seats reserved for the Depressed Classes out of general electorate seats in the provincial legislatures as follows:—Madras 30; Bombay with Sind 25; Punjab 8; Bihar and Orissa 18; Central Provinces 20; Assam 7; Bengal 30; United Provinces 20. Total 148. These figures are based on the Prime Minister's (British) decision.
- Election to these seats shall be by joint electorates subject, however, to the following procedure All members of the Depressed Classes registered in the general electoral roll of a constituency will form an electoral college which will elect a panel of tour candidates belonging to the Depressed Classes for each of such reserved seats by the method of the single vote and four persons getting the highest number of votes in such primary elections shall be the candidates for election by the general electorate.
- The representation of the Depressed Classes in the Central Legislature shall likewise be on the principle of joint electorates and reserved seats by the method of primary election in the manner provided for in clause for their representation in the provincial legislatures.

BATTLE OF KOREGAON

THE MARATHA WARS

While I can understand the desire of Dalits to home into that skirmish and claim that to be the be all and end all of all, skirmishes like this have to be grounded in the greater framework. The Maratha Empire brought to life by Shivaji attained its greatest strength by 1760.

And I should point out that Shivaji was not a Brahmin. While they claimed Kshyatriya status later on, there are some arguments that he was originally a Dalit, a Shudra to be precise. Finally, Shivaji's army was largely composed of people like him, so it was a Dalit Army anyway which got promoted, so to say. Then comes the first Anglo Maratha War 1777-1783 where first the Maratha's won and then the British won. In both cases, native soldiers were far too frequently Dalits. Anyway, more land was captured by the Brits and the power of the Maratha's was further reduced.

Peshwa Baji Rao II and his father basically got up to no good. In 1802, BajiRao went and sucked up to the British after being defeated by Holkars in the Battle of Poona. This pissed off the other Maratha warlords and they got into a bit of a fight with the British which ended with more loss of territory for the Marathas. Then comes the crucial 3rd War which our Dalit friends might now appreciate.

This relates to the 3rd Anglo Maratha War 1817-1818 or the Pindari War. The Pindari's were highly mobile cavalry units which were not on the payroll of any ruler but associated with rulers in return for protection and permission to plunder. Guess what?

These Pindari's were low caste, Ladul and also had quite a lot of Muslims (mainly Afghans and Pusthun). Anyway, all this plundering was not good for the British and a really very big army of 120,000 men and 300 artillery pieces was put into gear by Lord Hastings to exterminate these Pindari's. The attacks happened from the east in Bengal, from the South in the Deccan and from the west from Gujarat and Bombay.

THE IMMEDIATE PREDECESSOR TO THE 1ST JAN 1818 BATTLE OF KOREGAON

Once the British invaded Maratha territory to go after the Pindari's, there were skirmishes between the Peshwa's forces and the British forces such as the sack of the British Residency in Pune, and then the British routed another Peshwa force at Khirki.

Then the main battle was fought in the Battle of Khadki on November 5, 1817 where the Peshwa Baji Rao was routed pretty much comprehensively and then the British took over the Peshwa's seat at Shaniwarwada by November 17, 1817. The Peshwa, by this time, was running ragged. There was another battle between the Nagpur forces and the British at Sitabalsi on November 27 1817. The next battle to be fought was the Battle of Mahidpur on 20th December where the Holkar's fought and lost to the British, after being betrayed by one of the Pindari (who killed Tulsibai).

THE BATTLE OF KOREGAON

A good description of the battle can be found here. This is a book by WC Taylor, A Popular History of British India published in 1847.

Sounds like a pretty good bash. Taylor says that the Peshwa's forces numbered about 25,000 although it should be noted that counting was pretty vague at that time. Still, it wasn't 50,000.

But here's the crucial thing, the Peshwa's forces then retreated not because they were defeated by Captain Francis Staunton's forces, but because they got to hear that British reinforcements were coming over. The British forces lost 200 soldiers out of 500, and 6 out of 7 British officers. Good defensive battle without food or water at this village.

THE SOLDIERS

The soldiers who did most of the dying were Mahars. And again ironically, they got their start in being soldiers by no other than Shivaji to become scouts and fortress guards. They were highly mobile light infantry, which is the reason why they were in the 2nd Battalion, 1st regiment of 'Bombay Native Light Infantry' as part of the Maratha Light Infantry. The Peshwa's soldiers were also by and large lower caste soldiers including Mahars, in any case, not Brahmins.

So the fighting basically was between lower castes, only the people who were ordering them around were the British and the Peshwas.

This Mahar Regiment still exists and has provided two of the most brilliant Indian Army Chiefs: Gen (Retd) K V Krishna Rao and Gen (Retd) K Sunderji. Also, there is no caste element to the regiment from 1963 onwards and it is now a fully mixed regiment.

THE AFTERMATH OF THE BATTLE OF KOREGAON

There was another fight between the fleeing Peshwa's forces and the British at Ashti on February 20th 1818 and he remained under pressure till he surrendered to Sir John Malcolm on June 3, 1818 and was given the pension of an annual payment of 8 lakhs rupees. The Battle of Koregaon was celebrated by raising of an Obelix which commemorated this. So all in all, I am afraid what my research threw up was in sharp variance with the mythology is being provided.

It was frankly a small battle/skirmish in a much bigger war, the Peshwa's forces were not defeated in this skirmish, the British Army did not fight this battle expecting the worst because they had been winning every battle in this war, this battle of Koregaon was not really that important as fighting kept on happening for months after this battle and I am afraid there is absolutely no evidence that any kind of caste based ideology was involved in the fight.

So all in all, good myth but a rather more calm reading of the historical record tells differently. I can also see why the Dalit hotheads want to use this battle to burnish their credentials. After all, all revolutions need their battles. "Battle of Koregaon" to see how this myth is being built up, but I am afraid the reading is slightly different. If they do want to celebrate the success of lower caste soldiers, they should celebrate Shivaji, the Indian Soldier, the bravery that these soldiers showed to whoever paid them. But to bring this casteism into the Indian Army? Not really cricket, old chaps. But I am very happy to be corrected if I have not referred to any other source or documentation. Happy to learn more.

SELF-RESPECT MOVEMENT

The Self-Respect Movement was founded in 1925 by Periyar E. V. Ramasamy (also known as Periyar) in Tamil Nadu, India. The movement has the aim of achieving a society where backward castes have equal human rights, and encouraging backward castes to have self-respect in the context of a caste based society that considered them to be a lower end of the hierarchy. The movement was extremely influential not just in Tamil Nadu, but also overseas in countries with large Tamil populations, such as Malaysia and Singapore. Among Singapore Indians, groups like the Tamil Reform Association, and leaders like Thamizhavel G. Sarangapani were prominent in promoting the principals of the Self-Respect Movement among the local Tamil population through schools and publications.

A number of political parties in Tamil Nadu, such as Dravida Munnetra Kazhagam (DMK) and All India Anna Dravida Munnetra Kazhagam (AIADMK) owe their origins to the Self-respect movement, the latter a 1972 breakaway from the DMK. Both parties are populist with a generally social democratic orientation.

THE TENETS OF SELF-RESPECT

Periyar was convinced that if man developed self respect, he would automatically develop individuality and would refuse to be led by the nose by schemers. One of his most known quotes on Self-Respect was, "we are fit to think of 'self-respect' only when the notion of 'superior' and 'inferior' caste is banished from our land".

Periyar did not expect personal or material gain out of this movement. He used to recall in a very casual manner that as a human being, he also was obligated to this duty, as it was the right and freedom to choose this work. Thus, Periyar opted to engage himself in starting and promoting the movement. Periyar declared that the Self-Respect Movement alone could be the genuine freedom movement, and political freedom would not be fruitful without individual self-respect. He remarked that the so called 'Indian freedom fighters' were showing disrespect of self-respect, and this was really an irrational philosophy.

Periyar observed that political freedom as conceived by nationalists not excluding even Gandhi and Jawaharlal Nehru did not cover individual self-respect. To him neither revival of the original spirit of Hindu religion and ancient traditions which formed part of Gandhi's conception of freedom, nor complete liberation from the British rule which was considered by Nehru to be the meaning of freedom or both of them together could ensure individual self-respect or remove the ills from Indian societies. In his opinion the task of fulfilling the need for self-respect would have to be faced whatever be the extent of political freedom gained.

Pointing out that even the British monarch in a sovereign independent nation had no freedom to marry a person of his choice and had to abdicate his kingdom, Periyar raised a question whether Gandhi's vision of freedom or Nehru's concept of independence contained even an iota of individual self-respect.

Periyar believed that self-respect was as valuable as life itself and its protection is a birth right and not swaraj ('political freedom'). He described the movement as Arivu Vidutalai Iyakkam, that is, a movement to liberate the intellect. The terms tan-maanam or suya mariyadai meaning 'self-respect' are traceable in ancient Tamil literature considered a virtue of high valor in Tamil society.

Periyar once claimed that to describe the ideology of his movement, no dictionary in the entire world, implying that no other language, could provide a word better than or equal to suya mariyadai. Started as a movement (Iyakkam in Tamil) to promote rational behaviour, the Self-Respect Movement acquired much wider connotation within a short period of time. Periyar speaking with M.K. Reddy at the First Self-Respect Conference held in 1929, explained the significance of self-respect and its principles.

The main tenets of the Self-Respect Movement in society were to be: no kind of inequality among people; no difference as rich and poor in the economic life; men and women to be treated as equals in every respect without differences; attachments to caste, religion, varna, and country to be eradicated from society with a prevalent friendship and unity around the world; and every human being seeing to act just as to reason, understanding, desire, and perspective, and shall not be subject to slavery of any kind or manner. Equality with stress on economic and social equality formed the central theme of the Self-Respect Movement was due to Periyar's determination to fight the inequalities ingrained in the caste system and religious practices. Working on the theme of liberating the society from the baneful social practices perpetrated in the name of dharma and karma, Periyar developed the idea of establishing this movement as the instrument for achieving his objective.

ANTI-BRAHMANISM

Tamil Brahmins (Iyers and Iyengars) were frequently held responsible by followers of Periyar for direct or indirect oppression of lower-caste people on the canard of "Brahmin oppression" and resulted in attacks on Brahmins and which among other reasons started a wave of mass-migration of the Brahmin population.

Periyar in regards to a DK member's attempt to assassinate Rajagopalachari, "expressed his abhorrence of violence as a means of settling political differences". Eventually, the anti-Brahmanism subsided with the replacement of the DMK party by the AIADMK.

SELF-RESPECT MARRIAGES

One of the major sociological changes introduced through the self respect movement was the self-respect marriage system, where by marriages were conducted without being officiated by a Brahmin priest. Periyar had regarded the then conventional marriages were mere financial arrangements and often caused great debt through dowry.

Self-Respect marriages encouraged inter-caste marriages and arranged marriages to be replaced by love marriages. It was argued by the proponents of self-respect marriage that the then conventional marriages were officiated by Brahmins, who has to be paid for and also the marriage ceremony was in Sanskrit which most people did not understand, and hence were ritual and practices based on blind adherence.

MANDAL COMMISSION

The Mandal Commission was established in India in 1979 by the Janata Party government under Prime Minister Morarji

Desai with a mandate to "identify the socially or educationally backward." It was headed by Indian parliamentarian Bindheshwari Prasad Mandal to consider the question of seat reservations and quotas for people to redress caste discrimination, and used eleven social, economic, and educational indicators to determine backwardness.

In 1980, the commission's report affirmed the affirmative action practice under Indian law whereby members of lower castes (known as Other Backward Classes (OBC) and Scheduled Castes and Tribes) were given exclusive access to a certain portion of government jobs and slots in public universities, and recommended changes to these quotas, increasing them by 27% to 49.5%.

SETTING UP OF MANDAL COMMISSION

The plan to set up another commission was taken by Mr. Clooney and the Morarji Desai government in 1978 as per the mandate of the Constitution of India under article 340 for the purpose of Articles like 15 and 16. The decision was made official by the president on 1 January 1979. The commission is popularly known as the Mandal Commission its chairman being B.P. Mandal..

CRITERIA TO IDENTIFY OBC

The Mandal Commission adopted various methods and techniques to collect the necessary data and evidence. The commission adopted 11 criteria which could be grouped under three major headings: social, educational and economic in order to identify OBCs.

Social

- Castes/classes considered as socially backward by others.
- Castes/classes which mainly depend on manual labour for their livelihood.
- Castes/classes where at least 25 per cent females and 10 per cent males the state average get married at an age below 17 years in rural areas and at least 10 per

cent females and 5 per cent males do so in urban areas.

- Castes/classes where participation of females in work is at least 25 per cent above the state average.

Educational

- Castes/classes where the number of children in the age group of 5–15 years who never attended school is at least 25 per cent above the state average.
- Castes/classes where the rate of student dropout in the age group of 5–15 years is at least 25 per cent above the state average.

Economic

- Castes/classes where the average value of family assets is at least 25 per cent below the state average.
- Castes/classes where the number of families living in kuccha houses is at least 25 per cent above the state average.
- Castes/classes where the source of drinking water is beyond half a kilometer for more than 50 per cent of the households.
- Castes/classes where the number of households having taken consumption loans is at least 25 per cent above the state average. Also known as "Creamy layer," this criteria of separation is ignored by the government which is known as the most controversial issue of reservation.

Weighting Indicators

As the three groups are not of equal importance for the purpose, separate weightage was given to indicators in each group. All the Social indicators were given a weightage of 3 points each, educational indicators were given a weightage of 2 points each and economic indicators were given a weightage of 1 point each. Economic, in addition to Social and Educational Indicators, were considered important as they directly flowed from social and educational backwardness.

This also helped to highlight the fact that socially and educationally backward classes are economically backward also. It will be seen from the values given to each indicator, the total score adds up to 22.

All these 11 indicators were applied to all the castes covered by the survey for a particular state. As a result of this application, all castes which had a score of 50% (*i.e.* 11 points) were listed as socially and educationally backward and the rest were treated as 'advanced'.

OBSERVATIONS AND FINDINGS

The commission estimated that 54% of the total population (excluding SCs and STs), belonging to 3,743 different castes and communities were 'backward'. So the commission used 1931 census data to calculate the number of OBCs.

The population of Hindu OBCs was derived by subtracting from the total population of Hindus, the population of SC and ST and that of forward Hindu castes and communities, and it worked out to be 52 per cent. Assuming that roughly the proportion of OBCs amongst non-Hindus was of the same order as amongst the Hindus, population of non-Hindu OBCs was also considered as 52 per cent.

- Assuming that a child from an advanced class family and that of a backward class family had the same intelligence at the time of their birth, it is obvious that owing to vast differences in social, cultural and environmental factors, the former will beat the latter by lengths in any competitive field. Even if a backward class child's intelligence quotient was much higher as compared to the child of advanced class, chances are that the former will lag far behind the latter in any competition where selection is made on the basis of 'merit'.
- In fact, what we call 'merit' in an elitist society is an amalgam of native endowments and environmental privileges. A child from an advanced class family and that of a backward class family are not 'equals' in any fair sense of the term and it will be unfair to

judge them by the same yard-stick. The conscience of a civilized society and the dictates of social justice demand that 'merit' and 'equality' are not turned into a fetish and the element of privilege is duly recognised and discounted for when 'unequal' are made to run the same race.

- To place the amalgams of open caste conflicts in proper historical context, the study done by Tata institute of Social Sciences Bombay observes. "The British rulers produced many structural disturbances in the Hindu caste structure, and these were contradictory in nature and impact .... Thus, the various impacts of the British rule on the Hindu caste system, *viz.*, near monopolisation of jobs, education and professions by the literati castes, the Western concepts of equality and justice undermining the Hindu hierarchical dispensation, the phenomenon of Sanskritization, genteel reform movement from above and militant reform movements from below, emergence of the caste associations with a new role set the stage for the caste conflicts in modern India. Two more ingredients which were very weak in the British period, *viz.*, politicisation of the masses and universal adult franchise, became powerful moving forces after the Independence.

RECOMMENDATIONS

The report of the commission was submitted in December 1980. Following are the recommendations as stated in the report. It may appear the upliftment of Other Backward Classes is part of the larger national problem of the removal of mass poverty.

This is only partially correct. The deprivation of OBCs is a very special case of the larger national issue: here the basic question is that of social and educational backwardness and poverty is only a direct consequence of these two crippling caste-based handicaps. As these handicaps are embedded in our social structure, their removal will require far – reaching structural changes. No less important will be changes in the perception of the problems of OBCs by the ruling classes of the country.

Reservations

One such change in the attitude of the ruling elite pertains to the provisions of reservation in Government services and educations institutions for the candidates of Other Backward Classes. It is generally argued that looking to the large population of OBCs (52%), recruitment of a few thousand OBCs every year against reserved vacancies is not going to produce any perceptible impact on their general condition. On the other hand, the induction of a large proportion of employees against reserved vacancies will considerably impair the quality and efficiency of the Government services.

It is also stated that the benefits of such reservations will be skimmed off by those parts of OBCs which are already well off and the really backward parts will be left high and dry. Another argument advanced against this approach is that the policy of large scale reservations will cause great hurt burning to those meritorious candidates whose entry into services will be barred as a result thereof.

All the arguments are based on fairly sound reasoning. But these are also the arguments advanced by the ruling elite which is keen on preserving its privileges. Therefore, like all such reasoning, it is based on partisan approach. By the same token, while illuminating some immediate areas of concern it tends to ignore much larger issues of national importance. It is not at all our contention that by offering a few thousand jobs to OBC candidates we shall be able to make 52% of the Indian population as forward. But we must recognise that as essential part of the battle against social backwardness is to be fought in the minds of the backward people.

In India Government service has always been looked upon as a symbol of prestige and power. By increasing the representation of OBCs in Government services, we give them an immediate feeling of participation in the governance of this country. When a backward class candidate becomes a Collector or a Superintendent of Police, the material benefits accruing from his position are limited to the members of his family only. But the psychological spin off of this phenomenon is tremendous; the entire community of that backward class candidate feels socially elevated.

Even when no tangible benefits flow to the community at large, the feeling that now it has its "own man" in the "corridors of power" acts as a morale booster. In a democratic set-up every individual and community has a legitimate right and aspiration to participate in ruling this country.

Any situation which results in a near-denial of this right to nearly 52% of the country's population needs to be urgently rectified. Apprehensions regarding drop in the quality of Government services owing to large-scale induction of S.C./ S.T. and O.B.C. candidates against reserved posts may be justified only up to a point. But is it possible to maintain that all candidates selected on merit turn out to be honest, efficient, hard-working and dedicated? At present, top echelons of all the Government services are manned predominantly by open competition candidates and if the performance of our bureaucracy is any indication, it has not exactly covered itself with glory.

Of course, this does not imply that candidates selected against reserved posts will do better. Chances are that owing to their social and cultural handicaps they may be generally a shade less competent. But, on the other hand, they will have great advantage of possessing first hand knowledge of the sufferings and problems of the backward parts of society. This is not a small asset for field workers and policy makers even at highest level. It is no doubt true that the major benefits of reservation and other welfare measures for Other Backward Classes will be cornered by the more advanced parts of the backward communities.

But is not this a universal phenomenon? All reformists remedies have to contend with slow recovery along the hierarchical gradient; there are no quantum jumps in social reform. Moreover, human nature being what it is, a "new class" ultimately does emerge even in classless societies. The chief merit on reservation is not that it will introduce egalitarian amongst OBCs when the rest of the Indian society is seized by all sorts of inequalities. But reservation will certainly erode the hold of higher castes on the services and enable OBCs in general to have a sense of participation in running the affairs of the country.

It is certainly true that reservation for OBCs will cause a lot of heart burning to others. But should the mere fact of this heart burning be allowed to operate as a moral veto against social reform.... When the higher castes constituting less than 20% of the country's population subjected the rest to all manner of social injustice, it must have caused a lot of heart burning to the lower castes.

But now that the lower castes are asking for a modest share of the national cake of power and prestige, a chorus of alarm is being raised on the plea that this will cause heart burning to the ruling elite. Of all the specious arguments advanced against reservations for backward classes, there is none which beats this one about 'heart-burning' in sheer sophistry.

In fact the Hindu society has always operated a very rigorous scheme of reservations, which was internalised through caste system. Eklavya lost his thumb and Shambhk his neck for their breach of caste rules of reservations. The present furore against reservations for OBCs is not aimed at the principle itself, but against the new class of beneficiaries, as they are now clamouring for a share of the opportunities which were all along monopolised by the higher castes.

Quantum and Scheme of Reservations

Scheduled Castes and Scheduled Tribes constitute 22.5% of the country's population. A pro-rata reservation of 22.5% has been made for them in all services and public sector undertakings under the Central Government.

In the States also, reservation for SCs and STs is directly proportional to their population in each State. The population of OBCs, both Hindu and non-Hindu, is around 52% of the total population of India. Accordingly 52% of all post under the Central Government should be reserved for them, but this provision may go against the law laid down in a number of Supreme Court judgements wherein it has been held that the total quantum of reservations under Articles 15(4) and 16(4) of the Constitution should be below 50%. In view of this the proposed reservation for OBCs would have to be pegged at a figure which, when added to 22.5% of SCs and STs, remain below 50%.

In view of this legal constrain, the commission is obliged to recommend a reservation of 27% only, even though their population us almost twice this figure. States which have already introduced reservation for OBCs exceeding 27%, will remain unaffected by this recommendation.

With the general recommendation regarding the quantum of reservation, the Commission proposes the following over-all scheme of reservation for OBCs:

- Candidates belonging to OBCs recruited on the basis of merit in an open competition should not be adjusted against their reservation quota of 27%.
- The reservation should also be made available to promotion quota at all levels. Nitika goyal (3) Reserved quota remaining unfilled should be carried forward for a period of three years and deserved thereafter.
- Relaxation in the upper age limit for direct recruitment should be extended in the same manner as done in case of SCs and STs.
- A roster system for each category of posts should be adopted by the concerned authorities in the same manner as presently done in respect of SC and ST candidates.

The scheme of reservations in its toto should be made applicable to all recruitment to public sector undertakings both under the Central and State Governments, as also to nationalised banks. All private sector undertakings which have received financial assistance from the Government in one form or the other should also be obliged to recruit personnel on the aforesaid basis. All universities and affiliated colleges should also be covered by the scheme of reservation. To give proper effect to these recommendations, it is imperative that adequate statutory provisions are made by the Government to amend the existing enactments, rules, procedure, etc. to the extent they are not in consonance with the same.

Educational Concessions

Our educational system is elitist in character, results in a high degree of wastage and is least suited to the requirements of an over-populated and developing country. It is a legacy of the British rule which was severely criticised during the independence struggle, and yet, it has not undergone any structural changes.

Though it is least suited to the needs of backward classes, yet, they are forced to run the rat-race with others as no options are available to them. As 'educational reform' was not within the terms of reference of the Commission, we are also forced to trend the beaten track and suggest only the palliative measure within existing framework.

Various State Governments are giving a number of educational concessions to other backward class students like exemption of tuition fees, free supply of books and clothes, mid-day meals, special hostel facilities, stipends, etc. These concessions are all right as far as they go. But they do not go far enough. What is required is, perhaps, not so much the provision of additional funds as the framing of integrated schemes for creating the proper environment and incentives for serious and purposeful studies.

It is well known that most backward class children are irregular and indifferent students and their dropout rate is very high. There are two main reasons for this. First, these children are brought up in a climate of extreme social and cultural deprivation and consequently, a proper motivation for schooling is generally lacking.

Secondly, most of these children come from very poor homes and their parents are forced to press them into doing small chores from a very young age. Upgrading the cultural environment is a very slow process. Transferring these children to an artificially upgraded environment is beyond the present resources of the country. In view of this it is recommended that this problem may be tackled on a limited and selective basis on two fronts.

First, an intensive and time bound programme for adult education should be launched in selected pockets with high concentration of OBC population. This is a basic motivational approach, as only proper motivated parents will take serious interest in educating their children. Secondly, residential schools should be set up in these areas for backward class students to provide a climate specially conducive to serious studies.

All facilities in these schools including board and lodging, will have to be provided free of cost to attract students from poor and backward homes, separate Government Hostels for OBC students with the facilities will be another step in the right direction. A beginning on both these fronts will have to be made on a limited scale and selective basis. But the scope of these activities should be expanded as fast as the resources permit.

Adult education programme and residential schools started on a selective basis will operate as growing-points of consciousness for the entire community and their multiplier effect is bound to be substantial. Whereas several States are extended a number of ad hoc concessions to backward class students, few serious attempts have been made to integrate these facilities into a comprehensive scheme for a qualitative upgradation of educational environment available to OBC students.

After all, education is the best catalyst of change and educating the backward classes is the surest way to improve their self image and raise their social status. As OBCs cannot afford the high wastage rates of our educational system, it is very important that their education is highly biased in favour of vocational training. After all reservation in services will absorb only a very small percentage of the educated backward classes and the rest should be suitably equipped with vocational skills to enable them to get a return on having invested several years in education. It is also obvious that even if all the facilities are given to OBC students, they will not be able to compete on an equal footing with others in securing admission to technical and professional institutions. In view of this it is recommended that seats should be reserved for OBC students in all scientific, technical and professional institutions run by the Central Government as well as State Governments.

This reservation will fall under Article 15(4) of the Constitution and the quantum of reservation should be the same as in the Government services, *i.e.*, 27%. Those States which have already reserved more that 27% seats for OBC students will remain unaffected by this recommendation. While implementing the provisions for reservation it should also be ensured that the candidates who are admitted against the reserved quota are enable to derive full benefits of higher studies. It has been generally noticed that these OBC students coming from an impoverished cultural background, are not able to keep abreast with other students.

It is, therefore, very essential that special coaching facilities are arranged for all such students in our technical and professional institutions. The concerned authorities should clearly appreciate that their jobs is not finished once candidates against reserved quota have been admitted to various institutions. In fact the real task starts only after that special coaching assistance to these students, not only these young people will feel frustrated and humiliated but the country will also be landed with ill-equipped and sub-standard engineers, doctors and other professionals.

Financial Assistance

Vocational communities following hereditary occupations have suffered heavily as a result of industrialisation. Mechanical production and introductions of synthetic materials has robbed the village potter, oil crusher, blacksmith, carpenter, barber, etc. of their traditional means of livelihood and the pauperisation of these classes is a well-known phenomenon in the countryside. It has, therefore become very necessary that suitable institutional finance and technical assistance is made available to such members of village vocational communities who want to set up small-scale industries on their own. Similar assistance should also be provided to those promising OBC candidates who have obtained special vocational training. Of course, most State Governments have created various financial and technical agencies for the promotions of small and medium scale industries. But it is well known that only the more influential members of the community are able to derive benefits fro these agencies.

In view of this, it is essential that separate financial institutions for providing financial and technical assistance are established for the backward classes. Some State Governments like Karnataka and Andhra Pradesh have already set up separate financial corporations etc., for OBCs. Cooperative Societies of occupational groups will also help a lot. But due care should be taken that all office-bearers and members of such societies belong to the concerned hereditary occupational groups and outsiders are not allowed to exploit them by infiltrating into such cooperatives.

The share of OBCs in the industrial and business life of the country is negligible and this partly explains their extremely low income levels. As a part of its overall strategy to uplift the backward classes, it is imperative that all State Governments are suitably advised and encouraged to create a separate network of financial and technical institutions to foster business and industrial enterprise among OBCs.

Structural Changes

Reservations in Government employment and educational institutions, as also as possible financial assistance will remain mere palliatives unless the problems of backwardness is tackled at its root.

Bulk of the small land-holders, tenants, agricultural labour, impoverished village artisans, unskilled workers, etc. belong to Scheduled Castes, Scheduled Tribes and Other Backward Classes. "Apart from social traditions, the dominances by the top peasantry is exercised through recourse to informal bondage which arises mainly thorough money-lending, leasing out of small bits of land and providing house-sites and dwelling space to poor peasants.

As most of the functionaries of the Government are drawn from the top peasantry, the class and caste linkage between the functionaries of Government and the top peasantry remain firm. This also tills the socio-political balance in favour of the top peasantry and helps it in having its dominance over others."

The net outcome of the situation is that notwithstanding their numerical preponderance, backward class continues to remain in mental and material bondage of the higher castes and rich peasantry. Consequently, despite constituting nearly 3/4th of the countries population, Scheduled Castes, Scheduled Tribes and Other Backward Classes have been able to acquire a very limited political clout, even though adult franchise was introduced more than three decades back.

Through their literal monopoly of means of production of higher castes are able to manipulate and coerce the backward classes into acting against their own interests. In view of this, until the stranglehold of the existing production relations is broken through radical land reforms, the abject dependence of under privileged classes on the dominant higher castes will continue indefinitely. In fact there is already a sizeable volume of legislation on the statue books to abolish zamindari, place ceilings on land holdings and distribute land to the landless.

But in actual practice its implementation has been halting, half-hearted and superficial. The States like Karnataka, Kerala and West Bengal which have gone about the job more earnestly have not only succeeded in materially helping the Backward Classes, but also reaped rich political dividends into the bargains.

It is the Commission's firm Conviction that a radical transformation of the existing production relations is the most important single step that can be taken for the welfare and upliftment of all backward classes. Even if this is not possible in the industrial sector for various reasons, in the agricultural sector a change in this nature is both feasible and overdue. The Commission, therefore, strongly recommends that all the State Governments should be directed to enact and implement progressive land legislations so as to effect basic structural changes in the existing production relations in the countryside. At present surplus land in being allotted to SCs and STs. A part of the surplus land becoming available in future as a result of the operation of land ceiling laws etc. should also be allotted to the OBC landless labour.

Miscellaneous

- Certain parts of some occupational communities like Fishermen, Banjaras, Bansoforas, Khatwes etc. still suffer from the stigma of untouchability in some part of the country. They have been listed as O.B.Cs. by the Commission, but their inclusion in the lists of Scheduled Castes/Scheduled Tribes may be considered by the Government.
- Backward Classes Development Corporations should be set up both at the Central and State levels to implement various socio-educational and economic measures for their advancement.
- A separate Ministry/Department for O.B.Cs. at the Centre and States should be created to safeguard their interests.
- With a view to giving better representation to certain very backward parts of O.B.Cs. like the Gaddis of Himachal Pradesh, Neo-Buddhists in Maharashtra, Fishermen in the Coastal areas, Gujjars in J&K., it is recommended that areas of their concentration may be carved out into separate constituencies at the time of delimitation.

Central Assistance

At present no Central Assistance is available to any State Government for implementing any welfare measures for Other Backward Classes. The 18 States and Union Territories which have undertaken such measures have to provide funds from their own resources. During the Commission's tours practically every State Government pointed out that unless the Centre is prepared to liberally finance all special schemes for the upliftment of OBCs, it will be beyond the available resources of the States to undertake any worthwhile programme for the benefit of Other Backward Classes.

The Commission fully shares the views of the State Governments in this matter and strongly recommends that all development programmes specially designed for Other Backward Classes should be financed by the Central Government in the same manner and to the same extent as done in the case of Scheduled Castes and Scheduled Tribes. Regarding the period of operation of the Commission's recommendations entire scheme should be reviewed after twenty years.

We have advisedly suggested this span of one generation, as the raising of social consciousness is a generational progress. Any review at a shorter interval would be rather arbitrary and would not give a fair indication of the impact of our recommendations on the prevailing status and life-styles of O.B.Cs.

IMPLEMENTATION

All the recommendations of the report are not yet implemented. The recommendation of reservations for OBC's in government services was implemented in 1993. As on 27 June 2008 there is still a backlog of 28, 670 OBC vacancies in government jobs. The recommendation of reservations in Higher educational institutes is implemented in 2008.

CRITICISM

The National Sample Survey puts the figure at 32%. There is substantial debate over the exact number of OBC's in India, with census data compromised by partisan politics. It is generally estimated to be sizable, but lower than the figures quoted by either the Mandal Commission or and National Sample Survey. There is also an ongoing controversy about the estimation logic used by Mandal commission for calculating OBC population. Famous Indian Statistician, Mr. Yogendra Yadav who supports Reservations agrees that there is no empirical basis to the Mandal figure. According to him "It is a mythical construct based on reducing the number of SC/ST, Muslims and others and then arriving at a number." National Sample Survey's 1999-2000 round estimated around 36 per cent of the country's population is defined as belonging to the Other Backward Classes (OBC).

The proportion falls to 32 per cent on excluding Muslim OBCs. A survey conducted in 1998 by National Family Health Statistics (NFHS) puts the proportion of non-Muslim OBCs as 29.8 per cent L R Naik, the only Dalit member in the Mandal Commission refused to sign the Mandal recommendations. He said that there are two social blocks among the OBCs: upper caste (Jat and Gujjar) and upper OBCs (Yadavs, Kurmis, etc.) and Most Backward Classes (MBCs). He feared that upper OBCs would corner all the benefits of reservation. Here we shall present the study of the Mandal Commissions's list of the OBC for the state of West Bengal only for the sake of brevity. In this list, Urao (along with its synonyms Bandot, Haro, Karkata, Luidu, Shitheo, Tigga and Tirki) has been listed as an OBC (OBC No.176). On the other hand, it is already in the list of Scheduled Tribes for the state with a slight difference of spelling "Oraon" (ST 33).

Similarly, Scheduled Tribes Kharia (OBC 105; synonym of Lodha, ST 23 in the ST List), Kherwar (OBC 107; ST 17, with a spelling Kharwar), Koda (OBC 113; ST 20, spelled Kora), Bhotia (OBC 33; ST 5, spelled Bhutia), Brijia (OBC 39, ST 7, with a spelling Birjia), Gonda (OBC 68; ST 12, spelled Gond) and Lakra (OBC 123, and Lakar OBC 122, which is actually a surname adopted by many members of the Scheduled Tribe Munda), which are already declared STs for the state.

Tharu (OBC 171) is a widely studied scheduled tribe. Thapa (OBC 170) is a synonym of ST Sherpa (ST 5, same as Bhutia, Tota, Dukpa, Kagatay, Tibetan, Yolmo). Many famous ST surnames have been listed as OBC Mahato (OBC 129), etc. Other anthropologically famous scheduled tribes listed as OBC are Kuki (OBC 118), Lushei (actually Lushai; OBC 124), Koli (OBC 116) and Rohangia. Similar manipulation has been done with many Scheduled Castes also. For example in the state of West Bengal, Bhangi has been listed as OBC (No. 26), with a rider "excluding those in the Scheduled Caste".

On the other hand the SC list for West Bengal shows that Bhangi (at place no. 22 in the SC list) is an unconditional SC for the whole of the territory of the state. Halalkhor has also been listed as an OBC (No. 73) with a similar condition but this caste is also an unconditional SC (No. 21, spelled Halelkhor).

A sub-caste of Dom (Maghaiya-Dom) has been listed as OBC at place No. 126. Dom as a whole has been a Scheduled Caste (No.17 in West Bengal SC list) for ages. Bahelia (SC No. 2) has been listed by its synonym Chirimar (OBC 45). Bagal (OBC 11) is already there in the SC list at place number 1, with a spelling Bagll. Although Nat is an SC (No. 47), its sub-caste KarwalNat has been made an OBC (OBC 97).

Jaliya Kaivartta (SC 23) is just the Sanskritized name of Machua listed as OBC (OBC 125). All the Nav-Buddhists (Neo-Buddhist) have been include in the OBC list, which is again an anomaly, because the Nav-Buddhists enjoy their SC status. Not only synonyms or alternative spellings of the SCs and STs have been recorded as OBC, but also there are other types of manipulations like same OBC caste has been listed twice or sometimes thrice in the list of the same state.

An example of this type of manipulation is Kahar in Bihar list (No. 23 as well as No. 70), Kewat (at no. 115 as well as 84.) At any rate the list is vitiated by such inclusions. The Kuki tribes (ST) actually live in Nagaland, Meghalaya, Mizoram and Tripura, none of which are neighbouring to West Bengal. Even if any member of the tribe migrates to West Bengal or anywhere else in India, either it retains its ST status of the mother state or becomes General population.

It is difficult to believe that some Kuki tribes live in West Bengal as OBC. Lushai tribe (ST) live mainly in Mizoram and are the principal Mizo tribe. They are also found in Manipur as ST. Koli (ST) are found in a widespread area ranging from

Orissa to Rajasthan up to Karnatak. Rohangia ((OBC 158) are actually a distant tribe which mainly live in Myanmar but are also found in Bangla Desh-Myanmar-Tripura border areas). Introduction of such castes to the West Bengal OBC list seems to be an act of fertile brain and raises doubt whether any actual survey was done at all.

At any rate a small number of these tribes could be present in the former East Bengal (now Bangla Desh) in areas adjoining former state of Assam and Myanmar before partition. Some OBC caste names given in the list are obsolete of forward castes. Tyagi is an upper caste, which lives in UP, Haryana and Delhi. This caste was earlier called Taga. But with a general trend of all the North Indian castes to Sanskritize their names, Taga people adopted a new name Tyagi which was similar to Taga.

But still in the remote village especially by the illiterate people Tyagis are often called Taga. We find the name of Taga in Haryana Mandal list (OBC 74), Delhi (OBC 81) and Uttar Pradesh (OBC 109, as Taga-Bhat). The principles and norms set in the very beginning regarding the criterion for the Non-Hindu communities have been violated flagrantly, hence now the Roman Catholic is not a religion but a caste in the eyes of the Mandal Commission (Latin Catholic, OBC 106, Kerala). Anglo-Indians, who are the off-springs of the British rulers, have also been made an Other Backward Caste (OBC 6, Kerala).

Although it has been decided at the outset that only occupational castes among the Muslims and Christians and the castes bearing the same name as a Hindu OBC or SC will be included as a Muslim or Christian OBC caste, the set rule was violated wherever political expediency dictated. For example Kayastha (Muslim) has been made an OBC (OBC 93, Uttar Pradesh) which does not fulfill the criteria set for inclusion of non-Hindu castes. A last word about credibility of the Mandal survey.

Presence of obsolete and archaic caste names like Taga (for Tyagi in Haryana, Delhi and UP), Bhuihar (for Bhumi-har in Bihar), Domb (for Dom in all the southern states), listing of

Kuki, Lushai, Rohangia tribes in West Bengal which are not found in West Bengal today but actually some of each of them lived in East Bengal in undivided India neighbouring Tripura, Meghalaya etc., and many such factors cannot be explained unless it is assumed that the Mandal list is not result of a recent survey, but it has been compiled by editing the caste list of 1931 census.

But the editing was most inefficient. These names could not have crept in unless the old united Bengla caste list of 1931 was just copied and some named SC & ST, as well as well known forward caste names were just deleted, to arrive at the current OBC list of Mandal. Every state's OBC list has the same story. The entire list seems to be manipulated, but most carelessly and inefficiently manipulated.

Most famous scheduled castes like Dusadh (Dhari), Mochi, Domb (Dom) and Bhangi have been put as OBCs in many states. If the Government does not reject this whole Mandal list, all the SCs and STs listed as OBC will have to be deleted from the respective SC and ST lists.

Because the Mandal Commission was a constitutional body which had done a survey and this survey was done at a later date than the surveys for the SC and ST, which were done during the British period without the authority of our present Indian Constitution. Indeed any act (or survey) done under the authority of Indian Constitution automatically supersedes any act (or survey) of the British administration if there is an overlap or confusion.

PROTEST

A decade after the commission gave its report, V.P. Singh, the Prime Minister at the time, tried to implement its recommendations in 1989. The criticism was sharp and colleges across the country held massive protests against it. Soon after, Rajiv Goswami, student of Delhi University, committed self-immolation in protest of the government's actions.

His act further sparked a series of self-immolations by other college students and led to a formidable movement against job reservations for Backward Castes in India. First student to die due to self immolation was Surinder Singh Chauhan on Sep 24, 1990.

ARGUMENTS AGAINST RESERVATIONS

The opponents of the issue argue:

- Allocating quotas on the basis of caste is a form of racial discrimination, and contrary to the right to equality. Although the exact relation between caste and race is far from well established
- As a consequence of legislating to provide reservations for Christians and Muslim, religious minorities in all government education institutions will be introduced which is contrary to the ideas of secularism, and is a form of antidiscrimination on the basis of religion.
- Most often, only economically sound people (and rather rich) from the so-called lower castes will make use of most of the reserved seats, thus counteracting the spirit of reservations. Political parties know reservations are no way to improve the lot of the poor and the backward. They support them because of self-interest of the "creamy layer", who use the reservations to further their own family interests, and as a political flag of 'achievement' during election campaigns. In fact, several studies show that the OBC class is quite comparable with the general caste in terms of annual per capita consumption expenditure, and the top strata of OBC is ahead in a host of consumption areas.
- The quality of these elite institutes may go down, because merit is severely being compromised by reserving seats for certain caste-based communities.
- There are no efforts made to give proper primary education to truly deprived classes, so there is no need to reserve seats for higher studies. The government schools in India have absolutely no comparison to the public schools in the developed countries, and only about 65% of the Indian

population is literate. The critics argue that "reservation" only in higher institutions and jobs, without improving primary and secondary education, cannot solve this problem.

- The government is dividing people on the basis of castes for political advantages.
- The caste system is kept alive through these measures. Instead of coming up with alternative innovative ideas which make sure equal representation at the same time making the caste system irrelevant, the decision is only fortifying the caste system.
- The autonomy of the educational institutes are lost.
- Not everyone from the so-called upper classes are rich, and not all from so called lower classes are poor.
- The reservation policy of the Indian Congress will create a huge unrest in the Indian society. Providing quotas on the basis of caste and not on the basis of merit will deter the determination of many educated and deserving students of India.
- Multi-national companies will be deterred by this action of the government, and foreign investment in India may dry down, hurting the growth of the Indian economy. Doubtless, urgent actions to improve the lot of the majority, which has not benefited from development—not achieved after 55 years of reservations for scheduled castes—are essential. But this must not hazard improving the economy's competitiveness in a very competitive world.
- There are already talks of reservations in the private sector. If even after providing so many facilities to reserved categories during education, if there is no adequate representation of those people in the work force, there must be some problems with the education system.

Critics of the Mandal Commission argue that it is unfair to accord people special privileges on the basis of caste, even in order to redress traditional caste discrimination. They argue that those that deserve the seat through merit will be at a disadvantage. They reflect on the repercussions of unqualified candidates assuming critical positions in society (doctors, engineers, etc.).

As the debate on OBC reservations spreads, a few interesting facts which raise pertinent question are already apparent. To begin with, do we have a clear idea what proportion of our population is OBC? The Mandal Commission (1980) it is 52 per cent. The 2001 Indian Census, out of India's population of 1,028,737,436 the Scheduled Castes comprise 166,635,700 and Scheduled Tribes 84,326,240, that is 16.2% and 8.2% respectively. There is no data on OBCs in the census.

However, just as to National Sample Survey's 1999-2000 round around 36 per cent of the country's population is defined as belonging to the Other Backward Classes (OBC). The proportion falls to 32 per cent on excluding Muslim OBCs. A survey conducted in 1998 by National Family Health Statistics (NFHS) puts the proportion of non-Muslim OBCs as 29.8 per cent. The NSSO data also shows that already 23.5 per cent of college seats are occupied by OBCs.

That's just 8.6 per cent short of their share of population just as to the same survey. Other arguments include that entrenching the separate legal status of OBCs and SC/STs will perpetuate caste differentiation and encourage competition among communities at the expense of national unity. They believe that only a small new elite of educated Dalits, Adivasis, and OBCs benefit from reservations, and that such measures do nothing to lift the mass of people out of backwardness and poverty.

ARGUMENTS OFFERED IN SUPPORT OF RESERVATION

- Affirmative Action has helped many—if not everyone from under-privileged and/or under-represented communities to grow and occupy top positions in the world's leading industries. Reservation in education is not the final solution, it is just one of the many solutions. Reservations is a means to increase representation of hitherto under-represented caste groups and thereby improve diversity on campus.

- Although Reservation schemes do undermine the quality of education but still affirmative Action schemes are in place in many countries including USA, South Africa, Malaysia, Brazil etc. It was researched in Harvard University that Affirmative Action programmes are beneficial to the under-privileged. The studies said that Blacks who enter elite institutions with lower test scores and grades than those of whites achieve notable success after graduation. They earn advanced degrees at rates identical to those of their white classmates. They are even slightly more likely than whites from the same institutions to obtain professional degrees in law, business and medicine. They become more active than their white classmates in civic and community activities.
- Although Reservation schemes do undermine the quality of education but still they are needed to provide social justice to the most marginalized and underprivileged is our duty and their human right. Reservation will really help these marginalized people to lead successful lives, thus eliminating caste-based discrimination which is still widely prevalent in India especially in the rural areas. (over 60% of Indian population stays in Villages).
- But meritrocracy is meaningless without equality. First all people must be brought to the same level, whether it elevates a part or delevels another, regardless of merit. Only after that merit becomes meaningful. Privileged people have never known to go backward due to reservations or lack of "meritrocracy". Reservations have only slowed down the process of the 'forward' becoming richer and backward becoming poorer.

- In a perfectly functioning society the institutions and various walks of life must represent the many parts roughly in proportion to their share in population. In India it is clearly not the case and hence the need for reservations.
- India does not have the economic or institutional capacity for undertaking a grassroots based solution to the problem, so reservations remain the only practical solution for social antidiscrimination
- People who support reservations keenly invite all the anti-reservationists to lead the life of a backward class citizen and live within the means that they have for themselves. It is their contention that in a experimental setup like this the differences in achievement/ performance would disappear or reduce down to experimental errors/random error. Underlying idea being that everyone is born equal but into an unequal circumstances. And when the circumstances have been a result of a social system then the system either needs to be abandoned or reformed.
- Reservations are a political necessity in India because vast influential parts of voting population see reservations as beneficial to themselves. All governments have supported maintaining and/or increasing reservations. Reservations are legal and binding. As shown by Gujjar agitations (Rajasthan, 2007-2008), increasing reservations is also essential for peacekeeping in India.
- Reservations will go a long way in capacity building with regard to the human resource of the country. In the long run, it has tremendous economic benefits as it will raise the productivity of the majority of the potential workforce of the country
- The government of India, is bound and empowered by the constitution of the country to secure for all citizens equality in social, economic and political sphere.

NAMANTAR ANDOLAN

Namantar Andolan was started by Dalit Panthers. Namanter Andolan is a movement to change Marathwada University's name to Dr. B.R. Ambedkar University. Marathwada is made up of five districts—Aurangabad, Parbhani, Beed, Nanded and Usmanabad—out of 28 districts that were part of the earlier Hyderabad state ruled by the Nizam of Hyderabad.

The Marathwada part of the state was merged with Maharashtra after its trifurcation in 1956. As per the 1971 census, the population of this region was 8,058,347. This consisted of 80% Hindus; 9.52% belonged to Scheduled Castes; 11.8% Muslims, 7.2% Buddhists, and the rest were of other communities. Marathwada is an economically backward region of the state.

82% of the people are occupied in farming, as against the figure of 65% for the whole state. At that time (1971 census), industrial activity was almost nil, with only two persons out of 1,000 engaged in industry compared to 100 industrial workers out of every 1,000 in Mumbai. Further, Dalits comprised about 17% (9.5% of Scheduled Castes and 7.2% of the population compared to about 12% for the whole of Maharashtra.

About 75% of the Dalit population consisted of farm labourers, and 90% of the Dalit lived below the poverty line. The literacy rate among the Dalits in Marathwada was about 19% as compared to the general literacy rate of 35%. Among the Dalits, the Mahar community was supposed to be relatively better off and socially more conscious and with a higher rate of literacy.

Unemployment was a severe problem in Marathwada. For example, on 23 March 1974, 2,000 youths who came to Parbhani town looking for jobs were told that only 40 posts were to be filled up. There was no scope for the youths in farming or in industry. Thus education was the only field where there was a concentration of Dalit youths. After one united march with Panthers there was a split in the students' advisory committee, allegedly provoked by Panthers. The differences of opinion among the leaders of the committee were also caused by the meeting they had with Vasantrao Patil. Those opposing the renaming move organized themselves under the banner of 'Marathwada Vidyarthi Kriti Samiti'. This Samiti gave a call of colleges in Marathwada remained closed from 12 to 26 September 1977. The Samiti also organized a total Marathwada bandh on 19 September.

DALIT BUDDHIST MOVEMENT

The Dalit Buddhist movement (dubbed as Navayana by certain Ambedkerites) is arguably the most influential of a series of 19th and 20th century Buddhist revival movements in India.

It received its most substantial impetus from B. R. Ambedkar's call for the conversion of Dalits to Buddhism in the context of a caste based society that considered them to be at the lowest end of the hierarchy.

ORIGINS

Buddhism was once dominant through much of India, it had however begun to decline by the 12th century. The Buddhist revival began in India in 1891, when the Sri Lankan Buddhist leader Anagarika Dharmapala founded the Maha Bodhi Society The Maha Bodhi Society mainly attracted upper-caste people., most of whom did not identify themselves specifically as Buddhists, seeing no significant difference between Buddhism and Hinduism.

South India

In 1890, Pandit C. Ayodhya Dasa (1845-1914), better known as Iyothee Thass, founded the Sakya Buddhist Society (also known as the Indian Buddhist Association). The first president of the Indian Buddhist Association was the German born American Paul Carus, the author of The Gospel of Buddha (1894).

Thass, a Tamil Siddha physician, was the pioneer of the Tamil Dalit movement. He argued that Tamil Dalits were originally Buddhists. He led a delegation of prominent Dalits to Henry Steel Olcott and asked for his help in the reestablishment of "Tamil Buddhism." Olcott helped Thass to visit Sri Lanka, where he received diksha from Bhikkhu Sumangala Nayake. After returning to India, Thass established the Sakya Buddhist Society in Madras with branches in many places including Karnataka.

Thass established a weekly magazine called Oru Paisa Tamizhan ("One Paisa Tamilian") in Chennai in 1907, which served as a newsletter linking all the new branches of the Sakya Buddhist Society.

The magazine discussed traditions and practices of Tamil Buddhism, new developments in the Buddhist world, and the Indian subcontinent's history from the Buddhist point of view. Brahmananda Reddy, a Dalit leader of Andhra Pradesh, was also fascinated by Buddhism.

Uttar Pradesh

In the early 20th century, the Barua Buddhists of Bengal under the leadership of Kripasaran Mahasthavir (1865-1926), founder of the Bengal Buddhist Association in Calcutta (1892), established viharas in cities such as Lucknow, Hyderabad, Shillong and Jamshedpur.

In Lucknow, Bodhanand Mahastavir (1874-1952) advocated Buddhism for Dalits. Born Mukund Prakash in a Bengali Brahmin family, he was orphaned at a young age, and was then raised in Benaras by an aunt. He was initially attracted to Christianity, but became a Buddhist after a meeting with Buddhists monks from Ceylon at a Theosophical Conference in Benares. He later lived in Lucknow where he came in contact with Barua Buddhists, many of whom were employed as cooks by the British. In 1914, Prakash was ordained Bodhanand Mahastavir in Calcutta in the presence of Kripasaran Mahasthvir.

He began preaching Buddhism in Lucknow. He founded the Bharatiye Buddh Samiti in 1916, and set up a vihara in 1928. In his book Mula Bharatavasi Aur Arya ("Original Inhabitants and Aryans"), Mahastavir stated that the shudras were the original inhabitants of India, who were enslaved by the Aryans. Bodhanand Mahastavir wrote another book on Buddhist rituals called Baudha Dvicharya. His associate, Chandrika Prasad Jigyasu, founded the Bahujan Kalyan Prakashan. The two coauthored a book on the life and teaching of the Buddha.

Acharya Ishvardatt Medharthi (1900-1971) of Kanpur also supported the cause of the Dalits. He had studied Pali at Gurukul Kangri and Buddhist scripture was well knowr to him. He was initiated into Buddhism by Gyan Keto and the Lokanatha in 1937. Gyan Keto (1906-1984), born Peter Schoenfeldt was a German who arrived to Ceylon in 1936 and became a Buddhist.

Although Medharthi heavily criticized the Indian caste system, he didn't criticize Hinduism. He claimed that the Dalits ("Adi Hindus") were the ancient rulers of India and had been trapped into slavery by the Aryan invaders. He also claimed that the sanatana dharma was the religion of "Adi Hindus", and tried to reconcile Buddhism with the Sant Mat. Another Bhikkhu of Kanpur, Bhikshu Uttam, was a strong supporter of the Arya Samaj and the Jat Pat Todak Mandal, the anti-caste wing of the Arya Samaj.

B. R. AMBEDKAR

At the Yeola conference in 1935, prominent Dalit leader B. R. Ambedkar declared that he would not die a Hindu, saying that it perpetuates caste injustices. Ambedkar was approached by various leaders of different denominations and faiths.

Meetings were held to discuss the question of Dalit religion and the pros and cons of conversion. On May 22, 1936, an "All Religious Conference" was held at Lucknow. It was attended by prominent Dalit leaders including Jagjivan Ram, though Ambedkar could not attend it.

At the conference, Muslim, Christian, Sikh, and Buddhist representatives presented the tenets of their respective religions in an effort to win over Dalits. Buddhist monk Lokanatha visited Ambedkar's residence at Dadar on June 10, 1936 and tried to persuade him to embrace Buddhism. Later in an interview to the Press, Lokanatha said that Ambedkar was impressed with Buddhism and that his own ambition was to convert all Dalits to Buddhism. In 1937, Lokanatha published a pamphlet Buddhism Will Make You Free, dedicated to the Depressed Classes of India from his press in Ceylon.

In early 1940s, Ambedkar visited Acharya Ishvardatt Medharthi's Buddhpuri school in Kanpur. Medharthi had earlier been initiated into Buddhism by Lokanatha, and by the mid-1940s, he had close contacts with Ambedkar. For a short while, Ambedkar also took Pali classes from Medharthi in Delhi.

Bodhananda Mahastvir and B. R. Ambedkar first met in 1926, at the "Indian Non-Brahmin Conference" convened by Shahu IV of Kolhapur. They met on two more occasions and for a short while in the 1940s, where they discussed dhamma. Mahastavir objected to Dr Ambedkar's second marriage because his bride was a Brahmin. Later, his followers actively participated in Ambedkar's Republican Party of India.

Ambedkar's Conversion

After publishing a series of books and substances arguing that Buddhism was the only way for the Untouchables to gain equality, Ambedkar publicly converted on October 14, 1956 at Deekshabhoomi, Nagpur.

He took the three refuges and the Five Precepts from a Buddhist monk, Bhadant U Chandramani, in the traditional manner and then in his turn administered them to the 380,000 of his followers that were present. The conversion ceremony was attended by Medharthi, his main disciple Bhoj Dev Mudit, and Mahastvir Bodhanand's Sri Lankan successor, Bhante Pragyanand.

Ambedkar would die less than two months later, just after finishing his definitive work on Buddhism. Many Dalits employ the term "Ambedkar(ite) Buddhism" to designate the Buddhist movement, which started with Ambedkar's conversion and many converted people called themselves as "Nava-Bauddha" *i.e.* New Buddhists.

22 Vows of Ambedkar

After receiving ordination, Ambedkar gave dhamma diksha to his followers. The ceremony included 22 vows given to all new converts after Three Jewels and Five Precepts. On 16 October 1956, Ambedkar performed another mass religious conversion ceremony at Chanda.

He prescribed 22 vows to his followers:

1. I shall have no faith in Brahma, Vishnu and Maheshwara nor shall I worship them.
2. I shall have no faith in Rama and Krishna who are believed to be incarnation of God nor shall I worship them.
3. I shall have no faith in Gauri, Ganapati and other gods and goddesses of Hindus nor shall I worship them.
4. I do not believe in the incarnation of God.
5. I do not and shall not believe that Lord Buddha was the incarnation of Vishnu. I believe this to be sheer madness and false propaganda.
6. I shall not perform Shraddha nor shall I give pinddan.
7. I shall not act in a manner violating the principles and teachings of the Buddha.
8. I shall not allow any ceremonies to be performed by Brahmins.
9. I shall believe in the equality of man.
10. I shall endeavor to establish equality.
11. I shall follow the noble eightfold path of the Buddha.
12. I shall follow the ten paramitas prescribed by the Buddha.
13. I shall have compassion and loving kindness for all living beings and protect them.
14. I shall not steal.
15. I shall not tell lies.
16. I shall not commit carnal sins.
17. I shall not take intoxicants like liquor, drugs etc.
18. I shall endeavor to follow the noble eightfold path

and practice compassion and loving kindness in every day life.

19. I renounce Hinduism, which is harmful for humanity and impedes the advancement and development of humanity because it is based on inequality, and adopt Buddhism as my religion.
20. I firmly believe the Dhamma of the Buddha is the only true religion.
21. I believe that I am having a rebirth.
22. I solemnly declare and affirm that I shall hereafter lead my life just as to the principles and teachings of the Buddha and his Dhamma.

Nowadays many Ambedkarite Organisations are working for these 22 vows (*i.e.* 22 Pratigya). They believe that these vows only are responsible for the existence and rapid growth of present Buddhism in India.

The umbrella organization known as the 22 Pledges Practice and Propagation Movement (*i.e.* in Hindi- 22 Pratigya Aacharan aur Prachaar Abhiyan) is fully devoted for this purpose. This totally non-political movement is the brain-child of Arvind Sontakke, and comprises around 5,000,000 volunteers (Pracharaks) including many regional and local groups throughout India.

DALIT BUDDHISM MOVEMENT AFTER AMBEDKAR'S DEATH

The Buddhist movement was somewhat hindered by Dr. Ambedkar's death so shortly after his conversion. It did not receive the immediate mass support from the Untouchable population that Ambedkar had hoped for. Division and lack of direction among the leaders of the Ambedkarite movement have been an additional impediment.

The 2001 census, there are currently 7.95 million Buddhists in India, at least 5.83 million of whom are Buddhists in Maharashtra. This makes Buddhism the fifth-largest religion in India and 6% of the population of Maharashtra, but less than 1% of the overall population of India. The Buddhist revival remains concentrated in two states: Ambedkar's native

Maharashtra, and Uttar Pradesh—the land of Bodhanand Mahastavir, Acharya Medharthi and their associates.

Developments in Uttar Pradesh

Acharya Medharthi retired from his Buddhapuri school in 1960, and shifted to an ashram in Haridwar. He turned to the Arya Samaj and conducted vedic yajnas all over India. After his death, he was cremated just as to Arya Samaj rites. His Buddhpuri school became embroiled in property disputes. His follower, Bhoj Dev Mudit, converted to Buddhism in 1968 and set up a school of his own.

Rajendranath Aherwar appeared as an important Dalit leader in Kanpur. He joined the Republican Party of India and converted to Buddhism along with his whole family in 1961. In 1967, he founded the Kanpur branch of "Bharatiya Buddh Mahasabha". He held regular meetings where he preached Buddhism, officiated at Buddhist weddings and life cycle ceremonies, and organized festivals on Dr. Ambedkar's Jayanti (birth day), Buddha Jayanti, Diksha Divas (the day Ambedkar converted), and Dr Ambedkar Paranirvan Divas (the day Ambedkar died).

The Dalit Buddhist movement in Kanpur gained impetus with the arrival of Dipankar, a Chamar bhikkhu, in 1980. Dipankar had come to Kanpur on a Buddhist mission and his first public appearance was scheduled at a mass conversion drive in 1981. The event was organized by Rahulan Ambawadekar, an RPI Dalit leader. In April 1981, Ambawadekar founded the Dalit Panthers (U.P. Branch) inspired by the Maharashtrian Dalit Panthers. The event met with severe criticism and opposition from Vishwa Hindu Parishad and was banned.

In 2002, Kanshi Ram, a popular out-caste political leader from a Sikh religious background, announced his intention to convert to Buddhism on October 14, 2006, the fiftieth anniversary of Ambedkar's conversion. He intended for 20,000,000 of his supporters to convert at the same time. Part of the significance of this plan was that Ram's followers include not only Untouchables, but persons from a variety of castes, who could significantly broaden Buddhism's support. However, he died October 9, 2006 after a lengthy illness; he was cremated as per Buddhist rituals.

Another popular Dalit leader, Bahujan Samaj Party chief Mayawati, has said that she and her followers will embrace Buddhism after the BSP gains control of the government.

Maharashtra

Japanese-born Bhadant Nagarjun Surai Sasai is an important Buddhist leader in India. Sasai came to India in 1966 and met Nichidatsu Fuji, whom he helped with the Peace Pagoda at Rajgir. He fell out with Fuji, however, and started home, but, by his own account, was stopped by a dream in which a figure resembling Nagarjuna appeared and said, "Go to Nagpur".

In Nagpur, he met Wamanrao Godbole, the person who had organized the conversion ceremony for Dr. Ambedkar in 1956. Sasai claims that when he saw a photograph of Dr. Ambedkar at Godbole's home, he realised that it was Ambedkar who had appeared in his dream. At first, Nagpur folk considered Surai Sasai very strange.

Then he began to greet them with "Jai Bhim" (victory to Ambedkar) and to build viharas. In 1987 a court case to deport him on the grounds that he had overstayed his visa was dismissed, and he was granted Indian citizenship. Sasai is one of the main leaders of the campaign to free the Mahabodhi Temple at Bodh Gaya from Hindu control.

Organized Mass Conversions

Since Ambedkar's conversion, several thousand people from different castes have converted to Buddhism in ceremonies including the twenty-two vows. The Tamil Nadu and Gujarat governments passed new laws in 2003 to ban "forced" religious conversions. These laws were later withdrawn due to heavy opposition.

- 1957: In 1957, Mahastvir Bodhanand's Sri Lankan successor, Bhante Pragyanand, held a mass conversion drive for 15,000 people in Lucknow.

- 2001: A prominent Indian Dalit Buddhist leader and political activist, Udit Raj, organized a large mass conversion on November 4, 2001 where he gave the 22 vows, but the event met with active opposition from the government.
- 2006, Hyderabad: A report from the UK daily The Guardian said that some Hindus have converted to Buddhism. Buddhist monks from the UK and the U.S. attended the conversion ceremonies in India. In response, Hindu nationalists asserted that Dalits should concentrate on illiteracy and poverty rather than looking for new religions.
- 2006, Gulbarga: On October 14, 2006 hundreds of people converted from Hinduism to Buddhism in Gulburga (Karnataka).
- 2006: A Buddhist source claimed that "300,000 Dalits are estimated" to have converted to Buddhism as part of 50th year celebrations of Ambedkar's deeksha in 2006. Non-Partisan sources put the number of attendees (not converts) at 30,000. The move was criticized by Hindu groups as "unhelpful" and has been criticized as a "political stunt."
- 2007, Mumbai: On May 27, 2007 tens of thousands of Dalits from Maharashtra gathered at the Mahalakshmi racecourse in Mumbai to mark the 50th anniversary of the conversion of Ambedkar. The number of people who actually converted, however, versus the number of people in attendance was not clear. The event was organized by the Republican Party of India leader Ramdas Athvale.

Criticism of Conversions

Hindu critics have argued that efforts to convert Hindus to Ambedkarite Buddhism are political stunts rather than sincere commitments to social reform.

In addition, several Dalit leaders have stated that they are not against the upper castes *per se*. Leaders of the Dalit Bahujan Samaj Party have said that they are being branded as "anti-

Hindu" because of the publicity associated with the conversions is largely the work of "manuvadi vested interests, including political parties and parts of the media" and that they are only interested in peaceful dialogue with the Brahmins.

DISTINCTIVE INTERPRETATION

Dr. Gail Omvedt, an American-born and naturalized Indian sociologist and human rights activist:

- Ambedkar's Buddhism seemingly differs from that of those who accepted by faith, who 'go for refuge' and accept the canon. This much is clear from its basis: it does not accept in totality the scriptures of the Theravada, the Mahayana, or the Vajrayana. The question that is then clearly put forth: is a fourth yana, a Navayana, a kind of modernistic Enlightenment version of the Dhamma really possible within the framework of Buddhism?

Most Dalit Indian Buddhists espouse an eclectic version of Buddhism, primarily based on Theravada, but with additional influences from Mahayana and Vajrayana. On many subjects, they give Buddhism a distinctive interpretation. Of particular note is their emphasis on Shakyamuni Buddha as a political and social reformer, rather than merely as a spiritual leader.

They point out that the Buddha required his monastic followers to ignore caste distinctions, and that he was critical of the social inequality that existed in his own time. Ambedkar's followers do not believe that a person's unfortunate conditions at birth are the result of previous karma.

8

Dalits Social Groups and Political Parties

VIDUTHALAI CHIRUTHAIGAL KATCHI

Dalit Panthers of India (DPI) or Viduthalai Siruthaigal is a people's movement and political party mainly based in Tamil Nadu. It advocates for the rights and welfare of Dalits.

Its leader is Thol. Thirumavalavan. It won two MLA seats in 2006 state assembly elections on its own in alliance with AIADMK. Now it is in the DMK front. It was involved in a controversy involving the south Indian actress Kushboo.

BAMCEF

All India Backward and Minority Communities Employees' Federation popularly known as BAMCEF is an organization of educated employees from scheduled castes, scheduled tribes, Other Backward Classes, and converted minority communities in India.

In 1973, Kanshiram along with D.K. Khaparde, and their colleagues established the BAMCEF, which was relaunched on December 6, 1978 on the death anniversary of Dr. B. R. Ambedkar. BAMCEF celebrated its silver jubilee in the year 2008. BAMCEF has its mission to change the traditional Indian social system based on castes and varnas.

As an employee in the Defence Research and Development Laboratory in Pune, Kanshiram realised that the formation of the dalit bureaucracy was important if dalits' interest were to be served. He set about forming the federation, through which he worked his way in the higher echelons of bureaucracy by identifying a few zealous officers, and through them, influencing the lower staff. The motto of the organization was Pay back to society, to inspire the dalit bureaucrats to do their bit for the dalit masses.

In this way a continuous supply of brains, money, and talent was ensured. Kanshiram did not want to make the BAMCEF mere an employees' union, instead he wanted it to become the organisation of educated bahujan employees, "the think tank, talent bank, and financial bank of the bahujan samaj". BAMCEF undertook collection of funds for the purpose of supporting agitations and training; Kanshi Ram appointed state level convenors as well as mandal convenors to act as links between state and district levels.

Knowing the limitations of BAMCEF, Kanshiram formed Dalith Soshit Samaj Sangharsh samithi (DS4) in 1981. In 1984 Kanshiram dissolved the DS4 and formed a completely political wing Bahujan Samaj Party (BSP). This caused major strains in BAMCEF Ranks. In early 1986 major slipt took place. Kanshiram announced at that time that he was no longer will to work for any organisation other than BSP.

Without Kanshi Ram, D. K. Khaparde has registered BAMCEF in the Year 1987 in consultation with other colleagues. Since then one group of BAMCEF which was associated with Kanshi Ram was converted into a shadow organization helping BSP in electoral mobilization for the party, on the other hand the group of employees which had parted ways from kanshi Ram got itself registered and started mobilizing Dalits Independently without the help of any political clout..

BHARIPA BAHUJAN MAHASANGH

Bharipa Bahujan Mahasangh is a political party in India. The party was formed in 1999, through a split in the Republican Party of India. The party is led by Prakash Yashwant Ambedkar, the grandson of Dr. Ambedkar. The party fights for the rights of the Dalit community. BBM is primarily based in Maharashtra. In the 13th Lok Sabha elections during 1999 Party President Mr Prakash Ambedkar was elected from the constituency Akola. In the Lok Sabha election 2004 the party lost its parliamentary representation. In total the party had launched 16 candidates, all from Maharashtra.

In Akola Ambedkar was defeated by a Bharatiya Janata Party (BJP) candidate. In the elections to the Maharashtra state assembly 1999 BBM had put up 34 candidates. In total BBM got 606 827 votes, and won three seats. The complete name of the party is Bharatia Republican Paksha—Bahujan Mahasangh (Indian Republican Party—Majority Grand Union). Bharatia Republican Paksha is abbreviated BhaRiPa.

BAHUJAN SAMAJ PARTY

Bahujan Samaj Party (BSP) or Majority People's Party is one of the only five prominent national political parties of India, which is the largest democracy of the world.

BRIEF INTRODUCTION

The ideology of the Bahujan Samaj Party (BSP) is "Social Transformation and Economic Emancipation" of the "Bahujan Samaj ", which comprises of the Scheduled Castes (SCs), the Scheduled Tribes (STs), the Other Backward Classes (OBCs) and Religious Minorities such as Sikhs, Muslims, Christians, Parsis and Buddhists and account for over 85 per cent of the country's total population.

The people belonging to all these classes have been the victims of the "Manuwadi" system in the country for thousands of years, under which they have been vanquished, trampled upon and forced to languish in all spheres of life. In other words, these people were deprived even of all those human rights, which had been secured for the upper caste Hindus under the age-old "Manuwadi Social System".

Among the great persons (Mahapurush) belonging to "Bahujan Samaj", who fought courageously and with commitment against the brutal and oppressive Manuwadi system, for providing a level playing field to the downtrodden to help move forward in their lives with "self-respect" and at par with the upper castes Hindus, especially Baba Saheb Dr. Bhimrao Ambedkar's socio-political campaign later proved to be very effective in this direction. Though the contributions of leaders of the downtrodden communities like Mahatma Jyotiba Phule, Chhatrapati Shahuji Maharaj, Narayana Guru and Periyar E. V. Ramaswami have been immense in the fight against the obnoxious Manuwadi system, but the struggle of Baba Saheb Dr. Bhimrao Ambedkar, who was born in Scheduled Caste community, and that of Manyawar Kanshi Ram Ji later proved to be greatly effective and pregnant with far-reaching consequences.

Besides waging a spirited campaign against the Manuwadi Social System, Dr. Ambedkar instilled consciousness among not only the Dalits, but also among those belonging to other backward groups, which continue to be victimised and trampled under this oppressive and unjust Manuvadi Social System.

By virtue of his pivotal role in the framing of the Indian Constitution, these groups were given a number of rights in the Constitution on a legal basis to lead a life of dignity and self-respect. But he was fully conscious of the fact that these exploited parts of the society would not be able to get the full legal rights as long as the governments would remain dominated by the Manuwadi persons and parties.

That's why Dr. Ambedkar, during his lifetime, had counseled the "Bahujan Samaj" that if they wanted to fully enjoy the benefits of their legal rights, as enshrined in the Constitution, they would have to bond together all the Bahujan groups on the basis of unity and fraternity, bring them on a strong political platform and capture the "Master Key" of political power.

This was to be the modus operandi for the formation of Bahujan Governments at the Centre and in States. Only such governments could enforce all the constitutional and legal rights of the "Bahujan Samaj" and provide opportunities to its People to move forward in all spheres of life besides enabling them to lead a life of "self-respect". Keeping in view this observation and advice of Dr. Ambedkar, respected

Manyawar Kanshi Ram Ji founded the Bahujan Samaj Party (BSP), with the help of his associates, on April 14, 1984. For many years while he enjoyed good health, he prepared the "Bahujan Samaj" to secure the "master key" of political power, which opens all the avenues for social and economic development. However, being a diabetic and host of other serious ailments, his health did not permit him to lead an active political life for too long.

On December 15, 2001, Manyawar Kanshi Ram Ji, while addressing a mammoth rally of the BSP at the Lakshman Mela Ground in Lucknow, Uttar Pradesh on the banks of the river Gomti, declared Kumari (Miss) Mayawati Ji, then the lone Vice-President of the Party, as his only political heir and successor.

Moreover, on September 15, 2003, Manyawar Kanshi Ram Ji's health suffered a serious setback, and the entire responsibility of the Party fell on the shoulders of Bahan (Sister) Kumari Mayawati Ji. Later, on September 18, 2003, the Party, through a consensus and in keeping with its Constitution, made her its National President.

Being the National President of a National Party, Kumari Mayawati Ji in her address sought to assure that "I would like to make aware people of the country that my Party, the BSP, is committed to not only improving the socio-economic conditions of people belonging to the "Bahujan Samaj" but also of the poor among the upper caste Hindus, small and medium farmers, traders and people engaged in other professions. But people of the Manuwadi mindset, even if they are in different fields of life, are acting under a conspiracy to project the image of the BSP as if it is confined to championing the cause of Dalits alone and is opposed to the upper castes Hindus and other parts of the society.

Also, the BSP has nothing to do with the issues of national interest. However, on the basis of facts, I can say with firmness and conviction that all such talks are a bunch of lies, baseless and devoid of facts and are nothing else more than a slanderous campaign of the status quoits Manuwadi forces. The policies, objectives and ideology of the BSP are crystal clear and attuned to the welfare of the entire country and its vast population. On the basis of its ideology, the BSP wants to sound the death-knell of the "Manuwadi Social System" based on the 'Varna' (which is an inequality social system) and striving hard and honestly for the establishment of an egalitarian and "Humanistic Social System" in which everyone enjoys JUSTICE (social, economic and political) and EQUALITY (of status and of opportunity) as enshrined in the PREAMBLE of the Constitution.

Further, our Party Constitution very clearly states that "the chief aim and objective of the Party shall be to work as a revolutionary social and economic movement of change with a view to realise, in practical terms, the supreme principles of universal justice, liberty, equality and fraternity enunciated in the Constitution of India."

Such a social system is wholly in the overall interest of the Country and all parts of the society too. If, in this missionary work of "Social Transformation", people of the upper castes (Hindus) shed their Manuwadi mindset and join hands with the Bahujan Samaj, our Party, with all due respect and affection would embrace them. Such people will be given suitable positions in the Party organisation in accordance with their ability, dedication and efficiency, and there would be no distinction between them and those belonging to the Bahujan Samaj.

Also they will be fielded as Party candidates in the parliamentary and assembly elections, and if our government is formed, they will also be given ministerial berths. These are not hollow talks because the BSP in the past, during the three successive governments, had implemented all such promises. In Uttar Pradesh, Ms. Mayawati government was formed four times, and on each occasion, upper castes people were inducted in the Council of Ministers.

Even an upper caste person was appointed to an all-important post of Advocate General. They were given the Party ticket for Lok Sabha and Assembly elections and also nominated to the Parliament's Upper Chamber *i.e.* Rajya Sabha and state Legislative Councils. In addition, upper caste people have been given high posts in the Party organisation. For example, Mr. Satish Chandra Mishra was nominated to the Rajya Sabha and also was made national general secretary of the Party. In similar fashion, other castes of the Upper Castes (Hindus) were promoted.

Thus, keeping in view all these facts, it would be injudicious and fallacious to hold that the BSP works for the welfare of a particular group or part. Yes, the Party does give priority to those parts, which have been ignored and scorned all along by the Manuwadi governments in all spheres of life. In addition, the BSP has always contributed positively to all issues pertaining to the welfare of the Country.

The BSP has always taken an unequivocal stand on issues of the Country's welfare and never compromised on the issues related to the interest of the country whenever the need arose.

AIMS AND OBJECTIVES

The chief aim and objective of the party shall be to work as a revolutionary social and economic movement of change with a view to realise, in practical terms, the supreme principles of universal justice, liberty, equality and fraternity enunciated in the Constitution of India, to be followed by State in governance, and in particular summed up extract from the Preamble of the Constitution.

We, The People of India, having solemnly resolved to constitute India into a Sovereign Secular Democratic Republic and to secure to all its citizens:

- Justice, social, economic and political;
- Liberty of thought, expression, belief, faith and worship;
- Equality of status and opportunity; and promote among them all
- Fraternity assuring the dignity of the individual and the unity and integrity of the Nation;"

The Party shall regard its ideology as a movement for ending exploitation of the weaker parts and suppression of the deprived through social and economic change in keeping with the stated chief aim, and its political activity and participation in governance as an instrument of furthering such a movement and bringing in such a change. This being the chief aim of the Party, the strategy of the Party in public affairs will be governed by the following general principles:

- That all citizens of India being equal before law are entitled to be treated as equal in true sense and in all matters and all walks of life, and where equality does not exist it has to be fostered and where equality is denied it has to be upheld and fought for.
- That the full, free, uninhibited and unimpeded development of each individual is a basic human right and State is an instrument for promoting and realising such development;
- That the rights of all citizens of India as enshrined in the Constitution of India and subject to such restrictions as are set out in the Constitution, have to be upheld at all costs and under all circumstances;
- That the provisions of the Constitution requiring the State at Centre and in States to promote with special care and protect the socio-economic interests of the weaker parts of the society denied to them for centuries, have to upheld and given practical shape in public affairs as a matter of prime most priority.
- That economic disparities and the wide gaps between the 'haves' and the 'have nots' must not be allowed to override the political principle of "one man, one vote, one vote, one value" adopted by our republic.
- That unless political empowerment is secured for the economically deprived masses they will not be able to free themselves from the shackles of economic and social dependence and exploitation.

In particular and without prejudice to the generality of the aims stated the Party will work specially towards the following objectives:

- The Scheduled Castes, the Scheduled Tribes, the other Backward Castes, and the minorities, are the most oppressed and exploited people in India. Keeping in mind their large numbers, such a set of people in

India is known as the Bahujan Samaj. The Party shall organise these masses.

- The party shall work for these down trodden masses to.
  - To remove their backwardness;
  - To fight against their oppression and exploitation;
  - To improve their status in society and public life;
  - To improve their living conditions in day to day life;
- The social structure of India is based on inequalities created by caste system and the movement of the Party shall be geared towards changing the social system and rebuild it on the basis of equality and human values. All those who join the party with the commitment to cooperate in this movement of social change shall be ingratiated into the fold of the Party.

Towards the furtherance of the aims and objectives the organisational units of Party as designated in this constitution, shall be empowered to:

- Purchase, take on lease or otherwise acquire, and maintain, moveable or immovable property for the Party and invest and deal with monies of Party in such a manner as may from time to time be determined;
- Raise money with or without security for carrying out any of the aims and objectives of the Party;
- To do all other lawful things and acts as are incidental or conducive to the attainment of any of the aforesaid aims and objectives.

9

Globalisation and the Dalits

INTRODUCTION

The plethora of literature on globalisation paradoxically seems to induce more confusion than clearing out the true nature of its dynamics. For many, it is not at all a new phenomenon; it has been there in essence in the cross border trade that went on centuries ago and in an identifiable form in the nineteenth century capitalism insofar as it lent both labour and capital substantially mobile, gave fillip to international trade and when national economies were kept in kilter by the operation of the gold standard.

This attempt at universalising the theory as well as praxis of globalisation tends to imply futility of resistance to globalisation. Many proffer a TINA (There Is No Alternative) argument as per which despite adverse impact of globalisation on masses of people, there is no alternative for the world than adopting the globalisation model. This argument, while reflecting the admission of the adverse impact of globalisation and therefore sounding more credible, tends to indicate accrual of more benefits than costs.

It tends to neutralise the theoretical arguments against globalisation and therefore cripples the resistance movement much before its articulation. Then there are sponsored authorships that ceaselessly contribute multi-dimensional arguments in support of these policies.

They could range from out right theoretical distortions to empirical amplification. The sheer number of such studies claiming all kinds of success stories as attributes of these policies and all kinds of failures as due to absence of them overwhelms and enfeebles the truth to the contrary. The main theme of globalisation is pivoted on the promise of development and its "trickle down" to the subaltern parts of the society. Notwithstanding the total contrary evidence, the glitter created by the free markets misleads one into believing that the benefits of globalisation reached the weak and poor of the society.

After nearly a decade of adoption of these policies in our country and on the eve of the launch of so called second phase of Reforms, it is time that we examined the magnitude and direction of the impact of these policies on the dalits representing the oppressed people in India. This document seeks to attempt this task with the help of available statistics.

GLOBALISATION IN A HISTORICAL PERSPECTIVE

The doctrinal basis of today's globalisation is provided by the "neo-liberalism" that represented revival of economic liberalism propounded by Adam Smith in 1776 in his famous book titled, "Wealth of Nations". Economic liberalism advocated the abolition of the government intervention in economic matters; it considered fee trade was the best way for a nation's economy to develop.

These ideas were "liberal" in the sense of no controls. Underneath their democratic façade, promotion of individualism and encouragement of free enterprise, they came to mean free hand for the capitalists for exploitation of labour and to make huge profits at any cost. These ideas ruled the world through the 1800s and early 1900s till the great depression of the 1930s eclipsed them with the theory of a British economist named John Maynard Keynes.

This theory propounded that full employment is necessary for capitalism to grow and it can be achieved only if governments and central banks intervened to increase employment. It worked well through the post World War II reconstruction period and thereafter through the mid sixties. The USA which had emerged as the major economy of the world long before the World War II, immensely benefited from the state-coordinated wartime economy so as to assume the reigns of global capitalist order. It zealously guarded the capitalist system against the radical nationalism sprouting at many places, invariably with the use of force under the peculiar terminology of falsehood like "protection against the threat to stability" (a case of overthrow of the first democratic government of Guatemala in 1954 or a blatant military intervention planned in Italy in 1948 in the wake of election results sensing the undesired outcome). With over half of the world's wealth, the USA performed the role of world's banker in the post-World War II system.

However, with the increasing financial crisis of the debt-ridden countries, the Nixon administration decided to dismantle this system, giving rise to huge explosion of unregulated capital flows that totally marginalized the real economy.

The composition of the international financial transaction shifted from real economy to speculation. Within just two decades form 1971 to 1990, the percentage of transactions related to real economy came down from 90% to paltry 10% and further declined to 5% over next five years. The capitalist crisis over the last 25 years, with its shrinking profit rates, inspired the corporate elite to revive economic liberalism into neo-liberalism.

This neo-liberalism is opeartionalised through "the Washington Consensus". This phrase significantly refers to the structural adjustment programmes designed by the government of the United States and the international financial institutions that it largely dominates. These institutions are the core of a "*de facto* world government" representing the interests of transnational Corporations, banks and investment firms in a new Imperial age. With regard to the operational features of the neo-liberalism, none other than its patron saint Adam smith had exposed its inherent class bias.

Writing about the society of his times he pointed out that the "principal architects" of policy in England were "merchants and manufacturers", who used state power to serve their own interests, however "grievous" the effect on others, including the people of England. The "principle architects" of the neo-liberal"Washington Consensus" are the masters of the private economy, mainly huge Corporations that control much of the international economy and have the means to dominate policy formation as well as the structuring of thought and opinion. The institutional structure through which the globalisation is being promoted is basically subservient to the interests of big capital, particularly that of US who seeks to leverage its dominant role in global economy through essentially a short-term, profit-maximization model.

Its anti-labour, anti-people characteristics are deeply embedded in its architecture that is incapable of anything but perpetuation of poverty, inequality and environmental degradation.

'CRISIS DRIVEN' REFORMS: INDIA INTO GLOBAL ORDER

The Brettonwood institutions have been the main instrument to spread the wings of globalisation. However, it came be adopted by every nation state in the form of some kind of local initiative, euphemistically called as Reforms. The conditionalities accepted as a rescue package were declared here as economic reforms by the government. These Economic Reforms launched in July 1991 in India were in nature of a crisis management response to the economic and political crises that erupted in early 1991.

The economic crisis comprised a steep fall in the foreign exchange reserve, galloping inflation, large public and current account deficits and mounting of domestic and foreign debt. In politics, the fall of two governments in a short span of four months, from November 1990 to March 1991; deferment of presentation of the union budget, fairly long political interregnum till the elections, the assassination of a former prime minister Rajiv Gandhi in their midst and the emergence of a minority government with a leader sans charisma, reflected an unprecedented crisis.

These events led to a sharp erosion of confidence in India among lenders, down gradation of India's credit rating and consequently snapping of international credit lines from private or commercial sources. Indian Reforms thus, were essentially of a 'crisis driven' variety. They did not represent strategic choice with a vision of long-term development of Indian people.

The blue print for the Reforms was provided by the combination of macroeconomic stabilisation and structural adjustment programme of International Monetary Fund (IMF) and World Bank respectively, which had been adopted by many countries before in similar situations.

The typical measures under these programmes are:

Macroeconomic Stabilisation:

- Complete autonomy of the central bank to pursue independent monetary policy,
- Devaluation of currency for making exchange rate more realistic,
- Elimination/reduction of all subsidies,
- Introduction of financial structure reforms and free entry of foreign financial institutions,
- Reduction/elimination of fiscal and balance of payments deficits,
- Removal of all controls on prices, exchange and interest rate, and
- Withdrawal of restrictions on imports.

Structural Adjustment:

- Decontrol of industries,
- Privatisation of government-owned entities,
- Structural changes in the economy aimed at export-led growth,
- Free entry of foreign capital and technology without any let, hindrance or conditions,
- Free entry and exit of foreign firms including financial and services industries,
- Free cross border movement of capital and other funds,
- Legislative safeguards for protection of intellectual property rights,
- Creation of legal climate for enforcement of legal

contracts, private property rights, and free entry and exit of business, industrial and financial firms.

The underlying economic philosophy of these programmes stems from the theories of neoliberalism that propounds the rule of market, reduction in the role of State, cutting public expenditure on social services and eliminating the concept of public good; deregulation, and general replacement of public with private. It is based on the premise that the public sector leads to inefficient allocation and utilisation of economic resources and that the enterprise of private sector overcomes it through the dynamics of free market.

Dalits in India

Dalits, as the ex-untouchables prefer to be called, are a very distinct social group. While belonging to a broad class of have - nots they suffer an additional disability of social oppression. Economically, most of them are still the poorest of poor. The balance minuscule minority has managed to escape poverty limits and to locate itself on to a continuum ranging up to a reasonable level of prosperity. The main factor that has catalysed this transition is the reservation policy, which has provided them a basic opportunity to enter the modern sectors of economy.

In social terms however, all dalits, irrespective of their economic standing, still suffer oppression. This social oppression varies from the crudest variety of untouchability, still being practised in rural areas, to the sophisticated forms of discrimination encountered even in modern sectors of urban areas.

Although the statistics indicate that dalits have made a significant progress on almost all parameters during the five post-independence decades, the relative distance between them and non-dalits seems to have remained the same or increased. More than 75 per cent of the dalit workers are still connected with land; 25 per cent being the marginal and small farmers and balance over 50 per cent are the landless labourers. In urban areas, they work mainly in unorganised sector. Out of the total dalit population of 138 million, the number of dalits in services falling in the domain of reservations does not exceed 1.1 million; a mere 0.8 per cent.

Organisation of Study

Corresponding to dual disabilities of the dalits, the main body of the document is divided in two parts:

1. The impact on dalits as a part of the class of have-nots
2. The impact on dalits as a disadvantaged social group.

In the first part, impact of the Reforms in relation to the three most critical factors affecting the poor people is studied.

They are:

- Food security,
- Inflation
- Employment.

Poverty, which represents the combined influence of all deprivations, is also reviewed separately. In light of the vast data available on the impact of similar reforms in other countries, this part is subdivided so as to outline 'Indian experience' and 'international experience' separately. The second part focuses on the influence of the Reforms on the specific three disabilities suffered by the dalits in addition to their poverty.

They are:

- Educational backwardness,
- Discrimination in employment,
- Atrocities
- Socio-cultural suppression.

The last concluding part sums up the study with the observations regarding certain prerequisites for the Reforms to be more responsive to the problems of people, particularly the dalits.

IMPACT OF THE REFORMS ON THE POOR

Impact of the Reforms on poor people can be assessed along several dimensions but here the study confines itself to the three most predominant ones, *viz.*, food security, inflation and employment. Implementation of the Reforms over the last five years in India has generated huge data so as to enable meaningful and autonomous assessment of our native experience.

This is covered in the first part. The Reforms however were implemented many years before and in many countries. This vast treasure of information that is available can be used to validate or correct the inferences from the study. This is covered in the second part.

INDIAN EXPERIENCE

Food Security

Food security mainly relates with the production, distribution and pricing of food grains and thus brings agriculture, Public Distribution System (PDS) and the subsidy structure in to focus. The Reform measures that predominantly affect them are reduction in fiscal deficit, reduction in subsidies, devaluation of Rupee, export orientation and reduction in agricultural credit. Considering the pattern of the budgetary outlays of the government, the fiscal contraction inevitably resulted in a disproportionate cut in capital expenditure.

The capital expenditure slid from 5.10 per cent of GDP in 1990-91 down to 2.74 per cent in 1995-96. In terms of percentage of total expenditure, it fell from an average of 32.8 per cent during the preceding five years of the Reforms, to average of 22.05 per cent during the succeeding five years of the Reforms. In 1995-96 (BE), it was as low as 17.82 per cent. Agriculture sector also bore the share of this cut.

The average annual increase in public sector outlay on agriculture and irrigation during 1985-90 fell from ₹ 1.3 billion to an average of ₹ 0.68 billion during 1990-92. This cut is bound to have a depressing effect on the agricultural production in coming years.

The subsidy on fertilizer had played a crucial role in quadrupling food grain production from 46 million tonnes for a population of 363 million in 1951 to 170 million tonnes in

1991 for a population of 832 million. But, after the launch of the Reforms, the subsidy was reduced. It slid from 0.82 per cent of GDP in 1990-91 to 0.75 per cent of GDP in 1995-96. The prices of the phosphatic and potassium based fertilizers were decontrolled and that of nitrogen based fertilizers were reduced by 10 per cent.

The prices of phosphatic and potassium based fertilizers soared to international level resulting into sharp fall in their consumption. Consumption of phosphatic one fell from 3.3 million tonnes of nutrients in 1991-92 to 2.7 million tonnes in 1993- 94 and that of potassic fell from 1.4 to 0.9 million tonnes in the same period.

Some amount of substitution effect raised the consumption of nitrogen-based fertilizer from 8 million tonnes in 1991-92 to 10.8 million tonnes in 1995-96 resulting in skewing of the nutrient balance. As against the consumption ratio of a mix of nitrogenic, phosphatic and potassic fertilizer of 5.9:2.4:1 in 1991-92, closer to the deemed ideal of 4:2:1, it deteriorated to 9:3:1 in 1994-95.

This imbalance is said to have an adverse effect on soil quality and in turn on its productivity. The nutrient imbalance apart, a study of Andhra Pradesh, Maharashtra and Karnataka by Gaiha (1994) has noted a significant reduction in per hectare fertilizer consumption during the Reform period, which expectedly showed up in the decline in food grain production. This inherent threat to food security is further magnified by the devaluation of rupee by about 25 per cent effected in July 1991.

It resulted in making our food grains cheaper in the international market. As a result, even the ordinary (non-aromatic) rice (besides the usually exported superfine aromatic (basmati) rice was exported in huge volumes. The policy impetus to export of rice and wheat is reflected in the actual exports overshooting the targets.

For example, in 1995- 96 (October- September) actual rice export had reached 5.51 million tonnes as against the target of 2.5 million tonnes. Increasing exports and free market sales of foodgrains have contributed to a drastic reduction in the stocks of foodgrains with the public procurement agencies. For example, by September 1996, there was a whooping reduction of 10 million tonnes in the stock of foodgrains. In case of wheat, it dipped down to 10.36 million tonnes, even lower than the prescribed minimum norm of 13.1 million tonnes. The policy thrust on agricultural exports has moreover resulted in diversion of land to the export production of non-food primary products.

There has been a spurt in corporate farming for export horticulture and floriculture products, etc. As per one FAO report, this trend of shifting land for exportable non-food grain crops had already set in even in the decade ending 1991. The prospects for this trend lies in the fact that there is a huge demand in the developed countries for some 9000 varieties of edible non-food grain primary products which grow in sub-tropical and tropical regions of the developing countries.

Likewise, there is an exportable surplus of foodgrains and dairy products in the developed countries that craves for markets. Surely, as some economists apprehend, India may turn to be a net importer of foodgrains in not so a distant future. The international market for agri-products being a oligopsony of three to six giant companies whose control over the market extends to 80 to 90 per cent, export thrust in this area may not moreover be cost effective.

As the experience of some African countries shows, the increasing export of foodgrains for same level of foreign exchange earning certainly impairs the food security of people. The reforms in banking led to a severe squeeze on agriculture lending. The share of agriculture in net bank credit consistently declined and fell from 17.4 per cent to 12.4 per cent during March 1990 to March 1995.

Expressed in constant (1980-81) rupees, it fell from ₹ 81,470 million in 1989-90 to ₹ 70,500 million in 1994-95. Considering, the hike in input costs, the impact of this squeeze could have only been deleterious on food grains production. As a measure of ensuring food security to the large mass of Indian population, public distribution system was instituted in India in the wake of the calamity of the Great Bengal Famine of 1942-

43 and the World War-II. The system comprises over 4,24,000 fair price shops spread all over the country in rough proportion of the population. The food distributed through PDS is subsidised by the Government to the extent of the difference between the issue price of foodgrains and their economic cost to Food Corporation of India (FCI)—the agency that incurs the cost of transportation, storage and administration in respect of the stock of food grain.

It devours a significant part of the government subsidy. For example, in 1990-91 out of total food subsidy of ₹ 26,000 million, FCI -costs amounted to ₹ 10,000 million, which works out to a whooping 38.5 per cent. With the FCI-costs ever increasing, the impact of any reduction in subsidy has to hit the poor directly.

For ensuring supply of foodgrains to the PDS system in face of export attraction due to the devaluation of rupee, for maintaining their level of production in spite of sharp rise in input prices and for political consideration of assuaging the rich farmers' lobby, the government had to increase the procurement prices of rice and wheat.

The procurement prices of rice and wheat were raised by 67.56 per cent and 62.8 per cent respectively between 1989-90 and 1993-94. This rise was passed on to the consumers by increasing the issue prices of these commodities by 85.81 per cent and 75.14 per cent respectively between June 1990 and February 1994, apparently for reducing the food subsidy. The impact of this rise was reflected in a significant fall in the off-take of food grains.

After the Reforms, off-take of wheat and rice as a percentage of the allocation has shown considerable decline. In the years from 1990- 91 to 1992-93 this percentage was generally over 80 but in the next three years from 1993-94 to 1995-96, it came down to below 50 per cent in case of wheat and to little over 60 per cent in case of rice.

The export—attraction of wheat has already led to shortages from situation of surplus, which had to be met with expensive imports. The promising income from wheat crop has resulted in wheat extensively substituting coarse cereals—

the main food of poor people in many parts of the country, as can be seen from the dwindling output of the latter. The latest data show that it fell from 36.6 million tonnes out of a total foodgrains output of 179.5 million tonnes in 1992-93 to 30 million tonnes out of a total output of 185 million tonnes in 1995-96.

Since, the difference between the consumer-end PDS retail prices and market prices became marginal, the not-so-poor left the PDS and owing to unaffordable prices the poor cut their consumption. The resultant effect on nutrition and hunger had to be borne by the people in direct proportion to their poverty. One study revealed that the families of landless labourers and marginal and small farmers reduced their off-take by over 50 per cent.

Considering their extremely low level of food consumption, below or around the subsistence minimum calories defined by the poverty line, the impact of further reduction of intake by over 50 per cent may have led many people to starvation deaths. Recently, on the advice from the World Bank, the government has decided to make the PDS targeted at the real poor.

The real intention however appears to be the reduction in food subsidy. With the narrowing spread between the market and the PDS retail prices, the so-called non-poor are already out of its net. Even the back-of-envelope kind calculation will show that the people below the poverty line (at the 1991 level) require 46.5 million tonnes of foodgrains as against the actual distribution of only 16.6 million tonnes, a mere 36 per cent of the requirement.

The new scheme based on the executive reluctance to acknowledge poverty is bound to push many more people to starvation. The cumulative effect of the above could be clearly seen in a trend of falling per capita net availability of cereals per day for the Indian population.

During two years of the Reforms, there was 8.43 per cent fall in per capita availability of cereals and 12.02 per cent fall in that of pulses. Considering the acute inequality of Indian population, the impact of this declining trend on the poorer and particularly the disadvantaged parts like the dalits would be far more severe than revealed by the averages. Pulses being the only source of vegetable protein for poor people, a sharp decline in their availability certainly indicates malnutrition.

The incidence of malnutrition further would be disproportionately injurious to women and children because of the male preference in Indian tradition. The evidence of this disaster has already come in the form of malnutrition deaths of over 350 children in the Amaravati district of Maharashtra— the most industrialised and relatively progressive state in India.

Inflation

Inflation hits poor people the hardest. Being employed mainly in the unorganised sector, they do not have even the partial protection that their counterparts in the organised sector have by way of dearness allowance. Most of their earning is spent on the basic needs like food, clothing and shelter, and hence any price rise directly dampens their level of consumption.

The policy measures unleashed under the Reforms that directly contributed to inflation are:

- Reduction in the budget and fiscal deficit,
- Devaluation,
- Privatisation,
- Elimination or reduction in subsidies
- Export promotion.

The reduction in the budget and fiscal deficits predominantly resulted in curtailment of capital expenditure and consequently in the decline in capital formation. Between 1990-91 and 1993-94 the real fall in capital expenditure was 31 per cent.

The real gross fixed capital formation as percentage of GDP reflects a consistent decline from 21.3 in 1990-91 to 19.8 in 1993-94. Its fall for the public component is far more precipitous, from 8.6 to 7.8 for the same period. This could lead to fall in future output and with inelastic wages, would cause an inflationary pressure in the economy. Reduction in budgetary support to the public sector effected under the Reforms serves dual objective. One, it contributes to containment of the budgetary deficit and two; it constitutes a step in the direction of privatisation.

The budgetary support to the PSUs was reduced by 6.1 per cent over the balance budgetary period of nine months in the very first post- Reforms budget of 1991-92 and consistently thereafter. The budget prescribes the supplementary resources and their sources to the PSUs. For example, in 1992-93 it showed a marginal increase in the amount to be mobilised through sale of bonds but a growth of 320 per cent in the costlier funds obtained through commercial debts and suppliers' credit.

These methods are not always feasible and hence the PSUs had to resort to increasing prices of their products to make the two ends meet. For example, in the same budget, the impossible target given to Sail Authority of India to raise its internal generation from ₹ 4,910 million to 9,720 million was met by the 15 per cent increase in steel prices, giving significant fillip to the inflationary spiral in the economy.

Devaluation of currency directly contributes to inflation by raising the cost of imports that enter into domestic production or consumption. Large part of our import comprises petroleum crude and its products; chemicals, machinery, iron and steel, etc. which enter as raw or intermediate materials in our production processes.

Most of these products are of common use in the economy. Any escalation in their cost therefore directly contributes to the rise of general price level. The last administrative price rise of petroleum products could be a case in point. The devaluation of rupee made it dearer domestically, causing deficit in the oil pool account to mount.

Eventually, it entailed hefty price rise of petroleum products. Insofar as petroleum products are consumed directly or indirectly by all, their price rise impelled the general pricelevel to go up with a multiplier effect. All the studies on the Economic Reforms are unanimous in their conclusion that the Reforms have significantly contributed to inflation. A recent study by the EPW Research Foundation revealed significant price rise all across. Based on the wholesale Price Index (WPI), the price rise of the primary substances of consumption ranged from 42 per cent to 93 per cent.

The WPI for all substances increased by 44.4 per cent registering an annual compound growth of 10.3 per cent. In the decade preceding the Reforms (1980-81 to 1990-91) this increase was only 7 per cent, despite the 17 per cent growth in money supply. Prof. Kurien's study isolates four periods of significant price rise from 1950; *viz.,*

- 1964-65 to 1968-69,
- 1972-73 to 1976-77,
- 1979- 80 to 1983-84
- 1991-92 to 1995-96.

He clearly finds extraneous force majure situations being responsible for the price rise in the three periods before the Reforms but no such tangible reason for it in the fourth period. There were severe famines in the first and the third periods and huge increase in the international prices in the third period that caused the prices to rise. On the contrary, during the post-Reforms fourth period, there was an unprecedented long spell of good monsoons for continuous seven years, and relative stability in international petroleum prices. Therefore, the only inescapable inference Prof. Kurien reached was to attribute the price rise to the steps taken under the Reforms. For example, it is the Reforms that caused the price of chemical fertilizer to rise by 100.6 per cent, electricity by 65.9 per cent and coal by 58.1 per cent.

Devaluation of rupee and emphasis on the export-led growth caused pressure on the prices of products depending on their import content. The exact effect of simultaneous reduction of customs duty and excise duty is not easy to assess but as some micro studies indicate, they also added to the rise of general price level. For example, there being no significant customs duty on the imported medicines before the Reforms, the reduction therein did no difference to their prices. However, the devaluation of rupee pushed them sky rocketing. The aggressive export promotion of many primary substances also resulted in their price-rise in the domestic market. The increase in money supply resorted to thwart the revaluation of rupee in the face of huge inflow of foreign exchange during 1992-93 to 1994-95 also contributed to elevating the general price level. The price rise of food grains owing to the cuts in food and fertilizer subsidies and consequent adjustments have particularly been harsh.

In the preceding decade of the Reform the per annum price of rice had risen by 7 per cent and that of wheat by 3.3 per cent. But in the next four years of the Reform period, they registered the rise of 13.5 per cent and 18.1 per cent respectively. Other foodgrains also behaved approximately in similar fashion.

The price-rise for pulses has been 97.2 per cent; that for vegetables 163.4 per cent, for fruits 74 per cent; and for eggs, meat and fish group 102.5 per cent. The free market ethos unleashed by the Reforms also indirectly but significantly has contributed to the price rise.

Employment

The rate of growth of employment in the organised sector dropped from more than 1.7 per cent per annum in the late 1980s to 1.2 per cent in 1991-92 and to 0.6 per cent in 1992-93. Creation of jobs in the public sector fell from 11.0 million in the preceding four years to the 6.2 million in the succeeding four years of the Reforms.

For the Private Sector, the corresponding figures showed a slight rise from 2.08 million to 2.49 million on account of free market euphoria. In the Central Government establishment there were 4.03 million jobs on 1st March 1991, which went up next year to 4.14 million. But for the next two years, they came down to 3.97 million and 3.84 million respectively. Similar picture of declining employment opportunity is held out in the statistics of Employment Exchanges.

The notified vacancies had come down from 0.59 million in 1989-90 to 0.4 million in 1992-93 and to 0.38 million in the subsequent year. Similar decline is seen in the statistics of appointments. The appointments issued during the three years were 0.29 million, 0.23 million and 0.22 million respectively. The ratios of appointments to the notified vacancies for these years also shows a striking decline, *viz.*, 8.5 per cent, 7.9 per cent and 6.7 per cent respectively.

The contraction in public expenditure and the consequent reduction in aggregate demand could not but adversely affect employment in the unorganised sector, whether non-agricultural rural employment or urban informal sector employment, given the casual nature of such employment. The policy reforms made benefits of the small sector available to the big industrial houses.

National Council of Applied Economic Research had cautioned that the Reforms relating to deregulation of the big industries, withdrawal of the licence system and global reduction of custom duties would exert adverse impact on the small industries.

The statistics of the industrial sickness show a marked deterioration during the Reform period. For example, in 1990, there were 2,21,097 sick industries, which represented a 8.86 per cent decline from the previous year. But after the Reforms were launched, this figure went up to 2,23,809 in 1991 and further to 2,47,724 in 1992 indicating the 1.23 per cent and 10.69 per cent growth respectively, over previous years.

Entrepreneurship Development Institute of India, Ahmedabad had surveyed the impact of the Reforms on small scale industries in 1993, and saw clear deterioration in their situation.

It attributed this deterioration to three factors:

i. General recession in 1991-92,
ii. Reduction in the budgetary support to the public sector
iii. Liberalisation of imports of the capital goods.

The cumulative impact of these factors has been in the total collapse of demand for their products.

Small-scale industries based on imports had a tough time due to devaluation of rupee. Increasing competition, increasing costs and pressure on prices has made the very survival difficult for many. Today more than 4,00,000 small-scale industries are either sick or closed. The reforms in financial sector permitted the banks to charge interest as per the credit rating of debtors and manage their profitability. This also added to the difficulty of small-scale industries.

For, getting loans from banks at affordable interest rates now became a formidable task for them. One study clearly concluded that the Reforms had an adverse impact on the new job opportunities in the small-scale industries. In rural areas there has been a significant cut in the bank credit to the agriculture and nonagriculture industries. The bank credit to these sectors was 40 per cent till the launch of the Reforms. It came down to 38.7 per cent in 1992 and 35 per cent in July 1994. The bank credit to agriculture as a percentage of net bank credit fell consistently to 12.4 per cent in March 1995 from 17.4 per cent in March 1990.

It has had an adverse impact on these industries and in turn on rural employment. A study on the unemployment in 1993 estimated that out of 25 million unemployed, approximately 10 million came from the unorganised sector of urban areas and the non-agricultural sectors of the rural areas and were identified as the victims of the Economic Reforms.

The Economic Reforms lay excessive reliance on foreign investment not only for industrial development but also to solve the unemployment problem faced by the country. In this context, the observation of United Nations, in the Human Development Report of 1993 is quite revealing. It says that the TNCs and their associate companies had made significant investments in developing countries but it could not generate significant employment.

The amount of jobs created by the foreign investment in the entire third world during 1990 to 1993 is not even equal to the number of people entering the job market in India in a single year! The companies in the Fortune 500 list of 1992 together said to have had 5,472 billion dollars sales and 25 million jobs in 1992. Although this sales figure is 27 times

India's GDP, the employment figure does not reach even its one third. The impetus to export agriculture in the Reforms is bringing in corporate and contract system in the agriculture sector. The government has already declared that the Land Ceiling Act identified as the main obstacle in the process, would be suitably changed. Directionally, the emergent corporate farms will gobble up smallholdings of the marginal to middle farmers and push them into the herd of job seeking millions.

Corporatisation of agriculture always leads to depeasantisation and simultaneously reduction in labour absorption. The cropping pattern of these capitalist farms makes unskilled agricultural workers redundant. This emergent scenario is certainly going to aggravate the unemployment problem further rather than solving it. The theme of export-led growth emphasised by the Reforms will expose the Indian industry to the vagaries of international markets, which can have very negative effect on employment in the long run.

Export thrust, unmindful of the demands of the domestic requirements can be quite harmful as has been experienced in the case of cotton thread case. In this case, large scale export of the coarse cotton thread had catapulted 110 weavers in Andhra Pradesh to starvation deaths. There are many such case studies in the international repertoire of experience with such Reforms.

The import of modern technology and investment constitutes an important rationale for the economic Reforms. Many facilitating provisions have been adopted for attracting the same. It is a different matter that the flow of both technology as well as investment follows the capitalist logic of maximisation of long-term profits.

This logic is evident when Pepsi brings in its great technology to convert our potatoes and sell them in chip form at a price 80 times over. There is a virtual boom in strategic alliances, joint ventures, technological collaborations etc. that act as vehicles for bringing in foreign technology and capital. They invariably depend upon the marketing muscle of the foreign partner represented in their powerful brands. The influx of foreign brands is bound to displace Indian brands, not by virtue of their intrinsic superiority but because of their sheer financial and organisational muscle. The process will virtually spell deindustrialisation of the domestic industry. The modern factories replacing them cannot generate even a fraction of the employment lost in displaced manpower. The imperatives of global competitiveness moreover, will increasingly impel companies to re-engineer their business processes that necessarily results in 'down sizing' of the company rendering the millions jobless.

The relative mobility of capital vis-à-vis labour also holds an ominous prospect for future jobs. The buzzword of competition has suddenly awakened one and all in the business world to the necessity to restructure their companies. Since, this exercise is envisaged to prepare the companies to face global competitions, every one engaged a foreign consultancy firm that claimed the requisite experience and know how for millions of dollars. Already this phenomenon has threatened the well-meaning native consulting firms into seeking some kind of alliance with these foreign firms for sheer survival.

These exercises overtly aimed at creating sharper customer focus essentially end up in cutting jobs. Strangely, more than the private companies the State owned units operating as monopoly or oligopoly seem to feel greater pressure to so reorganise. Nationalised banks have already threatened to declare 4,00,000 persons surplus, Railways have stopped recruitment, Department of Post and Telecommunication intend to retrench 2,00,000 workers. The examples indeed are legion.

A study conducted by EPW Research Foundation in early 1994 found that the total employment which showed an increase in first two years of the Reforms, had slumped thereafter; that the bulk of employment had occurred in contract and other forms of non-regular employment, the share of which in total employment had gradually risen to one-third by March 1993, and that regular employment fell by 3.3 per cent in 1992-93 even as the value of fixed assets of the sample companies rose by some 27 per cent. The competitive pressure of the free market scenario has impelled managements to adopt labour flexibilisation strategies as noticed by the International Labour Organisation as early as 1989. The spurt in restructuring exercises in corporate India already reflects the trend towards 're-engineering' by concentrating on core or flagship businesses and spinning off non-core businesses through subcontracting or outsourcing.

It is reinforced with an HRD strategy that envisages workers to develop new skills and get exposed to various aspects of work so that they can become multi-skilled and can do varied tasks in a flexible work environment. This is leading to 'individual contact', thereby eliminating the vary basis of the trade unionism. The directional thrust of the Reforms is already evident in the tremendous growth of the informal sector, which is characterised by the rampant use of casual labour, hiring and firing practices, and all kinds of exploitation of labour.

Poverty

Poverty is a sum total of all the deprivations. In India governmental definition of poverty is based on the sole criterion of minimum food requirement for survival. Thus the poverty line is decided by the income sufficient to buy food equivalent of 2400 calories in rural and 2100 calories in urban areas.

The database for poverty estimates is provided by the quinquenial surveys of NSS. NSS also collects the consumer expenditure data by decile group on an annual basis. The Reforms have reversed the two decades long declining trend of poverty.

The rural poverty went up from the pre-reform low of 33.7 per cent to 41.7 per cent in 1992 and slightly declined to 40.2 per cent in 1993-94. The urban poverty also showed the same trend shooting up from the pre-Reform low of 36 per cent to 37.8 per cent and then coming down to 36.2 per cent. The ratio of ultra poverty (*i.e.*, extreme poverty) to total poverty showed a marked increase after the Reforms. In 1990-91, this ratio was 68.95%, it went up to 71.04% in 1991 and to 74.64% in 1992. The corresponding figures for urban area were 72.99, 73.14 and 74.20 per cent. In 1992, the rural workers in secondary and tertiary sectors showed a decline of 6.3% and 1.3% respectively from the pre-Reform level in 1989-90.

Curiously, the primary sector showed a hefty increase of 10.1% in the same period. In rural area nearly 50% farming households have less than one acre land. They need supplementary work in nonagricultural sector for meeting the two ends.

In absence of this work however, they land up engaging themselves with the sundry work related to their tiny farms and declare themselves as the agriculture workers. This increase in the primary sector jobs thus indicates partial unemployment of workforce.

The decline in non-agricultural jobs and the overall employment are attributed to the cut in the government expenditure on various poverty alleviation programmes, during the Reform period. Notwithstanding their extremely low transfer efficiency and ineffectiveness in targeting the poor, these programmes played a role in poverty reduction during the eighties.

They are operated on the 80:20 basis by the Centre and the State. In the first flush of enthusiasm the government effected drastic reductions in all of these programmes till it was alarmed by the havoc it created and its political implication in the ensuing general election. It attempted to reverse this trend in 1994-95 and 1995-96 budgets under the much-propagandised 'human face to reforms'.

Even after taking all these increased outlays into account its resultant effect barely equals provision of less than 20 days work at ₹ 21 for a person, in a year. The central transfers constitute a major resource for the states to conduct the programmes under the Social sector. These transfers show consistent decline during the Reform period on all the heads except for the payment of interest, over a period 1990-91 to 1993-94. This decline amounts to whooping 18.52 per cent. The central assistance to states for some specific schemes likewise has been on consistent decline from much before the start of the Reforms but the states seem to have managed the expenditure profile. However, the Reform-ethos has eroded this expenditure after 1990-91.

The maximum cut was effected in the expenditure on disease-prevention and control programme which relate with the poverty prone diseases like T.B., Malaria, Fileria, Leprosy etc. Its direct manifestation has been aplenty, in form of reemergence of the epidemics of Plague, T.B., Malaria, Jaundice, Influenza, Pneumonia and very recently, Dengue. Inequality is a corollary of growing poverty for the upper layers seldom suffer degradation.

Based on the available data on consumption expenditure, the share of the bottom 30% people, which was growing consistently from 1987-88 up to 1990-91, both in rural as well as in urban areas, had a sudden reversal soon after the Reforms were launched. In rural area, it was 15.57% in 1987-88, which rose up to 15.96% in 1990-91, but thereafter slid down to 15.79% in 1991 (July—December) and further to 15.60% in 1992 (July-December).

For the urban area, the corresponding figures are 13.33%, 13.74%, 12.74% and 13.17%, indicating a slight upturn in the terminal year. The share of the middle 40% population also dwindled in the same manner in both rural and urban area. The loss of these 70% population appears to have benefited the top 30% population. Their share for the pre-Reform period was on consistent decline, which has suddenly jumped up in the Reform period.

EXPERIENCE OF OTHER COUNTRIES

Many protagonists of the economic Reforms tend to discount the Indian experience as premature. Fortunately, there are many countries in which similar Reforms are being worked for many years.

There are numerous studies assessing their efficacy and impact on various parts of population. Most of them are unanimous in noting the precipitous fall in standard of living of the majority population of the subject country that has led to widespread riots and socio-political unrest. The thrust of the Reforms is on economic growth, which as per their apologists would 'trickle down' to the people. Notwithstanding the metaphorical argument that trickle can never be equal to outpour that may be required in terms of distributive justice to the poor, the growth generating capacity of these Reforms itself appears to be in question. In Latin America, after adoption of the Reforms economic growth rates had actually fallen.

In the pre-Reform period, Latin America's economic growth rates had exceeded the average growth rate of the industrial countries and that of USA for over a decade. But, it suffered a historical reversal soon after the Reforms were launched.

From 1980 to 1985, the average real growth rates of per capita income in Argentina, Brazil, Chile, Mexico and Peru were negative and per capita income levels had gone back by a decade to those prevailing in the 1970s. For Peru and Chile, they had slipped back even to pre-1970 levels. Although, the growth rates of GDP in cases of Argentina and Chile appear to have risen in 1992, the reasons therefor do not quite belong to the standard Reform-package.

In Chile, the government's huge investments in copper mines projects, forestry, and document projects; extension of cheap credit to the new export industries and other such interventions during 1973 to 1990 came to fruition, in form of the spurt in economic growth rates. In Argentina, a totally different phenomenon seems to have caused the economy to look up in 1992.

The fall in the American interest rates had caused the dollars stacked in the American banks by the Argentinean capitalists, to flow back to Argentina into its emerging financial markets. Besides these examples, there are many countries where the GDP-growth rate seems to have deteriorated in 1992. In Brazil, it fell down from 9.1% in 1980 to 7.9% in 1985 and further to—0.9% in 1992. For the same years, the GDP- growth rates for Columbia were 4.1%, 3.3% and 2.7%; those for Peru were 3.1%, 2.1% and -2.8% and for Mexico they were 8.4%, 7.9% and 2.6% respectively. In some other countries like Ghana, Indonesia, Ivory Coast etc., notwithstanding their individual economic characteristics, the growth rates appear to be simply erratic. Contrary to the assertions of the IMF and the World Bank, there is thus no concrete evidence that these type of Reforms really lead to incremental economic growth in the subject countries.

There is enough evidence however, that these Reforms have heaped many kinds of miseries on the majority of population of these countries. In Latin America between 1980 and 1984, open unemployment went up from 7 to 11 per cent. In Chile, Columbia, Peru and Venezuela, the unemployment rates jumped by 50 and 100%.

A sizeable decline has taken place in industrial wages in the same period in African and Latin American countries. It fell by 40% in Tanzania, 33% in Zambia and Mexico and 24% in Peru. This decline ranged from 30 to 60%, between 1980 - 87 in Argentina, Bolivia, Chile, Costa Rica, Egypt and Kenya. The real wages of the government employees have fallen almost everywhere. The decline is of the order of 30 - 40% in the African countries during 1975 to 1985 and between 10 - 120% in Latin America between 1980 to 1987.

Most of the countries (*e.g.*, Argentina, Brazil, Chile, Columbia, Ivory Coast, Mexico, Peru, Philippines etc.) that adopted these IMF/World bank sponsored Reforms showed a clear decline in Gross Domestic Investment during the period from 1980 to 1992. There was a sharp decline in the share of social expenditure in the Latin American countries and West Asia. In the former, it fell from 36% to 24.3% and in the latter, from 20.3% to 17.2% between 1980 and 1987. In terms of share of capital expenditure, investment in social infrastructure has suffered in Sri Lanka; the spending on health, education and food subsidy having declined from 38% of current expenditure in 1977 to 22% during 1980 - 82.

There was a relatively sharper decline in similar expenditure in Turkey, Guyana and Sudan. In Somalia and Tanzania the share of primary education in such expenditure further declined. Per capita expenditure on education and health was reduced by 11% and 5% respectively in Morocco, by 29% and 35% in Ecuador and by 20% in Chile. The former Soviet Russian countries and the east European countries have been implementing these Reforms since 1989.

Whatever may be the pitfalls of the socialist regimes in these countries, it had provided its entire people with basic necessities of living. What has become of these countries after the Reforms were launched is very well documented in a report published by UNICEF. In Bulgaria 53.6% families were living in poverty in 1992. In 1989, Hungary had 10.1% poverty, which within next two years of Reforms had more than doubled to 21.3% in 1991.

In Czech Republic it went up from 5.7% in 1989 to 18.2% in 1992. It jumped from 21.8% to 41.4% in Poland during the same period. It went up from 27.3% to 51.1% in Rumania; from 5% to 43.8% in Russia and from 8.9% to 30.2% in Slovakia. In Poland 57.6%, in Rumania 70.1% and in Slovakia 41.3%, children live in poverty. In Mongolia the Reforms catapulted 25% population below the monthly 10 dollars—poverty line. The mortality rate between 1989 and 1993 also increased significantly in these countries due to drastic decline in living standard.

Unemployment rates have soared in most of the east European countries. About 6.5 million people were registered as unemployed in December 1992—a rise from 5 million a year ago. Inflation is still a major problem. In Poland, which was the pet success story of the Reforms for free market advocates, more than 50% people say that the Communist system was better.

More than 16% are unemployed in industrial cities and more than that in the rural areas; almost 14% of the people in the country are on doles and about one third of the total families now live below the official poverty line. The notable exception is the experience of East Asian countries. The proportion below the poverty line in this region, comprising People's Republic of China, Indonesia, Korea, Malaysia, Philippines, Thailand and Indo-china declined from 35% to

10% over this period. The key social indicators, *viz.*, life expectancy, infant mortality, adult literacy and population growth for these countries also improved very impressively. However, it is not the Reforms that have caused this miracle. The real reasons have been analysed as their specific historical setting, their creation of pre-conditions for success and the strategies they employed.

For instance, almost all of them had undertaken effective land reforms, achieved high levels of literacy, particularly female literacy; and substantially better health standards. Better female participation in the labour force led to rapid increase in household and overall domestic saving rates. The higher level of social consumption with relatively better distribution of incomes and wealth vastly widened the demand of those economies and facilitated more broad based development.

Higher literacy and health standards were the most crucial factors in enhancing labour productivity, which in turn went to facilitate significant import substitution and export promotion. Under the influence of these Bretton Wood institution sponsored reforms, inequality in the world has been consistently growing. Between 1988 and 1993, the per capita income of the lowincome countries of the world fell by 35% from $ 584 to $ 380.

As against this the same for the rich countries went from $ 17,080 to 23,090. The share of the low-income countries in total income also fell from 5.44% to 4.83% in the same period. For the block of Latin American countries famous as the test bench for these reforms, the picture is strikingly dismal in terms of inequality.

In Brazil, the ratio of income or consumption of the top and the lowest 20% people increased from 26.1% to 32.1% between 1983 and 1989. In Columbia, between 1988 and 1991, the same had gone up from 13.3 to 15.5%.

In all these countries the consumption of the bottom 20% population as a share of total consumption ranged from paitry 2.1 to 8.7%. The gap between poor and rich of the world has increased by 30% over the last decade along with the spread of these kinds of Reforms. During 1987 to 1994, the number of billionaires in the world showed a remarkable increase. In USA, it went up from 49 to 120; in the Asia Pacific region, from 40 to 86; in Europe, from 36 to 91 and in west Asia and Africa, it went up from 8 to 14.

The brief life sketches of these billionaires given in the Forbes magazine of July 18, 1994 show how these Reforms have been instrumental in enriching them.

IMPACT OF THE REFORMS ON DALITS AS A DISADVANTAGED SOCIAL GROUP

The social disadvantage suffered by the dalits in India was taken note of in the Constitution of India, which was drafted under the chairmanship of Dr. Ambedkar—a person who had spearheaded the most momentous anti-caste movement of the depressed classes. It provided the dalits with many safeguards, *viz.*,

- Social, educational, cultural and religious safeguards,
- Economic safeguards,
- Political safeguards
- Safeguards for employment.

The free market ethos unleashed by the Reforms, conceptually can neither confirm to the democratic spirit of the Indian Constitution of 'one vote, one value', nor can it coexist with the system of positive discrimination embodied in these safeguards. For, the market grants moneyed person more value, and overtly believes in the jungle law of 'might is right'.

To a large extent, the primary motivation behind these Constitutional provisions was liberal democratic aspirations that characterised the freedom movement. However, these aspirations and the initial ideological zeal of the founding fathers withered away in no time and what survived was its utilitarian dimension for the electoral politics.

The sorry state of the executive compliance with these Constitutional provisions amply bears out the fangs of the intrinsically iniquitous Indian society. The Reforms will bring a kind of legitimacy to this attitudinal resistance of the upper castes and classes to the movements for change by the downtrodden. These safeguards will stand eroded as the Reforms gain in momentum.

Influence of the Reforms is bound to be all pervasive. However, only a few issues of importance to the dalit masses have been picked up for discussion here.

RESERVATION AND FINANCIAL ASSISTANCE IN EDUCATION INSTITUTIONS

Reservation in the educational institutions and the financial assistance in the form of scholarships and freeships constitute perhaps the most important factor in the development scheme for dalits. For, it is primarily responsible to make the basic input of education available and affordable to them.

Without education, all the constitutional safeguards including the reservation in services would be infructuous. Under this scheme the dalit students whose parental income is below a specified level, get freeship, reservation in admissions to all the colleges getting grants-in-aid from the government, and scholarships. Without this assistance, even today, it would be difficult even for the second-generation educated dalits to send their children to school. The Reforms have already resulted in freezing the grants to many institutions and in stagnating, if not lowering, the expenditure on education.

The free market ethos has entered the educational sphere in a big way. Commercialisation of education is no more a mere rhetoric; it is now the established fact. Commercial institutions offering specialised education that signify essential input from utilitarian viewpoint, have come up in a big way from cities to small towns.

Their product-prices are not only based on the demand-supply consideration in their market segment but also are manipulated by their promotional strategies. In a true spirit of globalisation, many foreign universities are invading the educational spheres through hitherto unfamiliar strategic alliances with non-descript commercial agencies, of course at hefty dollar equivalent prices. Many elite institutions like IIMs and IITs, suddenly facing fund crunch had to resort to raising their fee structure and other prices many fold. They were already beyond the reach of the dalits. When they eventually turn self-financing, their prices would be benchmarked against their international counterparts, which any way would be affordable to the same top market segment that constitutes the focus of all the Reform-talk.

As the job markets become acutely competitive, owing to a sharp decline in job opportunities, the polarisation between the elite and commoner would also sharpen. Various kinds of price barriers would be erected to thwart the entry of downtrodden to the portals of development. Even the sphere of primary education the coverage of which has been so miserably inadequate as to leave out multitude of children in villages as illiterate, could not remain unaffected, notwithstanding its already existing divide between the vernacular and English schools.

Corporatisation has entered this arena, transforming the education into an enterprise for profits. The quality of input these expensive schools will provide will benchmark the products in the contracting job markets. Even today, because of preponderance of the English language in business circles, the divide between village and towns is almost complete in the field of education.

It is so difficult for a village student, educated in vernacular medium to compete with his convent educated (now an understatement!) counterpart in cities and towns. If this is the situation of general village population, the plight of the dalits who besides being the poorest of the village population carry additional burden of social discrimination, is indeed a worrisome matter. Despite several kinds of State assistance, the dalits are plagued with alarming rate of school dropouts.

This may be explained out as much by the need for dalit children to supplement their meagre family incomes for making the two ends meet as also by the erosion of their faith that education could be the instrument to change the pathetic course of their lives. This sense of alienation is going to grow with the progress of the Reforms, giving rise to increasing lumpenisation and criminalisation of the dalit youth.

RESERVATIONS IN SERVICES

Whatever may be the other costs, the government policy of reservations in employment sphere has undoubtedly played an important role in the process of advancement of the dalits. The policy broadly envisages representation of the dalits in proportion to their population in all the public services, which includes the government, the public sector, autonomous bodies and other institutions that receive grant-in-aid from the government.

A cursory glance at the figures of this representation is enough to get a pathetic state of implementation of this policy. Howsoever, unsatisfactory the results of implementation may be, the importance of reservations from the dalit viewpoint cannot be overemphasised. As could be evidenced by the organised private sector, where it would be difficult to find a dalit employee (save of course in scavenging and lowliest of the similar jobs), without reservations the dalits would have been totally doomed.

The importance of reservations thus could only be assessed in relation to situations where they do not exist. Whatever be their defects and deficiencies, they have given certain economic means of livelihood and some social prestige to the sons and daughters of over 1.5 million landless labourers.

Whether they get real power or not, over 50,000 dalits could enter the sphere of bureaucratic authority with the help of reservations. More importantly these tangible benefits to few have instilled a hope in entire dalit people to strive for their betterment.

This hope predominantly manifests in the form of spread of education among them. Their emotional bond with the nation and its Constitution despite heaps of injustice and ignominy they bear every moment of their life may also be significantly attributable to the Reservation Policy. The winds of privatisation under the Economic Reforms have already shaken the very foundations of Reservations. The Reforms clearly envisage the minimalist State. Wherever the Reforms patterned on the Structural Adjustment Programme of the World Bank were carried out, denationalisation and privatisation of the public sector have come in a big way. Being a late starter, India has not reached the scales achieved by others, say, the Latin American countries.

However, the start has not been any less impressive. Within a short time, almost all the sectors of economy stand opened up for private investment. The disinvestment in existing public sector companies has already been allowed up to 49 per cent by the policy. The public stake being more than 50 per cent, the 'public sector' as such is not yet dismantled in the policy.

It continues to be the State as before, and hence attracts application of the reservation policy. However, the Reform package has already endangered, if not abolished, the reservations through numerous back doors. In the name of preparing the Public Sector Undertakings (PSUs) for global free market regime, the PSUs are being allowed/encouraged to have strategic alliances with private companies from India and abroad.

As such, over the last five years, many profit making PSUs have formed the joint venture companies (JVC). Most of the PSU investments continue to be channelled through the JV route despite repeated failures of the joint ventures. These JVCs are strategically structured so as not to fall in the ambit of the PSU-framework.

The typical equity stake for the PSU and private could be 49:51. There appears to be a great deal of receptivity for this scheme in the government circles. There are no policy barriers on the business to be pursued by these JVCs. Theoretically, an existing PSU can hive off its business divisions into private JVCs and transform itself into a financial holding company with a Board of Directors and skeleton staff. Even if such an entity technically remains a PSU and follows the reservation policy sincerely, it would still have little or no scope to absorb the dalits in its staff. Whatever may be the strategic considerations, the fall out of this process practically amounted to shutting the doors of these new age companies to the dalits and to potential neutralisation of the reservation policy. The policy of limited disinvestment of the PSUs not being in conformity with the spirit of the Reforms, is bound to be relaxed in favour of privatisation any time.

But still, all the PSUs may not get privatised at once. The better ones would be gobbled up by the bigger sharks. The worst ones may be closed down or distress-sold. And the middle ones may for quite some time, continue to be the relic of their past. Whatever the scenario, the residual structures of the 'reformed' PSUs are never going to be the same, as far as the dalits are concerned.

The ethos of privatisation and the excuse of global competition, superimposed on the traditional caste prejudice, will never allow reservations to happen, any more. Other public services are also bound to slip out of the reservation policy. Most of the sectors, which were the traditional domain of the government investment, have already been released for the private investment.

ATROCITIES

The caste atrocities are an integral feature of the dalit life. The government machinery keeps on collecting their statistics year after year and issues it in a report of its Commissioner for the SCs and the STs (now the National Commission for the SCs and the STs). There are at least three Articles (15,17 and 23) in the Constitution of India, which seek to mitigate the evil.

To give effect to these Constitutional provisions the following acts also have been in operation:

- The Untouchability (Offences) Act, 1955, later amended and retitled as the Protection of Civil Rights Act, 1955
- The Scheduled Castes and Scheduled Tribes (Prevention of Atrocities Act) 1989 and The Bonded Labour System (Abolition) Act, 1976

Despite this, the statistics of the registered atrocities read like a balance sheet of a blue chip company with consistent rise every successive year. It is pertinent to remember that owing to the dependency relationship of the dalits with the perpetrators of atrocities, not every occurrence of the atrocity gets registered.

Rather, it can be safely assumed that behind each registered atrocity over ten atrocity cases go unreported. As per the latest statistics, every day nearly 50 cases of atrocities are registered all over the country. Over three dalit women are raped and six are disabled on each day round the year. The National Commission analysed the causes of each of the atrocities in a sample of 45 cases.

The analysis shows that out of 45 cases 13 are clearly attributable to the economic reasons. The balance can also be explained out by some kind of weakness of the dalits. Coupled with the weakness of the dalits, their growing assertiveness and the refusal to submit to the casteist dictates of the village lords, rebellion ethos assimilated through the Ambedkarian struggle and the process of general awareness, also cause atrocities to increase.

Atrocities are basically a rude reassertion of power over the powerless by the powerful in the wake of threat. It is thus an expression of insecurity by the powerful who perceive power slipping their hand. In the pre-colonial closed loop production system of a typical village since everyone followed his or her calling under the divine authority of religion, there were no atrocities of the kind we experience in the saner age of globalisation today.

If any one questioned or defied this system, the religious code provided for the punishment. In this scheme, it was more important to fortify the religious control on populace than physically taming them to comply. Although the emphasis was on enslavement of mind, physical punishment did exist as a contingency measure.

Atrocities on the dalits today are in essence a physical punishment for their act of forsaking the bondage. The physical punishments or atrocities presuppose material power in the hands of perpetrators of atrocities. Not only that the dalits lit the fire of anger in materially powerful upper castes by defying their notion of caste authority but also they added fuel to it by coming in competition for partaking scarce resources. The emergence of the land owning middle castes during the post-independence development process who at the one end replaced the traditional upper castes and wore their mantle of superiority but who at the other end found itself in competition with the dalits for resources like education and employment moreover led to accentuation of atrocities.

These middle castes lacked the cunning and sophistication of the upper castes and enraged themselves into physical response on slightest provocation. They could not stomach the dalits who were utterly dependent on them in the village setting asserting their human rights or competing with them on equal platform for scarce resources and eventually winning them away in some cases with the help of reservations.

This commonplace experience is amplified by the vested interests of the ruling classes to make out all the dalits as robbers of the share of these middle castes. Thus, the essential ingredients for atrocities on the dalits can be identified as the existence of material power in the hands of perpetrators of atrocities, enduring sense of social superiority, increasing scarcity of resources, and growing pauperisation of the masses. The directional impact of the Reforms on the atrocities on the dalits therefore can be inferred from the effect it would have on the existing dependency relationship in the villages that the dalits are engaged in with the powerful middle castes; on the caste system itself; on the availability of certain critical resources like jobs; health care, education etc.; and on the income distribution to the people.

Atrocities are seen to occur where the dependency relationships are more pronounced. Villages, where the dalits as landless labourers depend upon landlords or rich farmers for their livelihood and where the traditional caste equations have a potential to yield economic surplus to the latter, provide ideal setting for atrocities. What impact would the new regime have on the socio-economic setting of Indian villages? In face of it, this relationship cannot be altered till the dalits get land. Can the new regime afford this economic empowerment of the dalits? Can it, for instance, grant them land? The answer to all these questions will be in negative. Instead of talking about land reforms, the new regime will promote depeasantisation of Indian agriculture and consolidation of their holdings to start corporate farming.

The capital influx in the rural areas will have natural ally in the rich farmers who have hegemonic hold over their areas. These parts will be the main beneficiaries of the improved terms of trade and capitalist development in the rural areas. The form that the new system may take will have the corporate structure of management and beneath the local vendors to provide various inputs and services.

While the rich farmers may assume the roles in this organisation as big or petty capitalist, the erstwhile landless labourers, marginal and small farmers shall together constitute the vast army of jobseekers. Although in notional terms the dalits might get rid of the old relationships, in reality they will still be dependent on their upper caste employers and certainly far more vulnerable than before.

With regards to impact of the economic Reforms on the caste system, the optimists and protagonists rely upon an old rhetoric of contradiction between feudalism and capitalism. The problem of annihilation of castes subsumes the change in the economic structure of the society in favour of the dalits and simultaneously a massive cultural movement to cleanse the minds of people of the caste notions and implant in its place the attitude of scientificism and virtue of liberty, equality and fraternity.

Having seen that far from striving for economic equality, the Reforms are going to accentuate the existing inequalities, we can just examine its attitude towards the caste system. Will the Reforms promote the cultural movement for social equality?

Does it have the wherewithal or motivation to catalyse struggles against the caste system? The answers to these questions will also have to be in negative. The old rhetoric that capitalism will completely displace feudalism evokes positive expectations in some people about the prowess of the Reforms to annihilate castes. They would argue that the unbridled capitalism inherent in the Reforms is not compatible with any feudal structure and hence implementation of the latter should remove these last blots of the caste system.

This simplistic thumb rule does not seem to be entirely validated by the developmental experience in India. The capitalism in India did not have to sprout through the bedrock of contradictions of feudalism as in Western Europe. It was planted in the fertile soil of the Indian feudalism. It has grown here on its nutrients. The caste institution has defied the classical mould of feudalism by possessing many unique features, the most important being its resilience and adaptability.

What we experience in the mysterious growth of casteist politics today in India is precisely this ability of caste to adapt to changing times. The vast army of unemployed created by the developmental dynamics of the economic Reforms will need appropriate instruments for being controlled. The history bears ample testimony to the fact that whenever the people tended to come together with a common identity, the ruling classes have deftly used the time-tested weapon of castes to divide them.

Caste with its divisive potential will never be abandoned by any iniquitous regime. Its resilience may diffuse its contours but in its essence the caste would coexist with the Reforms. Privatisation and free market components of the Reforms are certainly impacting very adversely on the job situation. Many resources for public consumption shall also be scarce, as they would be produced in private enterprises for profits. They would be beyond the reach of common people. The impact of the Reforms in terms of increasing inequality has been established beyond doubt.

Therefore, it can be inferred that the Reforms are potentially incapable to alleviate the pain of dalit masses. In sum, the atrocities on the dalits not only shall continue but may also be increased on account of the Reforms.

SOCIO-CULTURAL SUPPRESSION

Privatisation, which is the pivotal component of the Economic Reforms, will eliminate the very basis of the reservation policy in its present form. Since the Reforms envisage minimalist role for the State, the space for the public domain and therefore for the reservations shall be greatly constricted.

Reservation policy that represented the strategic response of liberal bourgeoisie to the aspirations of the dalit movement not quite unlike that of the colonial State at the time of its inception, was never swallowed by the civil society as rightful share of the dalits.

Its response initially reflected feudal magnanimity but once the first generation of the dalits started pouring out of the university portals into the job markets and claimed their share of pie, the reaction reflected feudal ferocity. The cunning of upper caste dominated State apparatus was evident in full measure in the manner the circulars proclaiming this policy were issued.

Their convoluted language facilitated the unwilling bureaucracy to thwart it to the possible extent and judiciary to be labour over several years on what should have been so evident. The broad statistic on the implementation of this policy is enough to reveal the extent of prejudice of the State machinery as well as the civil society. One of the provisions of the policy states that a dalit candidate qualifying without any concession should not be placed in the reserved seat, implying thereby that the percentage representation of the dalits in services or the educational institutions would be more than its prescribed value.

But, over the five decades of implementation of the reservation policy it refuses to reach even the prescribed levels confirming the casteist notion still prevalent in society that the dalits are intrinsically an inferior specie. Despite this vile attitude of the establishment the reservations by far has been the sole contributor to advancement of the dalits. Privatisation is meant to directly hit it. The benefits of the reservation policy to the dalit community have been more indirect than direct.

Directly it benefited a few but indirectly it has created hope for advancement in the entire dalit population. This hope is already faded even when not much of privatisation has happened so far.

Their ideological armour is proving insufficient to resist it. There is a visible alienation, hopelessness and dejection setting in among them, which is getting manifested in increasing lumpenisation and criminalisation of dalit youth. This trend portends doom not only for the dalits but also for the entire oppressed people thirsting for some radical change. For, no radical change is possible in this country without dalit participation. The dalit consciousness formed over centuries of struggle is getting obliterated by the contemporary compulsions created by the Reforms.

This phenomenon will catapult dalit masses back onto the vicious spiral of backwardness and fortify reactionary regimes in the similar proportion. This irrevocable loss would prove dearest to the dalits. While privatisation might set in slowly, the free market ethos that it engenders much before could hit the dalits really harder through the legitimacy it grants to the base instincts against any emancipation project. For, the likely victims of the privatisation is still a miniscule part of the dalit population but the impact of these social ethos would engulf entire dalit population.

Howsoever base the individual conviction might have been, the ethos of yesteryears had nearly forbidden them from surfacing openly. But, now the emergent free market ethos is not only permitting but also promoting the vilest and venomous discourse against the dalits and the minorities. The vehemence with which the reservations or any kind of subsidy or any positive discrimination are derided today has a qualitatively distinctive edge.

It is interesting to note that there is not yet a dalit voice raised against this fascist hegemony. It would indeed be difficult for the dalits to resist this onslaught. The emergence of right wing politics to national prominence is merely a corollary or consequence of this transformation. Social consequences of the economic miseries associated with these

Reforms are indeed ominous for the dalits. On one side they shall be subject to increasing pauperisation and on the other stand in competition with the multitude of masses in the job market. Increasing tendency of businesses to downsize, virtual abolition of the reservation system through privatisation, the strategies of flexibilisation and informalisation of labour; corporatisation and depeasantisation of farming etc. will release vast numbers of people to the job market. The resident caste prejudices in such situations will certainly get activated to the detriment of the dalits.

CONCLUSION

The economic reforms in the mould of macroeconomic stabilisation and structural adjustment programme of IMF and World Bank have essentially a pro-rich bias. Wherever they were implemented, they have worsened the situation of the masses of poor people in absolute as well as relative terms. Some contrary data to this general observation are rather attributed to the departures from the standard blueprint given by the Bretton Wood institutions.

The dalits in India, being the poorest of the poor have been hit the hardest. Their social disabilities, largely reinforced by and sustained on the economic deprivations, are bound to get accentuated with these policies. The Indian reforms were ` driven' and not 'strategy driven' when they were adopted. There have since been changes in the formation and key persona.

The new government for instance has imparted them a form of 'strategy' through their Common Minimum Programme. However, there has not yet been any evidence of this strategy being any different from the course followed by the previous government. The complete discourse of the Reforms appears to be either grossly off the mark of Indian reality or to assume out its momentous features.

The broad Indian reality is that India has too many poor. As per the Human Development Report, 1996, there are 229 million income poor but more than twice as many, 554 million are capability poor. In terms of capability poverty, its 61.5%

population is poor. Its rank just as to descending poverty among the 174 countries of the world is 135. Even today India is predominantly an agrarian economy, with over 70 per cent of its population living in villages. No statistics moreover can adequately capture the heinous socio-cultural inequality that is an abiding part of the Indian reality.

It has acute inequalities not only in economic terms but also in the socio-cultural terms. The free market oriented reforms ought to take this grave Indian reality into consideration. Unless there is a wide spread purchasing power in the economy the market can never be free and sustainable. The reform strategy thus should embody sustainable economic empowerment of the rural masses; investments to enhance their capability and effective measures for accelerated development of the disadvantaged parts like the dalits.

The pre-requisite to reforms therefore could be the radical land reforms, massive investments in rural areas into agriculture-related infrastructural projects, universalisation of primary education, primary health care system and reinforcement of positive discrimination in favour of the dalits. The devil of casteism could be tamed only by freeing general masses of the people from the anxieties and uncertainties about basic survival.

The general condition of deprivation has rendered them vulnerable to be the preys to the frequent machinations of the vested interests that make them see the enemy within their own class. The relative equality thus can be the bedrock for launching the socio-cultural offensive in the form of mass-education programmes. But this all may still not be enough. The policy of positive discrimination in favour of the dalits will have to be reinforced much more vigourously in all the sectors of economy, than ever before.

They need to be reframed and simplified for the effective implementation. Unlike the current provisions, this may be stopped once their representation in services comes on par with the general population. The specific reform package can be formulated in terms of the conditions existing then. There arises a question of capital. Where will the capital for the investment in basic reforms come from? Not an easy question to answer, indeed. But some pointers may not be impertinent. It is acknowledged since number of years that India has a parallel economy in black money. The recent spate of scams is a mere corroboration of this hypothesis. The Reforms appear to have given them a boost. Whatever little has surfaced can be likened to a tip of iceberg.

Some five years ago, an unofficial estimate by the World Bank had put the unaccounted money of Indians kept in various tax havens at $ 100 billion. As per Finance India, the range of capital outflows was from $ 1065 million to $ 370 million just in one single year—1993. Much of the $ 10 billion money in the non-resident account is said to be belonging to the resident Indians.

The evidence of this kind abounds. As against this vast sum of our own money, what the government aims at out of the Reforms is the paltry sum of some four to five billion dollars of foreign direct investment a year to come in the country! The size of the money that rightfully belongs to the people of the country may be good enough for the task. But to unearth this treasure certainly requires a political will. India does not need capital as much as it does the political will to better its destiny.

10

Ambedkar and Dalits

INTRODUCTION

Ambedkar came to forefront in Indian academics from the decade of nineties with the intensified struggles of Dalits. The struggles of the ordinary people forced the centres of power and knowledge to consider the importance of Ambedkar and his ideas in social reconstruction of the nation. With Ambedkar as the source of inspiration, Dalits are struggling to write their own history by interrogating the dominant Brahminical traditions. The project of De- Brahiminisation of Indian history has appeal among the Dalit scholars in writing Indian history, culture and philosophy.

The relevance of Ambedkar has to be read with the fifty years developments of post Ambedkar of post independent India. His approach to Indian society and its history are crucial in understanding contemporary India and the struggles of the oppressed.

The document will focus on the importance of historical method of Ambedkar in relation to the theories of contemporary historiography of India. Ambedkar's notion of history is identified with 'moral community' imbibed with the principles of equality, liberty and fraternity. His historical method borrows tools from Marxism in understanding the ancient history.

Rather than mechanically applying Marxism, he had creatively used it in keeping the specific context of Indian society. He approached Indian society from the point of religion and finds the religion as source for the different ideological position. For instance, Buddhism is considered as revolutionary and Hinduism as counter revolutionary. 'Rationality' is the guiding principle in evaluating the principles and practices of religion. For the claims of religion he applied rationalistic principle. He brings the religion as a focal point in reference to caste system. To construct the Indian history in proper, he avail all the convincing ideas of his times, from liberal to Marxist. This may go in tune of pragmatism. The pragmatism of Ambedkar differs from the context of western societies.

The pragmatic method of Ambedkar came out of his social responsibility and in presenting the history from the victim's point of view. In essence he made a serious attempt in constructing the Indian history in which one finds dignified place for 'sudras' and 'untouchable communities'. Ambedkar is a source of inspiration for contemporary dalit movement and so for constructing history from dalit point of view. Dalit historiography establishes its own method by challenging the colonial, nationalist, marxists and subaltern approaches of Indian historiography.

PHILOSOPHY OF HISTORY

Historians have always tried to provide rationally justified knowledge about past, cause and effects of events. Philosophy of history can function as a conceptual enhancement for working historians and also it can function as a source of rational criticism of specific methods or approaches within contemporary historiography. Historically, there are various attempts to read history from diverse ideological and methodological positions.

Many thinkers contributed to the philosophy of historical ideas. Many who have concerned themselves with questions about the nature of historical knowledge and interpretation of the past have spent a good deal of time studying the history of various historical concepts and ideas; and in doing so some have concluded that there are no absolute ideals of historical method or truth which can be isolated from their own peculiar historical and social contexts. Broadly there are two streams identified in approaching the historical knowledge- idealistic and materialistic. In the realm of epistemological understanding of truth value of historical knowledge-rationalistic and empiricist methods were followed. The empiricist views past as an ordinary object of empirical investigation. The rationalist views past as an object of rational reconstruction and understanding. There raised a basic questions what is history about? Kant, Hegel and Marx have common strand and answered this question differently. For Hegel, history is unfolding of human freedom.

Hegel's conception of history presupposes an abstract or absolute spirit. History of humanity becomes history of abstract spirit of humanity, a spirit above and beyond the real man. The clue to history, in Hegel's view, is to be found in the idea of freedom. 'World history', in his words, 'exhibits the development of the consciousness of freedom on the part of spirit, and of the consequent realisation of that freedom.' Marx answered in another way – that the underlying driver in historical change is the tension between the forces and relations of production or class struggle.

For Marx, the first premise of all human history is, of course the existence of living human beings. All historiography must begin with these natural bases and their modification in the course of history by men's activity. Unlike the idealist view of history, it does not have to look for category in each period, but remains constantly on the real ground of history, it does not explain the practice from the idea but explains the formation of ideas from material practice. The whole previous conception of history has either completely neglected this real basis of history.

Consequently, history has always to be written in accordance with external standard, the real production of life appears to be ahistorical. During the Nineteenth century the central concern is changed from metaphysical issues about 'direction of history' to epistemological issues about 'historical truth'. In twentieth century these concerns about truths in history focus on dispute between two views on question into what is history. A good part of the twentieth century was devoted to a debate sparked by the philosopher of science Carl Hempels claiming that historical explanations—to be legitimately scientific ones have to be developed from the physical sciences.

In contrast with Hempel's thesis, some, such as R. G. Collingwood and William Dray' have insisted that the historian is more concerned with understanding the motives of historical agents than with predicting events. Collingwood, author of 'The Idea of History' argues that all history is the history of thought. He replaced the 'positivistic' notion of history with one which treats thought as the fundamental concept of historical inquiry.

Philosophy of history-as-discipline has also addressed concerns about the justification and limitations of historical objectivity, the truth of historical claims, and the nature of historical explanations. Are there any proper methods in understanding history? Is it possible to find the historical method without any ideological and political positions? The discussion further continued that historians' ideological and political positions play a role either approaching the knowledge of past or constructing the ideas of past. The historians are selective in interpreting the knowledge of past. In other words, the contemporary demands force them to probe into the past.

As the historian Croce said 'all history is contemporary'. As Carl Becker declares, 'the facts of history do not exist for any historian till he creates them.' As E H Carr explains, 'history is a continuous process of interaction between the historian and his facts and unending dialogue between the past and the present.' 'All history depends ultimately upon its social purpose.'

HISTORIOGRAPHIES IN WRITING INDIAN HISTORY

This document gives emphasis on the historical method of Ambedkar in countering the dominant social groups' construction of the Indian history. Both in construction of history of India and in having its historical method- Colonial,

Orientalist, Nationalist, Marxists, Cambridge historians and Subaltern historians who played a vital role. History writing in India as a conscious exercise began with scholars of Colonial and Orientalist persuasion and followed by nationalist elite and others. At present four dominant streams in Indian historiography are important—Colonial, Nationalist, Marxist and Subaltern schools.

Each school has its historical social context in emphasizing its method in writing Indian history. Each school argued its case in relation to other. The decade of eighties is turning point in Indian history in bringing new epistemological positions corresponding to the struggles of Dalits, Women, Adivasis. In writing history, categories wise, caste, gender, region became reference points.

On the other hand, struggles rallying religious nationalism are trying to invoke the 'glorious past'. With the many contesting positions, to reach out historical objectivity is not an easy task. When researches into India's past began in the late 18th century and early 19th centuries, Orientalist ideas structured historical representations. Inspired by the romanticism and classicism of the time, Orientalists like William Jones and H.T. Colebrooke returned to the ancient past, discovered its greatness and defined a specific notion of a glorious classical age.

It was in this age, so the Orientalists told us, that the essence of Indian civilization – embodied in its language, laws, institutions and religious texts – came into being. Subsequent to this golden age there was a continuous or cyclical decline to a degenerate present before the British rule.

If India had to develop, its lost past had to be rediscovered, its essence had to be properly understood, its juridical and religious texts had to be translated and canonized, its poetry had to be recaptured. The Orientalists saw themselves as the mediators who would define this relationship between the past and the present. As codifiers and translators they would be the ones to discover the ancient texts and ascribe to them their true meanings. By the early 19th century, with liberalism gaining ground, Orientalist histories were questioned from within the fold of imperial thought. If Orientalists had glorified India's past, the liberals condemned it. From a veneration of classicality we moved to a phase of arrogant deification of modernity. Liberal histories idealized the modern West and the assumed principles of its order – individualism, freedom and democracy.

Other societies – of the past and present – were understood and characterized only in terms of the presence and non-presence of liberal values. While Orientalists had discovered in India's past a succession of golden ages, liberals like James Mill and Thomas Macaulay could see only shades of darkness. In the West liberal histories traced a series of great transitions – from darkness to light, irrationality to rationality, magic to science, superstition to reason.

Modernity had emerged from the age of darkness, through the Renaissance and Enlightenment into the modern age. In India and other 'dark continents', as the liberals saw it, this transition never took place. India had remained unchanged, constrained by the social institutions that defined it – caste, village community and Oriental despotism. The colonial historians were tried to construct the Indian history that suits their political interests. The colonial historians tried to show that Indian nationalism was nothing more than an unprincipled, selfish, amoral bid for power by a few Indian elites.

They had used the traditional bonds of caste and communal ties to mobilize masses for their own ends. The colonial assumptions of historical thought was enshrined by Hegel and expounded by Macaulay, Mill, Seeley, and many others. In the historical literature, colonial powers escaped serious interrogation outside of the specific contestations of the nationalist struggle until new critical inquiries were initiated by figures as various as Bernard Cohn, Edward Said, and Ranjit Guha.

Nicholas Dirks argues that British colonialism played a critical role in both the identification and production of Indian 'tradition'. Essentially colonial history of India is Eurocentric and imperialistic. The tendency to read Indian history in terms of a lack, an absence, or incompleteness that translates into 'inadequacy' is obvious in these excerpts. The British conquered and represented the diversity of 'Indian' pasts through a homogenizing narrative of transition from a 'medieval' period to 'modernity'. The terms have changed with time.

The 'medieval' was once called 'despotic' and the 'modern', the 'rule of law'. 'Feudal/capitalist' has been a later variant. While the nationalists mounted a critique of colonial ideas, they continued to accept many of the key categories through which imperial representations of Indian society were fashioned. But in their critiques, nationalists still borrowed from the Orientalists, transforming the founding Orientalist notions of India's past – the idea of classical golden ages and the corollary myth of a subsequent civilizational decline – into accepted orthodoxies of Indian history.

But most nationalist histories continued to periodize pre-colonial history through religious categories. They referred to ancient India as Hindu and medieval India as Muslim – as if a unitary religious essence permeated the entire age and the whole society. By the 1980s history writing in India saw a new phase of dramatic change. Influenced by the new social history in England and the cultural turn in social sciences, Subaltern Studies challenged the elitism of earlier histories that attributed historical agency to the elites and looked at the world from above.

Subaltern histories emphasized the need to understand the experiences and lives of the dominated – peasants and workers, tribals and lower castes, women and dalits – people who leave few written records, whose voices are difficult to hear, whose actions appear inconsequential.

The cultural turn in history writing all over the world shifted the focus away from economist and reductive reading of historical processes. Power and domination, economy and society, experience of work and leisure, identities and interests, were all seen as culturally constituted. The real break came with the rise of a much more sophisticated historiography from the 1950s and 1960s pioneered by scholars, to name few of the most important, like D.D. Kosambi, R.S. Sharma and Irfan Habib. There was a veritable paradigm shift, particularly in ancient and medieval Indian history. The historiography of the Hindu Right necessarily sticks to periodization by religion: in effect, the religion of rulers, for that is the only way through which the premise of medieval 'Muslim domination' or 'tyranny' can be made credible.

The only real evil for it is religious, cultural or political domination coming from sources it considers external and alien, because non-Hindu. The failure to go beyond the single evaluative standard set by the colonial/anti-colonial binary produces similar problems for histories of subordinate caste and Dalit protest. Arun Shourie's onslaught on Ambedkar typifies this tendency at its worst, but an indication of the difficulties is revealed by the interesting recent attempt by G. Aloysius to write an alternative history of modern India from a 'Dalit-Bahujan' perspective.

Its many virtues include a valid stress on the complicities between colonialism and continued or refurbished high caste domination, as well as on the numerous overlaps between 'mainstream' nationalism and Hindutva. Even Nehru's Discovery of India is revealed as being not entirely immune from such contamination. In the decade of eighties, a group of scholars identifying with subaltern historiography got prominence by differing with earlier nationalist and Marxist historiography.

This rise coincided with that of the Dalit movement which was taking aspiration from the philosophy of Ambedkar. Dalit movement, on the one hand, questions Brahminism and its basic assumptions and on the other hand finds 'faults' with Marxism in practice as an alternative to dominant classes. The scholars influenced by the Dalit movement are even critical about the subaltern studies especially their treatment of the issue of caste.

Subaltern studies came into prominence from the decade of eighties in projecting a new method of historiography by countering the earlier ones. This approach came along the line of 'history from below' approach of European history writing in 1970 and 1980s. It came in opposition to both colonialist and nationalist historiography. It is skeptical about the established orthodoxies of both liberal nationalist and Marxist historiographies. Writing history from subaltern point of view was to show that neither nationalist nor left progressive historiography had a place for autonomous historical actions of the subaltern classes. Rajit Guha in an introductory note to Subaltern studies: 'The historiography of Indian nationalism has for a long time been dominated by elitism- colonialist elitism and bourgeois-nationalist elitism.' The thrust of the argument is subaltern consciousness is distinct and autonomous. The histories of class divided societies have been written and preserved in accordance with interests of dominant classes.

Only rarely does subaltern consciousness appear in its autonomous form in these accounts. Subaltern consciousness evolved out of the experience of subordination, out of struggle, despite the daily routine of servitude, exploitation and deprivation. The subaltern consciousness can not be found in archival material conventionally used by historians, since it is prepared and preserved by dominant groups. For the most part, those materials only show the subaltern as subservient. It is only the moment of rebellion that subaltern appears as the bearer of independent personality. The subaltern studies are criticized by scholars on different grounds.

The criticism is on the agency involved in this project and on the method. Many complained that subaltern history was becoming bhadralok history, the history of elites. Sumit Sarkar in an substance, 'The decline of the subaltern in subaltern studies' argued that in the name of theory, a tendency emerged towards essentializing the categories of 'subaltern' and 'autonomy', in the sense of assigning to them more or less absolute, fixed, decontextualized meanings and qualities. They were not advanced further by pointing out the economic reductionism of Marxism.

What is conveniently forgotten is that the problems do not disappear through a simple substitution of 'class' by 'subaltern' or 'community' identifying tendencies can be actually strengthened by the associated detachment from socio-economic contexts and determinants out of a mortal fear of economic reductionism. The handling of the new concepts, further, may remain equally naïve. The subaltern studies, symptomatically has ignored histories of the left and of organized anti-caste movements throughout, and the line between past and present-day neglect can be fairly porous. He further argues that subaltern studies don't have ideological strength to counter the communal violence. There is another criticism by branding the subaltern school as idealistic. 'Guha masks his idealism by formulating a critique of official, liberal and left historiography.

Guha's idealism can be seen most clearly in his attempt to criticize the analysis of the social and economic conditions which generate rebellion. By accepting the basic premises of idealism, peasant consciousness is rendered supra-historical as it is not determined by any objective historical forces. It is at a par with the Hegelian 'geist' which is not determined by history, while the development of history is march towards the self realisation of this spirit. Guha's idealism consists not in emphasizing the importance of consciousness, but in placing consciousness beyond the pale of historical determination or mediation.

Definitely there is a breakthrough in methodology in constructing the history with much authenticity. Subaltern Studies becomes a blanket term for all subaltern communities like dalits, women, peasants, adivasis etc. in countering the hegemony of the dominance. Within the subaltern studies, if each community had its own logic and approach to history, then the project of subaltern studies is in trouble. For instance, the issue of caste is important in writing the history so as the historians/scholars from the dalit communities had altogether different approach in constructing/imagining Indian history. Immediately, it even dismisses the so called subaltern by dismissing them as elite/or non dalits.

Dalit historiography throws a challenge to colonial, nationalist, Marxist and right wing and even to the so called historians of subaltern studies. In this context, Ambedkar's method of constructing the history from dalit perspective is path breaking, and provides insights for contemporary historians of all shades. Infect, very few historians worked out in the field of ancient history with sound ideological commitment and with a purpose of liberating the oppressed masses from dominant social and philosophical systems.

AMBEDKAR: IN PURSUIT OF HISTORICAL TRUTH

One may derive Ambedkar's 'historical method' in all his major writings on Indian history, culture and philosophy. The writings on this kind of issues not only provoked the scholars, political leaders of nationalist movement and orthodox Hindus of his times but helped deconstruct the dominant construction of ideas of Indian society.

He made a systematic attempt to construct the histories and genealogies of the submerged social groups of Indian society by questioning the elite and dominant established Brahminical positions. He seems confident of his position by declaring it as 'fresh insights and new visions' in looking at Indian history and philosophy.

In the year 1946, Ambedkar identified five streams of thoughts among the Hindus of Indian society in his writing on 'who are Shudras'- Orthodox, Aryasamajists, respecters of law (Hindu social system is all wrong, but who holds that there is no necessity to attack it. Since law does not recognize it, it is dying, if not dead system) Political minded (Swaraj is important than social reform) and Rationalists (regard social reform as primary and even more important than Swaraj).

Among these five classes of Hindus, Ambedkar would like to identify his position with rationalist Hindus who were arguing for social reform as immediate agenda rather than any other. In the words of Ambedkar; "I claim that in my research I have been guided by the best tradition of the historian who treats all literature as vulgar- I am using the word in its original sense of belonging to the people –to be examined and tested by accepted rules of evidence without recognizing any distinction between the sacred and profane and with the sole object of finding the truth."

As has been well said, an historian ought to be exact, sincere, and impartial; free from passion, unbiased by interest, fear, resentment or affection; and faithful to the truth, which is the mother of history, the preserver of great actions, the enemy of oblivion, the witness of the past, the director of the future. In short he must have an open mind, though it may not be an empty mind, and readiness to examine all evidence even though it be spurious. The non-brahmin scholar may find it difficult to remain true to this spirit of historian. He is likely to import the spirit of non-brahmin politics in the examination of the truth or falsity of ancient literature which is not justifiable. I feel certain that in my research I have kept myself free from such prejudice. In writing about sudras I have had present in my mind no other consideration except that of pure history. Respect and reverence for the sacred literature cannot be made to order.

They are results of social factors which make such sentiments natural in one case and quite unnatural in another. Respect and reverence for sacred literature of the Hindus is natural to a Brahmin scholar. But it is quite unnatural in a non-Brahmin scholar. In the historical method of Ambedkar; man is the maker of history: Ambedkar evaluates the three different views on the causes of historical changes, Augustine, Buckle and Marx.

Augustinian, history is only an unfolding of divine plan in which mankind is to continue through war and suffering until that divine plan is completed at the day of judgment. Ambedkar pointed out that this is not acceptable to many except theologians. For Buckle, history was made by geography and physics.

As per Marx, history was the result of economic forces. Ambedkar finds the limitations of these three arguments by holding the opinion that none of these would admit that history is the biography of great men. Indeed they deny man any place in making of history. He considers there is a truth in Buckle and Marx, but their views do not represent the whole truth. They are quite wrong in holding that impersonal forces are everything and that man is no factor in the making of history. That these impersonal forces are a determining factor can not be denied, however, the effect of impersonal forces depends on man must also be admitted.' The methods employed by Ambedkar in reconstructing the history are unique and convincing.

In developing an historical method he followed Goethe, as he said 'the historian's duty is to separate the truth from false, the certain from the uncertain...' Ambedkar agrees with Goethe in bringing out the relevant and necessary facts to forefront. Ambedkar proceeds further and points out into what the duty of historian in reconstructing the authentic history in situations, where he confronts with many missing links, *i.e.* when no direct evidence of connected relations between important events is available.

He himself faced this kind of situation in explaining the origin of sudras and untouchables as in both cases no documentary evidences were available or its antiquity. "In case of reconstructing history where there are no texts, and if there are, they have no direct bearing on the question. In such circumstances what one has to do is to strive to divine what the texts conceal or suggest without being even quite certain of having found the truth.

The task is one of gathering survivals of the past, placing hem together and making them tell the story of their birth. The task is analogous to that of the archaeologist who constructs a city from broken stones or of the paleontologist who conceives an extinct animal from scattered bones and teeth or of a painter who reads the lines of the horizon and the smallest vestiges on the slopes of the hill to make up a scene."

Ambedkar appears very much aware of the role of historian's social affinity in dealing the material in relation to the problems of social history. In an introduction to 'who are the Shudras', he made this point more clear. He finds the difference between the non-Brahmin scholar and Brahmin scholar in treating the same source material of sacred literature of Hindus. The Brahmin scholar's attitude is identified as uncritical commendation, and where as the Non-Brahmins attitude in dealing this is unsparing condemnation. Ambedkar finds both the attitudes are harmful to historical research. It is often argued by many Brahmins that sacred literature has to be treated with reverence and respect.

Ambedkar staunchly believes that in pursuit of historical truth, there is nothing wrong in exposure of these very sacred texts which are responsible for the decline and fall of nation and society. It is the duty of a scholar to treat the literature without having any distinction of sacred or profane in pursuing truth. It is quite natural for Brahmin scholar to treat it as sacred with lot of respect and reverence. More over its object is to sustain the superiority and privileges of Brahmins as against the non-brahmins.

Since he finds the comfort and privilege, it is not possible for the Brahmin scholar to be critical about sacred literature. In fact, it is his whole production and finds livelihood on it. 'Knowing that what is called the sacred literature contains an abominable social philosophy which is responsible for their social degradation, the non-brahmin reacts to it in a manner quite opposite to that of the brahmin..... I am a non-brahmin, not even a non-brahmin, but an untouchable.'

Ambedkar had more focus on philosophy of religion in understanding the socio-historical phenomenon and the moral basis of Indian society, than exclusively depending on either religion or philosophy. He developed it as a method. It seems in evolving this method, he got influenced by John Dewey. Dewey is one of those pragmatic philosophers who wrote extensively on philosophy of religion from this perspective. In the west, religion is identified with faith, and philosophy is with reason/science/rationality, in the age of enlightenment. It is also understood as tradition and modernity dichotomy. Religion and science started considering adverse to each other. In this backdrop pragmatism of Dewey got importance by considering religion on practical utility.

Religion is an institution or an influence and like all social influences and institutions, it may help or harm a society which is in its grip. Religion not only crossed everywhere the wrap of Indian history it forms the wrap and woof of Hindu mind.

The life of the Hindu is regulated by religion at every moment of his life. Besides religion acts as a social force, and it stands for a scheme of divine governance. The scheme becomes an ideal for society to follow. 'The power of religious ideal depends upon its power to confer material benefit'. Ambedkar favours for religion that stand for reason rather negating religion. He felt that Hindu religion need to undergo a reform. Caste is a natural outcome of certain religious beliefs which have the sanction of shastras.

To abolish the sanctity and sacredness of caste, one has to destroy the authority of the shastras and Vedas. One has to destroy the religion of sruti and smriti. Ambedkar not only proposed the religion that should stand for reason, but also tries to link it up with the governing principle of politics. In simple terms, he thought reason and critical analysis as a method used for the study of religion.

CASTE AS KEY PRINCIPLE IN UNDERSTANDING INDIAN HISTORY

Ambedkar identified caste as an important institution, in understanding the Indian society. In evolving his political theory, one could not ignore the role of caste system in India. No political theory is possible without some understanding of the caste.

Ambedkar is the first thinker who systematized the conception of caste in analytical way. Earlier discussions on caste are ethnographic and descriptive in nature. His approach is more political rather etnographical. He made an attempt to understand the origin and functioning of caste in order to understand the lives of the victims of the caste system. He understood that whole Indian social system was founded on the caste and the beliefs, customs, knowledge all are centred around caste system.

All the human activities are determined by the caste. Caste has social, political and economical implications. In simple caste is the primary institution of Indian society and other institutions like family, state, nation, school are directly or indirectly related/influenced by it. Most of his writing occupied the discussions on caste. It is generally understood that Indo-Aryan society of ancient India was based upon varna system, where the society was divided into Brahmins, kshtriyas, vaishyas and sudras based on the principle of labour and heredity.

Some of the scholars would like to argue that chaturvarna system based on economic theory of division of labour and that the varna system is scientific. In later days where the people deprived of this varna system contesting it is argued that the individuals are defined as their innate qualities (guna) but not by birth. However, Ambedkar refutes the chaturvarna system and argued that it is not only divided the society but also divided the labourers.

Further, this chaturvarna is opposed to natural law and spirit of human development. Ambedkar argued that initially there were only three varnas in indo Aryan society. The shudras were not a separate varna but were part of kshatriya varna. There was a constant fued between sudra kings and Brahmins. Brahmins were insulted and tortured by these kshtriya kings.

Ambedkar believes that Brahmins began to take revenge upon kshtriyas through 'divinity' and 'infinity' ideas which later on came to be attached to religious laws continued in course of time as sacred laws. Brahmins hatred towards sudras culminated into a situation where Brahmins refused to invest the sudras with sacred thread.

The sacred thread in ancient India presupposed a higher social and economic status. Owing to the loss of sacred thread, the sudras were socially degraded and demoted to the rank of the fourth varna. Amedkar shows this point through the examples from Hindu mythology.

REINTERPRETATION OF MARXISM IN INDIAN CONTEXT

Ambedkar made an attempt to interprete Indian society by using Marxian methodology for his own convenience. Contrary to the opinion that ancient India doesn't have any history, Ambedkar tried to dig out its history with the help of

Buddhist literature. The rise of Budhism considered by him as a revolutionary against Aryan Brahminism in the history of India. More than religious revolution, it is social and political. The Brahmins were the custodians of religion by monopolizing the priestly profession and guided the people in all its moral and spiritual matters. They set the standards to be followed by all others. The Aryan community at the time of Budha was steeped in the worst kind of debauchery: social, religious and spiritual.

The Aryan religion never concerned itself with what is called a righteous life. In the Aryan society the shudra or low caste man could never become Brahmin. But Budha not only preached against caste but admitted them at the rank of bhikku. The phenomena of the decline of Budhism, followed by the triumph of Brahminism—was considered by him as counter revolution and attempted to situate the sudras, women in relation to this counter revolution.

In understanding this phenomenon, Ambedkar made an attempt to understand the Brahminic literature and mythology from historical point of view. He finds the riddles of Hinduism in its sacred literature. He questioned the very authority of vedic literature and its privilege of apaurusheya. 'Present day Hindus are probably the strongest opponents of Marxism. They are horrified at its doctrine of class- struggle. But they forget that India has been not merely the land of class struggle but she has been the land of class wars'.

The bitterest class war took place between Brahmins and kshatriyas. The classical literature of Hindus abounds in reference to class wars between these two varnas. Conceptual structures will grow only when they are used in everyday life and in the context of thought and when contemporary thinkers in India begin to articulate their experiences about man, society, and polity in terms of classical thought, a new direction will be given to concepts.

In a sense, Indian thinkers from the time of Ramamohan Roy have been trying to do this, but the focus has mostly been on matters primarily non intellectual and non conceptual in nature. Indian philosophy like Indian culture approached with either too much enthusiasm or total negation of it. To assess Indian Polity properly, one has to keep aside both positive and negative emotions. There are certain myths about IP and claimed as facts. The claim of spirituality was never put to the test. In fact it seems so self evident as to require any argument or evidence on its behalf. No body feels it to question the worthiness of this claim.

Amedkar's contributions are not only significant in writing Indian history but in evolving a method which is more relevant even for contemporary historians of different schools. On the one hand, he tried to prove that historian's social affiliation plays a role in interpreting the past. This he shows by citing the brahminical scholarship. On the other, he argues for objectivity in case of non-brahminical scholars rather carried by the romanticism of non-brahmin struggles.

He identifies the historical change with socio- economical, political and cultural struggles of the people. He observed that this historical phenomenon reflected as a whole in evolution of religion. He considers the religion on moral basis that stand for the reason. For Ambedkar, religion had become important category in constructing/interpreting Indian history. Further he proceeds by understanding religion in historical dialectical way.

He borrowed the tools of Marxism in understanding Indian history in this fashion. Buddhism had been considered as revolutionary strand against Brahminism and against the triumph of Brahminism. Moreover, he made a systematic attempt to bring in view the history of victims of Indian society, where one finds no trace of any historical evidence in official records or narratives of dominant brahminical class.

DALIT HISTORIOGRAPHY

There is a significant scholarship coming up from Dalits in writing their own history. Their intervention is crucial in many ways. The history writing came along with the dalit struggles. In search of their identity, they dig the past in all possible ways. In writing of dalit history or interrogating dominant history from Dalit point of view, Dalit scholars/

activists/writers may not be systematic, argumentative but are striking in their attack and provide an alternative forcefully. One may find many missing links in the construction of the dalit history or questioning the dominance from Dalit point of view. They are in vernacular languages. These writings are often reproduction of oral narratives. Some of them are in the form of autobiographies.

In this connection this document presents historical claims of dalits of Telugu society as a case study. The word 'Dalit' in telugu society become familiar with Dalit Mahasabha, which came into existence with Karamchedu massacre of 1985. Dalit movement had taken roots at popular level and oppressed Dalit masses started questioning the dominance and hegemony of the upper caste people. The newly emerged dalit middle class, however small, played a role in production of knowledge systems in the fields of literature, culture, politics, philosophy and history.

Dalit movement provided the spectacle through which they could uphold the culture, history and politics of the lower caste. Dalit intelligentsia is making serious attempt to construct their cultured past and history as against the upper caste Brahminical hegemony. The literature coming in the name of Dalit, shattered the existing canons of Telugu society. As a Telugu Dalit writer G. Kalyana Rao felt, 'We have to dig a lot and simultaneously bury a lot.'

The Dalit intelligentsia is active in this mission to strengthen the on going Dalit struggles. Of course, within Dalit movement, there exists a variety of political positions. However, caste becomes a reference point in understanding history, philosophy, culture and politics, with active Dalit struggles.

From the trained historians, though negligible, there exists significant number of historical writings. Kancha Ilaih's Why I'm Not a Hindu (Nenu Hindunetlaitha in telugu) is a prominent intervention from Dalit-Bahujan perspective against Brahmanism. It is a critique on hindutva, culture, politics and economics from a sudra perspective. He reflected on these issues from his social experience. He argues that dalit-bahujans have different food habits, culture, customs, and religious practices, which are unique, democratic and different from brahminical Hinduism. Dalit bahujans culture emerged from their involvement in labour. They are productive classes and so their culture is real, natural and authentic. The Dalitbahujan Understanding of Telugu culturtal and Literary History, he argues that construction of history taking place from two opposite and conflicting views: the brahminical and dalit bahujan.

He questions us to whether the brahminical writings (based on Sanskrit language, Sanskrit texts, and Sanskrit lipi, etc.) should really be called history at all? 'For brahminical people, history is a march of god on earth; where as for dalit *bahujans,* history is the march of people (that is, the dalit bahujan majority) on the earth.'

Further, the dalit *bahujans* history mostly lies in folklore/ oral tradition. The language of this folklore is far richer, humanitarian and democratic-perhaps that is the reason why it has been relegated to the margins by the brahminical historians. On the other hand, productive castes had their own Telugu language, but it never figured in the brahminical writings.

Though it is in autobiographical form, the arguments directly go against the dominant forms of knowledge systems. A. Sayanarayana, Professor in History made an attempt to write history from dalit bahujan perspective in his book Dalits and Upper Caste, Essays in Social History. He tried to construct dalit history by using the alternative literary discourses of dalits which are marginalized in the mainstream literary discourses. Y. Chinna Rao's doctoral dissertation Dalit Movement in Andhra, 1900-1950 captures the dalit struggles of colonial times.

This tried to establish that alternative struggles of dalits in colonial times rarely found mention in both colonialism and nationalism. To focus on the specific nature of resistance and struggles of dalits against the dominance, he uses the framework of James Scott's 'Weapons of the Weak.' The major argument is that contemporary dalit struggles are in continuation of these struggles. In other words, charging the mainstream historians for not documenting the dalit struggles. 'Dalit movements have not become a part of Indian historiography yet, even though their study is of immense importance in view of their inherent radical democratic identity and their interrelation with contemporary movements. The available studies on dalit movement in India suffer from lack of historical and written documentation, leaving scope for ambiguity.'

Moreover, there are attempts from the conscious Dalit activists also. From late nineties, there are considerable numbers of books on history. Katti Padma Rao, Sanskrit teacher and activist in rationalist movement turned to a leader of Dalit Mahasabha.

In the process of his active involvement in dalit struggles reflected on many issues in relation to the liberation of dalit community. His Dalitula Charitaconstructs the history of the dalits based on the sources of Sanskrit texts. His Caste and Alternative Culture makes an attempt to construct history and struggles of the untouchable and sudra castes against Aryan - Brahmin-Hindu culture.

He explores this theme from ancient times to contemporary times. He is even critical of the communist movement of contemporary times led by the upper castes like Reddy and Kamma communities and their silence on the issue of annihilation of caste. He explains the philosophical background of dalit movement. The matriarchal culture, Carvakas materialism, Budhist sangha philosophy and humanism are the foundation of dalit movement. He argues that in the Indian sub- continent, the makers of history are the dalit people.

Ancient Indian culture was matriarchal in character, founded on the principle of equality. The Aryans after arriving in India established Hindu kingdom and tried the culture of the ancient indigenous Indians. They introduced casteism, patriarchal culture and politico-economic dictatorship. Suppressing all the indigenous castes, they propagated their own Hindu culture in Indian society, and forcefully implemented Hindu way of life. Dr. Vijaya Bharathicame out with three books on Puranalu-Kulavyavastha. She has critically evaluates the puranas and their role in protection of caste system. Though the puranas are not considered as history, but are intend to cultivate ideal society to control the different social groups. On analysing the story of Satya Harischandra, though this story seems to uphold the truth, but its purpose is essentially to consolidate the varna system and controlling the women in the name of pativratyam.

She made her analysis based on Markandeya puranam, skandha puranam and Harischandropakyanam. 'If we observe the stories and the constructed ideology around the avataramurthi's of different yugas, the whole effort is to implement and introduce the sanctions of the varna systems in the lives of ordinary people. Dharmasamsthapanam means varna dharma samsthapanam. The stories of the shatchakravarties (Pururudu, Purukutsudu, Harischandrudu, Sagarudu, Naludu, Karyaveeryarjunudu) are made popular because they stand as the symbols in protection of varnadharma.

In a similar fashion the mythological god Rama represents the dominant brahminical system. Bonigala Rama Rao made an attempt to trace out history of untouchables. In his Antarani Jathula Charitra, he tried to establish that untouchable communities are not only the sons of the soil but also earlier ruling communities. Though weakened economically, they are protecting their culture and social ideology.

He proposes an argument that the names of the untouchable communities are nothing but the relics of the vanished kingdoms. To construct the history of untouchable communities he relied mostly on historical texts, books of linguistics and inscription rather *puranas* and epics. He further wrote Mala Kannamaneedu and Adiguruvu Acharya Chandala.

The writings of Kathi padma rao and Bonigala Ramarao hvae influenced the later writings on the history of dalits—this includes Dr. K. Lakshmi Narayanawho tried to explore history of dalits in the Aadibharatteyula Charitra (from 2500

BC to 2500 AD) and Pilli Rambabu's Adi Baratheeyulu. Apart from these, Dalit literature as a creative intervention of dalit intelligentsia played a significant role in constructing dalit history. The historical consciousness is very much internalized in the structure of their literary narratives. The importance of dalit writings lies in authentic representation of the community by questioning the existing brahminical and progressive writings.

The protest against the caste and class dominance is central to the dalit writings. Mostly, Dalit literary writings are autobiographical reflections of the community. Dalit writings are conscious effort of bridging the oral and written cultures. Dalit writings often invoke social memory as the source of their knowledge system. This also helps in maintaining the historical continuity.

Dalit literature enriched with content and description of dalit struggles for human dignity. There has been constant effort from dalit writers in translating the condemned life styles and practices of marginalized people into symbols of protest and pride. In the process of writing their own history, they thoroughly interrogated the existing histories of dominant caste/class groups in their literary writings. As Dalit writer, Sivasagar marking the assertion of dalits in writing their own history against the brahminical history centred around advaita of Sankara.

With a smile on his face/Shambhuka is slaying rama/with his axe/Ekalavya is cutting drona's thumb away/with his small feet/Bali is sending Vamana down to pathala/With needles in his eyes/and lead in is ears/Manu, having cut his tongue is seen rolling on the graveyard/standing on the merciless sword of time/and roaring with rage/The chandala is seen hissing four hounds on Sankaracharya/Oh..!/The history that is occurring today/Is the most Chandala history

CONCLUSION

The historical writings and method employed by Ambedkar had serious implication for writings of colonial, nationalist, Marxist and even subaltern historiographies on

Indian history. As against the colonial writings, he showed that Indians had a tradition of rich democratic struggles throughout its history and overcomes the dichotomy of tradition and modernity created by the colonial scholarship.

He countered the nationalist historiographies. In order to counter colonial rule, the nationalist projects Indian spiritual tradition of their glorious past. Ultimately, the elite Brahminical ideology valorized through the writings of nationalists in the name of nation.

Ambedkar was critical against this kind of brahminical scholarship by showing the other worldview of oppressed groups. He totally dismisses the glorious past of vedic and upanishadic times. He is critical about the brahminical past and at the same time he valorizes the democratic past of the oppressed parts of India.

Altogether he gave different meaning for nationalism of oppressed. Although Ambedkar was lenient towards Marxism, he is against mere economic reductionistic approach of it. He forcefully argues that other factors like culture and religion too influencing the world view of people. This may come as a parallel to Frankfort school of late sixties and cultural studies of contemporary times. He argues Marxism had to creatively interpret by considering specificity of Indian context rather than mechanically interpreting it. He throws a challenge to Marxists on understanding the issue of caste. The subaltern studies are much concentrated on modern Indian history.

It masks the socio-economic realities in the name of consciousness. In the context of communalization of history with the rise of hindutva forces, theoretically it does not have strength to counter it. As subaltern studies argue in favour of indigenous culture, this may be appropriated by right wing politics.

But Ambedkar's method had potential to counter religious nationalism of hindutva kind and in place of it proposes democratic nationalism of the oppressed. Ambedkar's idea of history came out of the struggles of the oppressed communities and had the imagination of better future by owning the reasoned/democratic past.

11

Violence against Dalits Women in Modern India

INTRODUCTION

Vulnerably positioned at the bottom of caste, class and gender hierarchies, Dalit women experience endemic gender-and-caste discrimination and violence as the outcome of severely imbalanced social, economic and political power equations.

Their socio-economic vulnerability and lack of political voice, when combined with the dominant risk factors of being Dalit and female, increase their exposure to potentially violent situations while simultaneously reducing their ability to escape. Studies on violence against Dalit women in India presents clear evidence of widespread exploitation and discrimination against these women subordinated in terms of power relations to men in a patriarchal society, as also against their communities based on caste. This is a widespread phenomenon found in India, Nepal, Pakistan, Bangladesh and Sri Lanka where caste-based discrimination subjects millions of Dalit women to inhumane living conditions and systematic human rights violations.

In India the Dalits constitute about 16.20 per cent of Indias population in 2001 with little less than half being women, which means that 80 million Dalit women face multiple forms of discrimination in this country alone. Violence against Dalit women reinforces caste norms wherein they are seen as available for all forms of violence, especially sexual violence.

Indias National Commission for Women, "In the commission of offences against... [Dalit] women the [dominant caste] offenders try to establish their authority and humiliate the community by subjecting their women to indecent and inhuman treatment."

Further, when they transgress caste norms such as those prescribing caste endogamy or untouchability practices, or assert their rights over resources or public spaces, violence is unleashed on them.

The UN Special Rapporteur on Violence against Women has noted that Dalit women "face targeted violence, even rape and death from state actors and powerful members of dominant castes, used to inflict political sessions and crush dissent within the community..." Similarly, in its 2007 Concluding Comments the CERD Committee noted its concern about the alarming number of allegations of acts of sexual violence against Dalit women primarily by dominant caste men.

FORMS AND FREQUENCY OF VIOLENCE AGAINST DALIT WOMEN

There are nine major forms of violence against Dalit women; six being violence in the general community – physical assault, verbal abuse, sexual harassment and assault, rape, sexual exploitation, forced prostitution, kidnapping and abduction; and three being violence in the family – female foeticide and infanticide, child sexual abuse and domestic violence from natal and marital family members. The more frequent forms of violence that are perpetrated against the majority of Dalit women are verbal abuse, physical assault, sexual harassment and assault, domestic violence and rape, in descending order.

Child sexual abuse in terms of particularly early child marriages and sexual relations with minor Dalit girls below the age of 16 years is also prominent. A recent three-year study of 500 Dalit womens experiences of violence across four Indian states revealed that the majority of Dalit women faced one or more incidents of verbal abuse (62.4%), physical assault

(54.8%), sexual harassment and assault (46.8%), domestic violence (43.0%) and rape (23.2%).

LOCATION OF VIOLENCE

The majority of Dalit women face violence in public spaces – streets, womens toilet areas, fields, etc. – in and around their villages and towns. The next most common place for violence is within the home.

Aside from domestic violence, a number of women face physical assaults, verbal abuse, sexual harassment and sexual assaults in their very home from non-family members. Violence in the workplace ranks third in terms of common locations for violence.

Finally, government spaces become grounds for violence where women are forcibly incarcerated, verbally abused, sexually harassed or raped in police stations. Otherwise, verbal abuse is the most common form of violence meted out in government spaces from a range of government actors including the police, district administration officials and doctors. Social Status of

PERPETRATORS OF VIOLENCE IN THE GENERAL COMMUNITY

Within the wide range of identified perpetrators of violence against Dalit women in the general community, dominant caste landlords emerge as the most prominent group. Police also emerge as key perpetrators of violence against Dalit women.

They are not active perpetrators; they also act in a significant number of cases in collusion with the perpetrators by failing to enforce the law when violence against Dalit women takes place. Two other groups of perpetrators whose numbers are significant belong to the professional category, namely doctors and teachers.

In addition, there are a large number of "other dominant caste persons" as perpetrators. Moreover, often this violence is committed by these perpetrators not only as individuals, but also as group violence involving people of the same status (or different status Finally, a number of "other Dalit persons" are either active perpetrators of violence against Dalit women, or colluders in the violence.

CASTE BACKGROUND OF PERPETRATORS OF VIOLENCE IN THE GENERAL COMMUNITY

While in some instances the perpetrators of violence belong to one homogenous dominant castes, there are instances where they cut across all dominant caste lines, that is, backward castes and forward castes. This is particularly so where the Dalit woman is seen to transgress established caste norms, for example, by asserting her rights in defiance of „untouchability practices.

The punishment meted out, therefore, takes on the form of collective punishment that is both expressive of caste outrage as well as instrumental in terms of teaching the woman and her community a session of „obedience to caste norms. Otherwise, sexual violence against Dalit women often takes a collective caste aspect, in terms of gang rapes or forced prostitution.

CAUSAL FACTORS FOR VIOLENCE

VIOLENCE IN THE GENERAL COMMUNITY

- The primary identified factor for violence in the general community relates to the issue of Dalit womens sexual or bodily integrity. Accompanying Dalit womens low caste status and the socio-economic and political power of the dominant castes is the latters view of their superior caste and gender status and accordingly a perceived right over Dalit womens bodies. Sexual violence is a tool utilised by dominant caste men to reinforce the caste „impurity of both the Dalit woman and her community, given the hegemonic discourse of women symbolising the group identity and bearing the honour of their community.
- A second frequent causal factor for violence in the

general community directly links to gender inequality and the „natural caste hierarchy as often manifested in untouchability practices, and Dalit womens counter discourse of equality, rights, dignity and self-respect.

- Almost as frequently identified a causal factor for violence in the general community lies in the area of Dalit womens civil rights.
- A fourth causal factor for violence in the general community, given the aspect of economic exploitation built into the caste system, related to economic resources – land, or other economic resources/capital such as wages, payment for services, etc. – and particularly Dalits asserting their rights to own or utilise resources.
- In the realm of political rights, several Dalit womens assertions of their basic political rights provoke violent dominant castes backlashes. The issues that led to violence are Dalit women contesting panchayat elections; Dalit women exercising or attempting to exercise political authority as elected panchayat representatives.
- Finally, violence also takes place when Dalit women sought justice and the protection of the law for violence-done to them, or to forestall such action

VIOLENCE IN THE FAMILY

Similarly, Dalit women face violence in the family over a range of issues, suggesting the assimilation of the larger patriarchal caste systems norms by particularly Dalit men, with negative implications for Dalit womens personal lives and interactions in their community.

When it comes to domestic violence, however, the causes for this violence are much more nuanced and varied. Gender inequality and norms of female subordination formed a major category of causal factors for violence meted out by natal and marital family members to Dalit women.

Impunity for Violence Against Dalit Women

The systemic nature of violence against Dalit women is accompanied by equally systemic patterns of impunity. In 2006, the official conviction rate for Dalit atrocity cases was just 5.3 per cent.

The study of 500 Dalit womens cases of violence revealed:

- In less than 1% of cases were the perpetrators convicted by the courts
- In 17.4% of instances of violence, police obstructed the women from attaining justice.
- In 26.5% of instances of violence, the perpetrators and their supporters, and/or the community at large, prevented the women from obtaining justice.
- In 40.2% of instances of violence, the women did not attempt to obtain legal or community remedies for the violence primarily out of fear of the perpetrators or social dishonour if (sexual) violence was revealed, or ignorance of the law, or the belief that they would not get justice.

One negative implication is that violence against Dalit women is legitimised, spurring further violence.

RECOMMENDATIONS

Affected governments are encouraged to:

- Follow-up on recommendations relevant to the promotion and protection of Dalit womens rights of UN Special Procedures, particularly the Special Rapporteur on violence against women, UN Treaty Bodies, the Universal Periodic Review, etc.;
- Enact and implement national legislation to eliminate practices such as dowry, devadasi/jogini, manual scavenging, caste-based discrimination and "untouchability" in accordance with recommendations by the UN Committee on the Elimination of all forms of Discrimination against Women (CEDAW);
- Cooperate fully with the UN Special Rapporteurs by responding to their questions and accepting invitations to country visits;

- Provide disaggregated data on the incidence of crimes against Dalit women, as well as police and judicial handling of such cases (as per CERD General Recommendation XXIX, 2002) and include the following parts in periodic reports to UN treaty bodies:
  - The extent of domestic violence against Dalit women, and on the legislative and other measures taken to address this phenomenon, including facilities and remedies provided for victims;
  - The situation of women and the extent to which they enjoy the right to own land and property independent of their male relatives;
  - Annual data, disaggregated by age, sex, caste, ethnicity and religion, as well as specific benchmarks, to enable adequate monitoring and evaluation of the progress achieved.

NATIONAL DEMANDS

Affected governments should:

- Recognize Dalit women as a distinct social group rather than subsuming them under the general women or Dalit category, and accordingly evolve and implement a specific focus and activities on Dalit womens rights within the broader framework of the Dalit and womens empowerment agenda.
- Ensure full and strict implementation of laws in place to protect Dalit womens rights and implement measures to ensure the abolition of „untouchability practices, and implement strict sanctions against anyone preventing or discouraging victims from reporting incidents of violence or accessing the criminal justice system, including police and other law enforcement officers.
- Ensure the implementation of national penal codes in its jurisdiction, and that law enforcement officials, judges, lawyers, social workers and medical

professionals are duly trained on the serious and criminal nature of domestic violence;

- Evolve a national perspective plan aimed at specifically accelerating efforts to reduce the development gap between Dalit women and the rest of the population within fixed time-bound targets.
- Introduce affirmative action policies to increase Dalit womens participation in the police, judiciary, legal professions and education.
- Produce and disseminate disaggregated data on the status of Dalit women, particularly in government plans and development programmes.

Bibliography

Ahuja, R.: *Violence against Women*, Pune: Pune Publication, 2000.

Bandhu, P.: *Dalit Women's Cry for Liberation: My Rights are Rising Like the Sun, will you Deny this Sunrise?*, New Delhi: Long Life Publication, 2003.

Bhargav, G.: *Human Rights of Dalits: Societal Violation*, New Delhi: Long Life Publication, 2005.

Chakravati, V.: *Reconceptualising Gender; Phule, Brahmanisam and Brahminial Patriarchy*, Mumbai: Rohit Publication, 2003.

Chitnis, V.: *Human Rights of the Vulnerable Groups*, Pune: Futuristic Digital, 2005.

Fromm, E.: *Dalit Human Rights Report of the Proceedings of International Conference on Dalit Human Rights*, London: Kogan Page, 2000.

Jogdand Mahipal, P.: *Indian Social Reality and Inequality in to the Human Right Violence of Dalit*, Mumbai: Kamal Publication, 2003.

Jogdand, P.: *Dalit Women, Issues and Perspectives*, New York: Cambridge University Press, 2000.

Kale, R.: *Life of Dalits*, New York: Cambridge University Press, 2006.

Kumar, N.: *Dalit Policies, Politics and Parliament*, Banglore: Shipra Publication, 2004.

Kumar, S.: *Human Watch Report*, New York: Cambridge University Press, 2000.

Mahipal: *Women in Panchayats*, Pune: Pune Publishing, 2005.

Mary, G.: *The Struggle of Dalit Women, Resource Sheet Paper Presented in Dalit Theology Seminar, Barmingham*, New York: Cambridge University Press, 2004.

Michael, S.: *Dalits in Modern India, Vision and Values*, Toronto: Thomson Nelson, 2008.

Omvedt, G.: *Dalit Women and Communalism*, Pune: Saakshi Publication, 2004.

Pal, R.: *Human Rights of Dalits: Societal Violation*, New Delhi: Long Life Publication, 2000.

Pandit, V.: *Handbook on Prevention of Atrocities (SC/ST)*, Maharashtra: Vidnayak Sansod Prakashan, 2002.

Paswan, S.: *Encyclopedia of Dalits in India*, Banglore: Banglore Press, 2002.

Pillai, T.: *Ambedkar's Daughters: A Study of Mahar Women in Ahmednagar District of Maharashtra*, New Delhi, Vistar Publication, 2005.

Punalekar, S.: *On Dalitism and Gender*, New Delhi: Long Life Publication, 2004.

Raj, M.: *Dalit Leadership in Panchayats*, New York: Institute of Modern Studies, 2006.

Rao, A.: *Gender and Caste*, New York: Orgone Institute Press, 2003.

Sainath, P.: *Dalit's and Human Rights: The Battles Ahead*, Toronto: Thomson Nelson, 2003.

Sequeira, L.: *Human Response to Dalit Women Today*, Boston: Houghton Mifflin, 2002.

Singh, Sumit: *Unmusical Chairs*, New York: Julian Press, 2003.

Thorat, S.: *Caste, Role and Discrimination, Discourses in International Context*, New York: Orgone Institute Press, 2004.

Tirmare, P.: *Violation of Human Rights of Dalit Women: Issues and Facts*, Maharashtra: College of Social Work, 2000.

Umakant: *Caste, Role and Discrimination, Discourses in International Context*, New York: Orgone Institute Press, 2004.

Webstar, J.: *Who is Dalit?*, Pune: Vistar Publication, 2004.

Zelliot, E.: *Dr. Ambedkar and the Empowerment of Women*, Mumbai: Mumbai Publication, 2003.

Index